SARIS ON SCOOTERS

SARIS ON SCOOTERS
How Microcredit Is Changing Village India
SHEILA MCLEOD ARNOPOULOS

DUNDURN PRESS
TORONTO

Published under arrangement with Groupe Librex Inc., doing business under the name Éditions internationales Alain Stanké, Montreal, Quebec, Canada.

Editor: Jennifer McKnight
Designer: Jennifer Scott
Printer: Marquis

Library and Archives Canada Cataloguing in Publication

Arnopoulos, Sheila McLeod
    Saris on scooters : how microcredit is changing village India / by Sheila McLeod Arnopoulos.

Includes bibliographical references and index.
ISBN 978-1-55488-722-4

1. Microfinance--India. 2. Rural women--India--Economic conditions. 3. Women in rural development--India. 4. Rural development--India. 5. Arnopoulos, Sheila McLeod--Travel--India. I. Title.

HG178.33.I4A75 2010   332.7082'0954   C2009-907459-1

1 2 3 4 5   14 13 12 11 10

 Conseil des Arts Canada Council   Canada    ONTARIO ARTS COUNCIL
du Canada   for the Arts   CONSEIL DES ARTS DE L'ONTARIO

We acknowledge the support of the **Canada Council for the Arts** and the **Ontario Arts Council** for our publishing program. We also acknowledge the financial support of the **Government of Canada** through the **Book Publishing Industry Development Program** and **The Association for the Export of Canadian Books**, and the Government of Ontario through the **Ontario Book Publishers Tax Credit** program, and the **Ontario Media Development Corporation**.

Printed and bound in Canada.
www.dundurn.com

Dundurn Press
3 Church Street, Suite 500
Toronto, Ontario, Canada
M5E 1M2

Dundurn Press
3 Church Street, Suite 500
Toronto, Ontario, Canada
M5E 1M2

Dundurn Press
2250 Military Road
Tonawanda, NY
U.S.A. 14150

To India's courageous Dalit women for their trailblazing
achievements and their spirit of community

TABLE OF CONTENTS

FOREWORD

I invited Sheila to the Women's World Banking Global Meeting in New York City as a special observer. She was working on a book about how microfinance is transforming village India, and I thought it would be valuable to her to join our meeting of 41 microfinance institutions and banks from 29 countries, including India, that make up the Women's World Banking network. Sheila had spent 21 months between 2001 and 2008 living in villages in India, observing firsthand the richness of the lives of very poor people and learning about microfinance. Now at the WWB Global Meeting in New York, she was observing a network of roughly 200 people — mostly women but many men, too — committed to one vision: enhancing women's access to financial products and services to help them move themselves and their families out of poverty.

The meeting focused on the economic crisis and its effect on microfinance worldwide, how to mitigate risk and manage a microfinance institution in the current economic climate, and how to continue to expand microfinance's reach despite the capital-constrained environment that threatens to make substantial growth in the near future all but impossible. Microfinance and the WWB Global Meeting are not only about poverty and access to financing, however. With access to financing comes responsibility, opportunity, and empowerment.

In India, perhaps more than in other places, microfinance is a disruptive force (in the good sense) because of the country's caste system. Women who had been "untouchable," without opportunity, destined to continue living at the bottom of the social and economic ladder, now have an option, an opportunity, to access financial products and services that can enable them to improve their situations and the lives of their families. The social, political, and economic ramifications of this development in India, and around the world, are not well understood. To help us — both the general reader and microfinance expert — begin to understand, *Saris on Scooters: How Microcredit Is Changing Village India* provides its readers with firsthand accounts of exactly how microfinance is transforming lives and society in villages across India.

Saris on Scooters focuses on the stories of strong figures like Ela Bhatt, who began organizing women in the slums of Ahmedabad in the early 1970s; of Saraswati, who became a self-appointed ombudsman as she ran a municipal sand contract; and of Puriben, who was starving in the desert before joining the Self Employed Women's Association (which grew out of Ela's organizing), and became a key manager in helping to develop an international embroidery company.

Ela, Saraswati, and Puriben are all remarkable women. But why the focus on women? As CEO of Women's World Banking, I'm often asked, why women? The answer is simple, really. Women pay back their loans at higher rates than men, which makes them a more reliable investment. Women invest in the welfare of their families significantly more than men, spending more on children's education and health, which is critical to long-term economic development.

Unfortunately, despite all the evidence that women are a smart investment, not to mention the human rights issue of equality, women are still disenfranchised in many countries around the world, especially when it comes to financial decisions. Yet progress has been and is being made. In 1975, women from around the world gathered in Mexico City at the first International Women's Year conference. Amidst all the talk about women's rights, one visionary group realized that economic independence allows women to choose and affect their own education, opportunities, and well-being. This small group of women went on to found Women's World Banking in 1979 "as an organization that would truly be able to meet the challenge of the coming decades and influence the economic and professional growth of women throughout the world." In many ways, the forces changing village India today are a continuation of the women's economic empowerment movement, burgeoning at that first International Women's Year conference, in which rural women with hard, life-earned business skills and a deep belief in community are coming together to transform their lives.

Judging from most news coming out of India today, it is easy to understand how one may have missed the transformation currently underway in village India. Media coverage of India typically focuses on the nation as a rising superpower, fuelled by a growing urban middle class supported in large part by the country's booming information technologies industry. Yet, despite its ongoing economic growth, India is still a largely rural country, in which 260 million smallholder farmers live on less than 1 dollar a day and 80 percent of its 1.1 billion people live on less than 2 dollars a day, representing 40 percent of the world's poor. What do these figures tell us? They tell us that what is happening in India's villages — away from the cities, IT call centres, and 21st century urbanism — is as important if not more so to the future of India as the growing urban classes.

Hidden from the spotlight of the media are women in India's 600,000 villages, working everyday to provide for themselves, their families, and their communities. *Saris on Scooters* tells their stories, but the same kinds of stories can be found in the Middle East, Africa, Eastern Europe, and Asia. Books on microfinance are often dry, technical treatises, written for the microfinance practitioner, the specialist, or the academic. *Saris on Scooters* is for everyone interested in learning more about what microfinance means on a personal level for the lives of the vibrant women Sheila illuminates for us, and how microfinance is literally changing the world.

Mary Ellen Iskenderian, President and CEO
Women's World Banking, June 12, 2009

INTRODUCTION

In late 2001 when I flew to India to start a book on village women and how microcredit was transforming them, I had been immersed in writing a novel about life on the mean streets in my home town of Montreal. While living with my street kid characters, who were struggling with family breakdowns and inner city poverty in our own Third World, I also became fascinated with life in contemporary India.

My interest in the country was sparked by my friendship with Vithal Rajan. An Indian who came to Montreal in the late 1960s, he became a Canadian and fell in love with Canada. But in the late 1970s he returned to his birth country and stayed to make a mark as a "development volunteer" working among very poor, low-caste women in the state of Andhra Pradesh.

During the 1990s, while I was teaching journalism at Concordia University in Montreal, from time to time Vithal would blow into the city en route to and from far flung places for meetings about environment and development. I would invite him to talk to my classes about low-caste women he knew in India that were dirt poor but saving money through self-help groups and taking loans that were lifting them out of abject poverty and into promising enterprises.

I discovered through him that in many rural areas throughout the country, social and economic advancement was being spearheaded by community-spirited women, many of them Dalits formerly called untouchables at the bottom of the Hindu caste hierarchy.

By 2001, Western journalists like Thomas Friedman of the New York Times were writing about the "shining India" of call centres and information technology and predicting the rise of a new superpower. But in this country of over a billion people, only about 150 to 200 million in cities were on a roll into the consumer society that typified the West.

Another 750 million individuals, 250 million of them very poor, inhabited the fabled 600,000 villages of rural India where electricity was sporadic and television a luxury. Without a better deal for the millions of poor living outside the cities, how could India truly flourish?

Quickened by Vithal's stories of women's successes in the face of colossal odds, particularly in the state of Andhra Pradesh, I decided to plunge into a world of huts and villages where microcredit was linked to organizations of women on the march. This was to be a book about the empowerment of Indian women at the bottom of the ladder. In the end, these public-minded women who were daring enough to take on the Goliaths of their world ended up empowering me.

Dalit women in Andhra Pradesh, a state of about 75 million people that was becoming famous for its self-help groups of women, showed me the power of women's solidarity and the meaning of community that I believe we in the West have almost completely lost.

As a journalist, I had met hundreds of high-profile and accomplished people over the years, but the non-schooled village women I encountered in India over four extended trips between 2001 and 2008 taught me more about the resilience and capacity of the human spirit than anyone.

To take a step back, my first taste for the country came in 1971 when I was travelling around Asia with my husband during a year's leave from the world of daily journalism in Canada. By accident I landed in Calcutta during the Bangladesh crisis and ended up writing about the refugee camps for the *Montreal Star*, but my foray into the camps was a lapse.

I was in India to take time off from my life as a social issue journalist writing about women's rights, minority questions, exploited immigrants, and poverty in Montreal. The year before I had gone through the painful "October Crisis" during the build-up of nationalism in Quebec, and I needed a break.

Determined to remain a casual traveller, I went from Calcutta to Darjeeling in the Himalayas, and then to the Taj Mahal, the pink palaces of Jaipur, and the erotic temples in Khajuraho. In the holy city of Benares I sailed in a boat down the Ganges past the smoking funeral pyres. Just like all the other tourists, I rode a camel and climbed aboard an elephant. But I never experienced any of the country's legendary villages or the women who formed the backbone of labour on the small farms that dominated rural India.

Now, 30 years later, I was back in India, alone this time, to explore the India I had missed so many years before. For my first six-month trip, I landed in the wake of the 9/11 crisis, much to the dismay of some of my friends who thought this was not the time to be in Asia where Afghanistan was burning, and where the ruling Indian Hindu fundamentalist party was attacking its large Muslim population; but I was determined to go.

I could not have done it without Vithal Rajan and his wife K. Lalita, a well-known Indian feminist and co-editor of a marvellous anthology of Indian women's writing from 600 B.C. to the present. They received me in Hyderabad, the high-tech capital city of Andhra Pradesh. Their daughter Diia who had lived in Montreal when she attended McGill University was also very helpful.

I arrived in November 2001, intent on exploring the work Vithal had accomplished with 5,000 Dalit women in 70 villages in an organization he founded called the Deccan Development Society (DDS), but first he sent me off to look into the activities of women associated with government anti-poverty initiatives and other non-government organizations.

Insisting to his friends that I was worth the bother, he opened doors into a network of organizers in community development who took me into the Telugu-speaking villages where the busses didn't go. Through these people I was able to see beyond high-tech India into a world of unsung heroines using savings and loans to propel themselves out of poverty.

I quickly discovered that the power of microcredit lay not only with basic poverty alleviation, but also with the creation of groups of women who eventually started to mobilize for social and economic change.

Women taking small loans in villages usually met under the umbrella of non-government organizations (NGOs) or microfinance institutions with links to banks. From its beginnings, microcredit concentrated upon women because they had proven to be more reliable than men at repaying loans.

Early in the morning or after supper, loan officers who were often also community organizers would arrive in the villages to dole out money and receive weekly payments. In the beginning, the weekly meetings of women in microfinance circles, also called thrift and credit or self-help groups, concentrated on very small loans of up to 100 dollars for new mini businesses.

Soon the women who shared information about life in their villages began taking action on social issues. India had passed a host of laws around child labour, child marriage, dowry prohibition, and widow abuse, for example, thanks to the mobilization of feminist and human rights activists who had succeeded in placing equal rights for women in the Indian constitution, but the laws were often ignored. Bonded labour was illegal but rampant. Health services were often non-existent. Sometimes teachers at state schools didn't bother to show up to teach, and Dalit children arriving in bare feet with no school bags were harassed.

Once the women started to assemble, they became unofficial human rights enforcers, making sure that children were at school and not in the fields. A refreshing brand of thatch hut justice promoted by dynamic poor women began to slice into caste-bound discrimination imposed by landowners, moneylenders, and local politicians. Eventually many microcredit circles federated into influential cooperatives that became instruments for more extensive economic and social empowerment.

In the villages, at first the men were wary of letting their wives escape the house to gather in groups. Under the aegis of a mother-in-law and the extended family of their husbands, women were used to being restricted to the home unless they were working in the fields. Assemblies of women operating outside family control created suspicion. Attitudes softened when some husbands became the recipients of loans that their wives took on their behalf so they, too, could start businesses. The outlook of the whole family improved and the men saw the economic gains of microcredit.

At the same time, women gathering in groups started to undergo the kind of consciousness-raising that I had seen in the women's movement in the late 1960s and early 1970s in my own country. Right from the beginning, however, the Indian women I met fought for a better life for their families and social justice for their communities. They also grappled with a range of complicated Indian development and population questions; sustainable organic agriculture, the environmental shock of huge dams in the Himalayas, the impact of globalization, and ethnic conflict between Hindus and Muslims were among them.

As I became involved in the lives of very poor women that were rising out of marginality and accomplishing amazing things, I began to forget about the despair and isolation of the forgotten souls lodged in the fabric of my own country. During the 21 months I lived in India, I became so involved with the lives of the women that sometimes they treated me as *apne*, which in Hindi means "one of ours."

My journey to meet the women took me from Hyderabad in Andhra Pradesh in the south, to Ahmedabad in Gujarat in the west, and Dehradun in the Himalayan state of Uttaranchal.

Along the way I got to know Narsamma, who ran away at the age of nine when her mother tried to marry her off, but who ended up running a women's radio station geared to Dalit women farmers.

I watched ladies in burqas in the old city of Hyderabad form a chain to stop a riot provoked by police outside their mosque.

In Ahmedabad, street vendors, rag pickers, and head loaders had succeeded in starting what had become the most comprehensive and socially-advanced poor women's bank in the world.

In a small village in Andhra Pradesh, Meerabai Rao described how she had been confined to her house, living in virtual purdah, until she was married at 15. After being disowned by her landlord father, she learned how to escape poverty when she took loans to launch a successful recycling business with her husband in another state.

At 26-years-old, Saraswati Wagmari figured out how to deal with hoodlums and demands for bribes when her Dalit cooperative battled to make money running a municipal sand contract.

In 2008, during my last trip, this time to the desert areas of Gujarat, I was privileged to spend time with Puriben, a master embroiderer and barefoot manager that has been a key player in developing an embroidery company now selling gorgeous clothes and home accessories to upper-class India and the world.

These women and the hundreds of others that I met are a testament to a burgeoning Third World women's liberation movement that isn't being recognized, where rural women with hands-on skills and a belief in community are quietly gathering together without fanfare to make a difference.

In 2006, Muhammad Yunus won a Nobel Peace Prize for supplying microcredit to poor women through his much-publicized Grameen Bank in Bangladesh. Since then, the benefits of microcredit have created mounting interest across the world.

By the end of 2008, organized microcredit in India was, according to a report on the microfinance sector by Indian development economist N. Srinivasan, reaching about 55 million households across the country, and mostly through women's self-help groups. But the number expands to 115 million when those taking small loans through commercial banks and primary cooperative societies are included. According to Subir Roy, a leading Indian financial journalist, this means that microcredit in India was reaching 20 percent of the 600 million working poor.

In calculating the value of Indian rupees in Canadian dollars I have used currency postings from the Bank of Canada. Between 2001 and 2009 the rate ranged from 30 to 44 rupees. See yearly averages in the appendix.

But as I saw in Andhra Pradesh, where 12,000 women were launching a dairy, and in Gujarat, where 3,500 embroiderers started their own embroidery company, some groups of grassroots women have soared way beyond the economic confines of their local villages. The story of the Indian powerhouse was not going to be restricted to IT call centres and the car and steel tycoons.

To make sure I saw village life up close, I slept on floors in huts with village families, but I also experienced the life of high-caste people in villas with servants. In an ashram in Rishikesh on the Ganges I encountered monkeys that grabbed food from my hands. Outside a big hotel in Ahmedabad I glimpsed elephants from a temple wandering around begging for food. In towns, friendly small hotels serving fiery chili curries were blessed with merciful air conditioning, but mostly I roasted in Andhra Pradesh and Gujarat and froze in the Himalayas. I travelled by foot and autorickshaw, motor scooter, train, and overnight bus, as well as the occasional hired car with a driver. At every turn India exploded with life and colour, but it was a great adventure because of the spirited and brave women I encountered. Here are their stories.

1
PAMTRAMPALLI
MEETS THE BOOTLEGGER

Saraswati, named after the Hindu Goddess of learning, was my introduction to the sparkling brand of Indian rural women's activism that carried me into the dramas of life in Indian villages. Like many of the people I met she used one name only. At the age of 23, she had led a group of women in her village of Pamtrampalli to expel the local bootlegger. I met her in November 2001 when I arrived in her village from the city of Hyderabad in a government car to meet a group of women that took loans in self-help groups under a state program called DWCRA, or the Department of Women and Children in Rural Areas.

As we pulled into the village on a narrow dirt road edged with mud-and-thatch huts, I glimpsed a lively group of about 50 women in long black braids holding huge garlands of tropical flowers and wearing one-of-a-kind, brilliant-coloured saris. Decked out in jewellery — often an Indian woman's only assets — they looked as though they were going to a wedding or perhaps waiting to greet the premier of the state. But this, I slowly discovered, was how Indian women always dressed, even when out in the fields.

To my great astonishment the person they were waiting for was me. I stepped out of the car in my dark blue Canadianized *salwar kameez*, consisting of a long tunic over baggy pants, with no jewellery at all, looking, in comparison to their colourful opulence, like a poor cousin. With delightful abandon, as though as I were some long lost village returnee, they tossed garlands of flowers around my neck.

It was my initiation to the characteristic warmth of the women in even the simplest Indian village.

I was ushered into an outdoor meeting space on the edge of the forest and sat down with them on the ground. Knocking around villages, I quickly learned that chairs were few and far between. Occasionally I was offered one, and to my embarrassment I was usually the only one perched in the air, making me feel like some 19th-century colonial visitor rather than a 21st-century journalist.

They began telling me through a translator from the regional Telugu language to English what they and their self-help groups, referred to as SHGs, had been up to. Mostly landless, or with small plots of land, the women had taken loans to buy milk buffaloes, raise chickens, lease land, or start small flower-raising businesses. Some were making plates and mats from coconut and banyan leaves, which was what they were doing while they talked to me. They told me that eventually they would also like to set up a match factory and a cardboard box enterprise.

Husbands, I was told, were potters, carpenters, cobblers, and makers of *bidis* (small tobacco cigarettes), but they were prone to alcoholism, a problem I would hear more about later from Saraswati.

Until they started their thrift and credit groups, the women were dependent upon moneylenders who were charging as much as 120 percent interest per year. Borrowers, who took loans for marriages or dowries, or to tide them over during the dormant part of the agricultural season, could lose their property if they couldn't pay.

After listening to the women talk and exchange, I picked out Saraswati as a natural leader and asked if I could interview her. In India nothing is ever done alone, so along with about 15 of her closest village women friends we gathered to talk on a multi-coloured mat in the small court-yard of her simple two-room, pink cement house. Though adorned inside with pictures, her house was, to my Western eye, not much more than just a shelter with no running water or a regular toilet. Her husband, who was a tractor driver for one of the village landlords, stood quietly in a corner.

At 30-years-old, with 10-year-old twins, Saraswati had been in a self-help group in her village for seven years. But at the time of the story she was about to tell, when she was 23, there were no women's self-help groups in Pamtrampalli.

From a young age she was used to life at the bottom of the ladder. As a Dalit at school, she had been forced to sit apart from upper-caste kids. One of five children, she finished grade five and had learned to read and write, thanks to a teacher that supported her and told her mother she was a good student.

Her own father had been a drunk, and she described how seven years before she had been appalled at the chaos in the village caused by alcohol. The last thing she wanted in her own house, or those of her friends, was an alcoholic man. Prohibition was the law, but an illegal brewer was coming to the village and selling strong bootleg liquor to their husbands, including hers.

"Women were getting beaten and were constantly crying," she said. "So I went to the bootlegger and told him to sell elsewhere." The men in the village, including her own husband, who from his corner in the courtyard didn't flinch as she told her tale, objected.

The next day she gathered her friends together, and, as their pre-school children gleefully watched, they grabbed the liquor from their huts and openly poured it on the ground with all the defiance of Katharine Hepburn facing Humphrey Bogart in *The African Queen*.

"The brewer used filthy language when he saw what we were doing," she said, "so I grabbed him by the collar and told him to get out, and fast."

He threatened to set her house on fire. "My husband," she said, "was afraid and refused to talk to me for a week." Around her, she added, she had heard the cries of her women friends who were being beaten by irate husbands that didn't want their supply of alcohol to be cut.

As she told her story, with all the drama of a true storyteller, her women friends sitting with her nodded in sympathy and excitement because some of them had gone through this experience with her.

She took a deep breath and told me how she had come up with a plan. She went to the nearby town of Chittoor and spoke to her cousin who was in the police force. He set a trap and arrested the bootlegger. There was going to be a court case and the women, along with Saraswati, were gearing up to testify against him.

Then, everything changed when the high-caste wife of the bootlegger came to Pamtrampalli and in desperation asked Saraswati and her women friends not to go after her husband. The woman told them that she would be ruined along with him and promised that her husband would never darken the road to their village again.

So, in their version of what I would come to see as "thatch hut justice," Saraswati and her friends — this time in sympathy with another woman in trouble, even if she were a high-caste woman — went along with it.

Dalit Leader Saraswati succeeded in pushing the village bootlegger out of her community.

At the time, Pamtrampalli was an interior Dalit village with no women's groups at all. A government community organizer heard about the trouble in the village and proposed that the women who had formed the anti-bootleg campaign become a group. So in 1995, with Saraswati as leader, a group under DWCRA was set up.

When the group began, the women first saved a small amount of rupees each month and built up a bank account. Once they had demonstrated they could save, the DWCRA program gave them a small grant out of which they could take loans for small enterprises.

In the state of Andhra Pradesh, in 2001, 5.5 million women in thrift and credit groups, each composed of about 15 women, had saved about 10 billion rupees, or about $300 million Canadian. By the end of 2009, the amount of women had expanded to 10 million in over 900,000 state-sponsored self-help groups.

The groups were formed in order to improve the members' economic situation, but a strong sense of community was always present, as Saraswati's story so clearly illustrated.

Dalit Indian village women have seen dowry deaths, rape, prostitution, bonded labour, and their children bullied at school, like Saraswati was. Quite frequently they face hunger. This is totally apart from catastrophic floods, earthquakes, and tsunamis, all of which took place in some part of India when I was there.

Hinduism stresses karma and enduring your assigned place in life, but for the past 25 years in various parts of India, notably in the state of Andhra Pradesh where I was travelling, low-caste, poor women have been assembling to save and take loans and rise above their lot. Among the women a sense of community also propelled them to improve life in their villages.

In Pamtrampalli, all the self-help groups were gathering once a month in order to talk about how they could deal with misfortunes in the village. Out of that process a community hall was built, and the women stopped behaving simply as chattel born only to be unloaded in marriage; they were becoming entrepreneurs and leaders while remaining within traditional three-generation households.

The women, for example, ganged up on the landlords and won double the daily wages they had received for labouring in the fields. Family planning, increased adult literacy, and the desire of the women to get into politics were also on the rise. In a nearby village, two women had recently won village council seats.

Though a white western journalist coming from such a different culture, the women in the villages made me feel as though I were a part of some bigger project that we were all in together. Most importantly, they made me feel like one of them. It was a privilege to be among them, watching, laughing, and sharing.

My first experience in Pamtrampalli made me recognize that as a white lady with a notebook and a camera, and an un-Indian way of dressing and walking, I would be an event in any village. The appearance of a woman alone, especially moving around after dark, without the protection of a husband, was unusual.

On one trip, the driver of the car I had hired asked the male community organizer accompanying me this: "What kind of a husband does Sheila have that he lets her move around all by herself?"

The answer, I had to say, was that I had no husband. In another village I explained to a totally different group of women that even in the West, husbands would revolt if a wife set out to go away for six months as I was doing. I'm here, I told them, spending time with you, because I live on my own. At which point they gathered around to laugh and joke and pat me on the back saying what a good deal I had being a free woman and able to travel and meet new people.

With no television or movie theatre, and everyone already knowing everyone's business, when I arrived in a new village I was the day's visiting soap opera with all eyes glued to me.

Vithal Rajan emphasized that in villages it was important not to become a story. "You're there to *get* a story, not to *be* one," he said, "which means you're an ordinary person, married with a religion, not divorced and a doubter, for example." This was counsel that I ignored when I was in small groups of women who felt like friends.

When I explained what my life was really like back in Canada it brought me closer to the women. I saw them enthusiastically imagining another way of being. It reflected their enormous capacity to jump in and become full-fledged players in India doing untraditional and different things in their own society. Although I was there to ask questions, I was never just the journalist from a foreign country. We related to one another as women from a common clan.

2
HUT BUILDING FOR SINGLE MOMS

Listening to Dalit and Tribal people tell stories about their struggles, I spent the next few weeks in the same district trekking around the countryside mostly with community organizers from the Andhra Pradesh government's District Poverty Initiatives Program (DPIP). Funded by the World Bank, DPIP was designed help the poorest of the poor in six districts of Andhra Pradesh and worked primarily with women in self-help groups that were taking loans and initiating small businesses.

One day, in the village of Pedha Thayyur, I was standing on land that Dalits living there thought belonged to them. In 1973 they received a certificate from the government saying they owned it. This was followed by challenges from a landlord who had lost in the courts but who wouldn't give it up.

When the Dalits sowed crops on this land, the local landlord who claimed the land was his tore them out. I watched as this landlord with a scowl on his face walked along the road next to this land. "It is very difficult for Dalits here," said an organizer from a group that monitored such problems. "There is nobody here to protect them."

Later in the village of Jakkidona Adi Andhrawada, I heard other stories concerning landlords. In this hamlet of 16 families, one third owned one or two acres of forest where they could harvest certain nuts and fruit and get firewood. But in order to feed their families, they had to work as day labourers for landlords with the men making a little more than a dollar a day and the women making half that.

"If you're a Dalit coolie like me," said a father of three, "and you're on your knees in the field, when the landlord shows up, you better stand up quickly, or risk getting beat up. And if you should stay home from work to look after a sick child, like I did once, watch out for the landlord showing up with a stick.

"Some of our families have leased lands from the landlords, and we have to give them 50 percent of the crop," he said. "But when other caste people lease, they get 75 percent of the crop, and only 25 percent goes to the landlord."

Down the road the next night, I was under a tamarind tree in the village of Gantavaripalli, situated on the edge of a landlord's sugar cane field talking to a group of Tribal people. They worked as agricultural labourers sowing and cutting cane as well as running machinery that extracted sap from the stalks. One of them strung up a single light bulb to a tree with a wire going back to a hut so that I could take notes.

"Untouchability," said one of the men, referring to the problems of their neighbours in the next village, "is a real problem. We work alongside people in Dalit villages, and we see how difficult it can be for them."

The people in these two villages tried to help one another whenever they could. For example, when the Dalit villagers heard their neighbours in the nearby Tribal village had no space for kitchen gardens to grow vegetables with seed provided by DPIP, they set aside a patch for them.

Within the villages too, people went out of their way to help those facing special difficulties.

In Equvakannikapuram Tribal village, I arrived at dusk to see a throng of barefoot villagers busy building thatch huts for two homeless single mothers whose husbands had left them.

I was reminded of stories from colonial times in Canada where settlers banded together for barn-building to help a farmer whose barn had burnt down.

"The women had been going from one village to another selling baskets," explained one of the men as he heaved some palm branches up to the roof. The local landlord, in an act of generosity that seemed rare, donated a small parcel of land, and the villagers found the building materials and donated their labour.

In all these villages women were active in self-help groups. "In the past, we used to feel confined to our homes," said one woman who observed that at first their husbands tried to prevent them from leaving the house to organize meetings and confer with groups in other villages.

In more than one village, several men told me that they had been alcoholics who often beat their wives. Now, many exhibited barely concealed admiration for their women who were mobilizing to get loans for micro-enterprises and attacking village social problems.

"Clearly the women are learning that they have talent, wisdom, and maybe even power," observed a community coordinator in the area who was finishing up a Ph.D. in anthropology. "There is no mental poverty in these villages."

Once highly critical, some men were now working with their wives in small businesses like carpentry and construction, but also fighting problems like child labour and trying to create collectives of various kinds; and, of course, hoping that one day they'd have some land that would allow them to really prosper.

At night, in between visits to villages, I returned to a town and stayed overnight with Nirmala, a woman of 25 with a university degree who was a community coordinator for DPIP. She took me around and translated to English from Telugu, one of India's 23 officially recognized languages.

In a pastel-painted, villa-like place with an internal courtyard filled with plants, she lived in a tiny two-room abode on a second floor reached by an outdoor winding staircase. One room was crammed with files documenting the activities of all the self-help groups she monitored. In the second room she had a sink and no furniture and we slept on the floor on mats.

At the foot of the steep winding staircase, a toilet and a shower served three or four other tenants of the villa. In a small, smoky, stone room, a steel tub of water warming over a wood fire provided the hot water available once a day to a short lineup of people. My daily hot shower consisted of dipping a plastic jug into the tub and pouring two or three jugs of water over myself, being careful not to waste a drop.

Early in the morning I would sometimes accompany a girl from the downstairs room to the town pump to carry several heavy pails back and forth to the compound for the day's supply of water. Large numbers of women gathered at the town pump, and as I walked along children would call out "auntie" to me, the usual name for an adult woman that isn't their mother.

3
SAVING GIRLS FROM "GOD'S CROP"

It was now the day before Christmas, and I was standing under the blazing sun in a cotton field outside the village of Thogapur. A 27-year-old agricultural school graduate was supervising intricate work on cotton seed plants alongside a landless, illiterate Dalit woman in a bright green sari with a long thick braid down her back. I had heard about these fearless cotton-seed growers who weren't going to be pushed around by anyone, and decided I wanted to meet them.

Anjilamma Sangamkoti was one of nine women farmers from Dalit, and so-called backward castes, who had formed a thriving cotton-seed collective that everyone was talking about. In conversation with this vivacious 35-year-old farmer, I learned that she had been a destitute homeless woman whose husband had deserted her. "Now," she said, "because I was able to lease some land for this cotton seed project, I have enough money to buy a house of my own."

For 10 years cotton landlords around the village had been using superstitions to justify hiring child labour at 10 rupees (30 cents Canadian) a

Homeless Anjilamma joined a cotton seed collective that enabled her to make enough money to buy a house.

day. To shut out local adult women who could demand higher wages, the cotton landlords declared cotton-seed cultivation "God's crop" and proclaimed that pests would ravage cotton tended by women who had already entered puberty.

At first the women felt powerless to do anything about it. With only one or two acres of difficult-to-cultivate land of their own, they too were working for poverty wages in the cotton fields of landlords who paid when they felt like it, with the result that the women were turning to ruthless loan sharks in order to feed their children.

But word of this reached a federation of women's self-help groups in 35 villages in the area, and in 1998 the federation discovered that 800 girls were involved in child labour in the municipality. It mobilized to get the girls either back to school or enrolled in two "bridge school" programs designed to bring them up to the grade-seven level so that they could move into regular high schools.

But, in Thogapur, landlords were still hiring child labour. To combat it, the women's federation encouraged women from the self-help groups in the village to come forward for the 2000–01 season to do cotton seed cultivation on their own small plots of land in a model way.

The president of the federation was Eshwwamma Myathari, a 40-year-old woman from Thogapur on the executive committee of her village organization. A busy homemaker with three sons and a daughter, she rose to the challenge, and was now one of the village cotton seed farmers.

No child labour was their first rule. The second was to use local botanical insect repellents like neem seed. To help them work ecologically, they followed guidelines set by Integrated Pest Management, a program that worked in five Andhra Pradesh districts with 639 farmers in 22 villages, one of them Thogapur.

Their methods paid off. Using botanical products that they could get for free was more cost-effective than spending hard-earned cash on chemicals. All of them said they were showing profits. In addition, they were providing employment to 50 women from the village.

Despite all the efforts of the women, child labour was still thriving in their area. On our way back to the village from the fields, I was shocked to see 20 skinny child labourers, most of them girls, using bare hands as they worked under the direction of a hefty man with a huge heap of chemical fertilizer. Some looked no more than six years old.

A woman from the cotton seed collective stood next to me and listed the illnesses that child labourers exposed to chemicals could face. "Headaches, stomach aches and vomiting, skin diseases, burning sensations in the eyes — sometimes even death — not to mention the denial of the opportunity to attend school."

According to the 2001 census, there were over a million child labourers in Andhra Pradesh and 65 million across India. Despite efforts to stamp it out, as late as 2006, UNICEF reported that Andhra Pradesh cotton plantations were employing 200,000 children, most of them girls.

The next night, in the village of Chandravanka, I had my Christmas dinner at the Bala Karmika Vidya Vikasa Kendram "bridge" school, which housed 60 girls who had dropped out of school to become child labourers but were now at this catch-up school. I sat under a tree with them and ate slippery vegetarian chili with my fingers from a tin plate. Because they were all Hindus, no one I ate dinner with that night knew this was a special night for me.

I didn't miss the huge Christmas turkey with all the trimmings back in snowy Canada. Here in India, in the fragrant countryside, I experienced the Christmas message in the caring attitude of the women cotton growers, and in the dancing, hopeful eyes of these little girls who were former child labourers.

On duty at the school that night was 19-year-old Buggamma Urdigalla who started working at the school two years before, after completing grade 12 and a concentrated teacher training course. Along with six other teachers who lived at the school, Buggamma instilled into the children the value of education and its potential to lift them out of poverty. "We keep track of what happens to these children after they leave this school and none of them is returning to child labour," she said proudly. Three hundred had gone through the program.

The determination of rural women who have been exploited and ignored for centuries was the most impressive thing I witnessed in Thogapur and other villages.

The women, however, were not doing this alone. Supporting them were people like Buggamma, fresh out of college in disciplines ranging from social work to engineering. They were committed to helping rejected Dalits and "backward castes," as well as Tribal groups burst out of poverty.

In the countryside, the bright-eyed young community coordinators, like Nirmala from DPIP who took me around, were winning the confidence of the poorest grassroots women and, slowly, the rural men who had never had any confidence in the government.

Started in 1998 by the Andhra Pradesh government's Society for the Elimination of Rural Poverty, the DPIP program was designed to lift 3 million people out of destitution in villages across six of the state's poorest districts. Empowerment of women was seen as the most effective way to accomplish this.

My Christmas night ended with one of the former girl child labourers showing me one of the thatch hut classrooms where she would be studying the next day. There were no desks or chairs but the blackboard was covered in Telugu words. The little girl took a piece of chalk, wrote her name, and then took my hand and escorted me back to Buggamma outside.

4
VILLAGE WOMEN PICK UP THEIR PENS

It was week four of my swing through poor villages in the Chittoor District of Andhra Pradesh and now I was en route by car to the temple city of Tirupati to interview 20 Dalit village women who were learning to be journalists by publishing a quarterly social issue newspaper.

The official from the government's flagship anti-poverty agency who was taking me there explained that they were having a day-long training session. "You know," he said, about 20 minutes before we arrived, "we would really like it if you could give the journalists a workshop." I tried not to show any surprise, when he then added, "for about three hours."

Women from so many villages had given me hours of their precious time. Officials had transported me around, given me free nights in state guest-houses, and now it was my turn to do something for them. The village women I had come to identify with had always encouraged me to share and be one of them. I could not fall back upon playing the detached Western observer/journalist that soaks up information and disappears. I would have to figure out a way to do what he asked.

Teaching journalism at Concordia University in Montreal for years, I had conducted hundreds of workshops for students with 13 years of education behind them, but this would be completely different terrain.

In comparison to my Canadian students back home, what could I expect from these Indian village journalists?

The official explained to me that the women I would be meeting had, at most, finished grade six and had no family history of education, let alone literacy. Most, he said, worked nine hours a day as agricultural labourers in the fields in addition to taking care of families. They spoke and wrote only Telugu, and I would have to communicate with them through a translator.

What could I talk about with these women? All the worst clichés associated with a Western middle class woman that had just arrived in a developing country flashed up at me. I felt like an actress forced to go on stage with no lines at all.

When I arrived I sat down with the supervisor of the group — Kiran Kumari, a journalist, women's community activist, and specialist in Telugu literature who served on the DPIP Chittoor executive board. A child bride herself, Kiran had gone to university after she'd had a child at the age of 16, and she had an understanding of the kinds of issues the journalists had experienced and wanted to write about.

Together we looked quickly through two issues of the journal they were publishing called *Navodayam*, meaning new sun rising. There were success stories about women's self-help groups and how they built a road, constructed a school, and created a fair price shop, for example. Home health care remedies and special diets for people with certain illnesses were featured, but there was also a song about a widow lured into bed by the town potter and then dropped when she became pregnant. Other stories touched upon aspects of child labour, dowry harassment, abusive alcoholic husbands, equal wages, and the evil effects of superstitions. The span of issues showed a high-level of understanding about their communities of which I had not seen among my students back home.

With a very slim game plan, I went into a room where 20 women in colourful saris, ranging in age from about 19 to 45, wore welcoming smiles but they were there to improve their skills and did not want to waste their time. I went around the room and asked each woman to talk about a significant situation she had observed that week in the villages she was responsible for covering.

I soon recognized that these women were journalistic naturals. What could I talk about with them? Well, subjects like landlessness, malnutrition, bonded labour, child marriage, and more. My head swirled with their grasp of these questions and the detail they were able to provide.

One of the most affecting stories a woman told the workshop was about a 34-year-old woman with four children whose father remarried after her mother had died. "Later, when her father died, the daughter performed certain death ceremonies that are supposed to be done by a man," said the woman telling the tale.

"The villagers told her to go to the temple and shave her head, and when she tried to return to the village, they wouldn't allow her in. Her father had in his will left his daughter some land, but the stepmother said it was hers. She has gone to the police," the storyteller told a hushed room of colleagues who were nodding as though they had already heard a story like this before. "But police told her to go away." She paused for a moment, and then, with bitterness, said: "The curse of being a woman."

From the age of consciousness, these women had absorbed stories of death and drama worthy of a Rohinton Mistry novel. Wise and knowing, they understood the intricate workings of the most poignant aspects of their communities.

It was the beginning of my own questioning about the nature of formal education, including my own, which included an M.A. in sociology that in the light of what I was learning from women in India seemed of no consequence. Life experience, I realized, had been a great educator. Unlike my students back in Montreal who came mostly from privileged and sheltered backgrounds, these women revealed sharp sociological, political, and economic knowledge about their surroundings. In addition, thanks to self-help women's groups, where they could discuss and analyze in freedom, they had developed the kind of compassion and humour combined with outrage that made for the best kind of journalism. What a treasure-trove of investigative social issue stories they were following! And how well they could tell a story!

In the workshop we discussed how to protect vulnerable interviewees, find human-interest material — clearly not a problem — and locate background research material at NGOs and government organizations.

We also talked about using fiction — the short story, for example — as a way of exploring a volatile issue without naming anyone.

I had just finished reading about the shattering experiences of a landless man and his wife in the celebrated novel *Nectar in a Sieve* by Kamala Markandaya. Written in the 1950s, it was the first Indian novel to so beautifully illustrate the plight of the poorest in villages. Many of the stories the women in the workshop were telling lent themselves to fictional treatment and I encouraged them to experiment.

While I listened to them I furiously took notes. This "workshop" was proving to be a terrific way for me to get material, but I felt there was very little I could teach them. In fact, they had a lot to teach me, not only about village life, but also about the value of immersion in a community. This was something I resolved to encourage in my journalism students back home.

Finally, as a last assignment I asked the women to go into two groups, with each reporting back on a major story they thought should be explored.

The result? A consensus among all the women that they should comb the villages in each of the municipalities they were covering and gather material on the issue of bonded labour, an illegal but widespread practice. One of the journalists reported that out of 75 families in her village, four had a member in bondage. She told the following story.

A poor man borrowed 10,000 rupees from a landlord for a daughter's marriage, but found he was unable to pay back the loan from crop profits. To pay the debt, the man had to give his son as a labourer to the landlord, who then announced that because he was feeding and clothing the son, the work on the land wouldn't cover the money owed. Later a grandson was born, and when the boy was five, the landlord demanded he take the child in order to cover the outstanding debt. The father of the child wanted to send the boy to school, but the landlord took the son by force and the child found himself in perpetual bondage.

There was great excitement around the prospect of working on this issue and everyone agreed that they should not only document the numbers of bonded labourers, but also return with one strong human interest story that would illustrate the nature of the problem. "After that," said one of the women, "we need to have a team meeting to decide what to highlight."

I felt humbled in the face of the passion and commitment written on the faces of these women and I ended up by telling them that the best investigative journalist from the *New York Times* would have been impressed. They had never heard of the *New York Times*, but they got the message.

Village women's meetings often started and ended with a song and I was asked to close the workshop by singing. Sing a song! How could I do that? I don't know many songs and a hymn or a Christmas carol didn't seem right. But carried along by the euphoria of the moment I announced: "Okay, this song is for all of those of you who believe in love marriages." The issue of arranged marriages versus love marriages where the woman could choose her own husband had been a hot topic.

Amazed at myself, I launched into "Let Me Call You Sweetheart." When they shouted, "more, more, and more" in Telugu I countered with: "This is for all of you that have to put up a smile in spite of terrible problems," and I tucked into the old First World War song, "Pack up your Troubles in Your Old Kit Bag and Smile, Smile, Smile."

Before I left, a young woman called Manjula, who later became the editor of the paper, came up and asked me to spend the weekend with her family in her village. I said yes, even though there would be no translator.

The government official later dropped me off at a village of thatch and mud huts, and this became my introduction to sleeping overnight in a village.

When I arrived, Manjula, who usually worked all day in the fields, introduced me to her husband, a truck driver, and her two children, a boy and a girl aged six and seven, both attending an English school. Manjula, who knew only a few words of English, said with a flourish: "Meet family," and she patted the head of her daughter, "and planning," she smiled, taking the hand of her son. She raised two fingers. This was her way of saying very proudly that this household would remain a two-child family.

Research has shown that educating women in developing countries leads to smaller families, but expansion of economic possibilities through participation in these self-help groups is also a factor.

Manjula lived in a two-room hut and did her cooking outside over a wood fire. Eager to make sure I liked the food, she had the government official provide her with some plain chicken, which was expensive for villagers, and some salad, which I ate sitting on the floor with the family, Indian-style.

That night I sat on the ground outside at a meeting of her women's self-help group where she acted as the secretary. I also sat in on a men's self-help group meeting.

Wanting me to be as comfortable as possible, she housed me at the home of her aunt who had a bed off the floor. There was no mattress, just a sheet over some tin coils. I had a room to myself, but in the next room the aunt and her family spent the night on mats on the floor.

I had brought with me a bottle of mineral water, and I had a coconut with a hole in it that Manjula's son gave me in case I got hungry in the middle of the night and wanted a coconut drink. And of course I had my flashlight in case of a visit to the bushes along with my lace-up shoes as a protection from snakes. In the morning I was greeted by four or five young women who trekked me through the fields on a path to the great village outhouse — meaning the open fields. After a while I told them I was okay on my own.

In 2006, during my third trip to India, I returned to spend time in a different village with another group of rural women journalists producing a monthly paper called *Snehah*, meaning friendship, under the same Andhra Pradesh government anti-poverty organization, by then expanded and called Indira Kranthi Patham (IKP).

By this time seven social issue community papers had been launched so that grassroots women could learn how to be journalists. Two of them — *Navodayam* and *Snehah* — had become monthlies producing first-rate stories.

Snehah, with 17 reporters, operated closer to the capital city of Hyderabad. In Ranga Reddy district we met in Chilkoor village in a large room where we sat on the floor. In the back stood piles of tin cots that the women used if they stayed over.

The women were mostly in their 20s, and like the women of *Navodayam*, had had only six years of schooling. They'd produced

15 issues of *Snehah* so far in Telugu. Their pay was 750 rupees ($19 Canadian) monthly plus 200 rupees to cover travel, for 950 rupees.

To research and produce their stories they didn't have to work every day and the pay was equal to working in a field for a month for 25 rupees (62 cents Canadian) a day, which was what they said they earned in the fields as day workers, or coolies, as they called themselves.

Most were landless and had been married by the age of 15 and now had four or five children, but they were all against child marriage. Under the law, 18 was the legal age of marriage for girls, but the law was flouted everywhere.

The village women who work on a rural newspaper produced under an Andhra Pradesh government anti-poverty program have won prizes for their journalism.

All the reporters had arrived with stories written in Telugu by hand on paper. Typewriters or computers were unavailable, though their supervisor, a man who worked for years as a sub-editor for Telugu papers, said that would come. He wanted to create a syndicated rural

wire service in the Ranga Reddy area with stories produced by journalists from *Snehah*.

I went around the room and asked the women to talk about the stories they had written and the issues in their villages where they also operated as activists and community grassroots workers.

Four women talked about child marriages being nipped in the bud,
and each one said she would write about these cases for the next issue of
Snehah. They explained that ministers, priests, and imams in the villages
weren't stopping child marriages, and that the state wasn't demanding
proof of age for marriage.

One woman said she heard about a child being forced into marriage
in her village of Ebbanur. To help the girl she gathered some of the village youths together in a meeting, and collectively they stopped the marriage. "After that," she said, "it was decided that any young people getting
married had to register with this village youth group."

Another woman said that a 12-year-old girl went to one of the self-
help groups in her village to report that against her wishes her parents
wanted her to marry. "She had seen a video against child marriage," said
the woman referring to a video that I later discovered had been produced by the women from *Navodayam*. "That's why she had the courage
to complain." The SHG, she reported, went to the parents and stopped
the marriage.

A woman from the village of Medapally talked about a family that
was starving because the husband was an alcoholic and worked only
occasionally as a coolie. The mother, she said, sent the children, aged six
and eight, to beg in the village. So the journalist went out and found the
mother a job as maid, and then took the children to school.

Another reporter told a story about some Tribal children living in
a *tanda*, meaning a habitation outside the village, who were working
as coolies in the fields. Some of the women in a self-help group got
together and took the children who were around 10 years old to a hostel
and school in a nearby village with the agreement of their parents.

The women I met all had high hopes for their children.

On my way back to Hyderabad, one of the women joined us in the government car. She had three children that were teenagers and she wanted

them to go to university. She herself had only a grade one education, but she had managed to upgrade her skills and had been given money by an uncle to go to the Open University where she had completed one year.

But then her aunt made her uncle stop giving her further money and she had to quit. "My dreams are now for my children," she said , but I told her that she had a right to follow her dream as well.

Back in Hyderabad I discovered that the women journalists from *Navodayam* that I had met in 2002 had become famous.

An executive with Indira Kranthi Patham had taken the *Navodayam* journalists to join journalism students in a workshop at a university. Prizes were given out at the end of the course to the students that produced the best stories. The village journalists won! Later, *Navodayam* won a coveted best rural women journalists award given by a feature writing wire service in the state.

Emboldened by success, the *Navodayam* journalists then produced an investigative story about government officials with their hands in the till. "After that was published, the shit really hit the fan!" the executive told me. "A lot of the government people were really mad!"

But the courage and capacity of these village journalists had paid off, and four of the 20 I met had found mainstream journalism jobs working at Telugu language papers. Given half a chance, and with some support, the Dalit women were eager to persevere and take risks in the manner of dedicated investigative journalists.

By 2008, 10 village women were working full time as reporters for *Navodayam*, making a very respectable salary of 3,000 rupees a month and a travel allowance per month of 1,500 rupees. The circulation of the paper had expanded to reach 20,000 self-help groups in the area and about a quarter of a million women.

I had thought that the purpose of the government's anti-poverty Indira Kranthi Patham program, funded by the World Bank, was to help women not only escape abject poverty, but also to move into the middle class by breaking into long-term, better paying jobs. However, sources at Indira Kranthi Patham admitted that the government was not willing to allow the paper to be managed and owned by the women, but that IKP would continue to control it. Nor was IKP willing to create a field placement program tied to established papers so that more of these talented individuals willing to expose corruption could propel themselves into the mainstream.

The message I picked up — and I witnessed it later in connection with other endeavours — was that there was only so much support for empowerment of bottom-caste women from higher-caste men in power. In India, caste, class, and gender restrictions were loosening, but not that fast.

Another example of this can be seen in the evolution of the community radio station set up in the late 1990s at the Deccan Development Society NGO which works predominantly with poor Dalit women farmers in the Medak district. With money and equipment from UNESCO, the station's programs were produced by Narsamma, a former child labourer educated at the NGO's "green school" that incorporated regular academic work with training for rural living.

Coached by DDS director, P.V. Satheesh, who had broadcast experience, Narsamma and a small team under his aegis made tapes containing stories on agricultural issues and distributed them weekly to the Dalit self-help groups. For years Narsamma, who was known for her persistence and nicknamed "General," pressured the government for a licence. Finally in 2008, the government gave in and awarded the station a licence to broadcast in the Medak district.

But the station remains under the thumb of the donor-funded Deccan Development Society. Real empowerment for "General" Narsamma — and a co-producer also called Narsamma — would be full-time jobs with regular salaries covering rural issues for a mainstream radio station away from the net of a development organization. The DDS Sangham Radio station, as it is called, could keep on broadcasting in the area, and Satheesh could continue to train Dalit women reporters so that they could eventually jump into mainstream journalism.

However, as I saw over the years I was in India, once they are on a roll, Dalit women go into overdrive to learn and to break down barriers. The village print journalists I met were mastering the basics of journalism and learning how to write about important rural issues. In addition, they had become members of the India's Network of Women in Media which is exposing them to top women journalists from across the country and the possibility of being hired by established publications. No one, I believe, will be able to stop these Dalit dynamos. We will be hearing from them in the future.

5
MAKING THE DESERTS BLOOM

I was now in Gangwar, a small village of mud and thatch huts, sitting with village seedkeeper Anjamma on the floor in her open-air verandah facing a small courtyard where bullocks, cows, and a goat with two kids, quietly shuffled about. The sun was shining and the air smelled fresh and fragrant. Spread around Anjamma, in several small clay pots, were a sampling of her treasured seeds. She dipped her fingers into a pot containing a kind of chickpea called red gram and let some of the seeds drip through her fingers.

"I save the seeds in special baskets with a combination of straw, wood ash, neem seed, dung, and vitax leaf with a special layer of clay on top," she said, and glanced behind her to a large stack of them. "Of course, I dry the seed first.

"This seed bank which contains 54 varieties of traditional seeds will allow everyone in our sangham to continue to have the best kind of food." Sangham is a Sanskrit word meaning coming together.

Anjamma, 45 and a Dalit Christian, was a member of a sangham, or self-help group, of about 35 Dalit women. Of those women, 15 owned land like her and another 20 were landless. Her 10 acres of land overflowed with a Garden of Eden of millets, pulses, leafy greens, and oil-yielding plants that she and her husband cultivated.

She was the first woman farmer I met in a village sangham under the Deccan Development Society composed of 5,000 Dalit women spread over 70 villages in the Medak district of Andhra Pradesh.

Thanks to Vithal Rajan, the society had taken off over 20 years before. Along with a group of friends, he helped poverty-stricken women rise above starvation on scrub land in Andhra Pradesh's drought-ridden Deccan plateau that was yielding only scanty crops.

Vithal inspired the women to start village sanghams. "At that time," he pointed out, "the men had left the land for the cities and the women were practically starving."

In the villages he sat around with the women and talked. With his encouragement, the women began to save from their meagre earnings so they could take loans from their own money and avoid moneylenders.

"We also helped them to abandon the use of hybrid seeds and chemical fertilizers and pesticides that were drying up their barren land," he said.

Through the use of chemicals, the famous Green Revolution had dramatically increased yields in many parts of India. But it devastated dryland areas like the Deccan Plateau spread across four states where the land was poor and crops depended upon on erratic monsoon rains. Starting in 1997 in several regions, notably in Andhra Pradesh, thousands of Indian farmers who had borrowed to buy hybrid seeds and whose crops had failed were committing suicide by ingesting pesticides.

"Through loan programs set up by DDS with donor money," said Vithal, "the husbands in the villages were hired by the women to develop the land to do sustainable agriculture and families started to work together.

"The real leadership, however, came from the women themselves," said Vithal, who by 2006 was combining development work with capturing Indian village life in a series of published books of fiction.

"A long time ago I asked one of the DDS Dalit women why they hadn't taken action a long time before. I said I couldn't see what guys like me really contributed since all the good ideas were theirs. The woman said: 'When 10 of us are together, God is with us.' This," said Vithal, "is almost a traditional saying. So what we did at DDS was contribute a safe space where they could meet."

"Come," Anjamma said. "Let me show you my land."

Salome Yesudas, a nutritionist with DDS who became a friend, served as my trusty translator for Anjamma and other village women at DDS who spoke only Telugu.

As we walked through the village of mud and thatch huts, Anjamma mentioned her two married daughters who farmed land with their husbands 30 kilometres away in other villages, but in her fields her two sons and their wives worked alongside Anjamma and her husband. In her sparkling clean four-room hut with virtually no furniture, but adorned with painted Christian symbols, all eight, including two grandchildren, lived together.

We wove our way through her fields patched with millet, lentil, chickpea, and oil seed crops, all mixed in a way that allowed the land to thrive. Like other members of her sangham, she fertilized with a combination of dung and green manure. Pests were kept under control through intercropping and pest repellent concoctions made out of neem leaves. She pulled water from the village pump, had electricity, and was considered among the most prosperous in the village.

But it was not always thus. "I got married at the age of 10," she said, "with a sickle, a baby goat, and one sari. My husband was a bonded labourer. We were the poorest family in the village."

At first she worked as a coolie on other people's land, but by the time she was 18 she was a member of the village sangham and eager to provide more for her growing family.

Through her sangham thrift and credit program she first took loans for food and clothes. Then, with a knack for breeding and a loan to buy goats, she turned the kid that she brought to the marriage into 20 goats that she sold. Through DDS programs and her own savings, she leased land. Finally, by watching every rupee, she had saved enough to buy land and build a house. She fed her family completely from the fruits of the land and was able to sell red and green gram on the market.

As I looked over her personal Garden of Eden, I inadvertently broke the spell by asking what I thought was an ordinary question. "What about your children, Anjamma, did you send them to school?" I knew that she herself could write only her name, and was non-literate.

She drew herself up tall, and without an ounce of apology said: "No, I did not send my children to school." Glancing over the land that she had worked so hard to make fruitful, she looked up to the sky, and with a passion I will not forget, said: "The earth goddess teaches us more than anyone ... we worked on the land together and learned."

Anjamma looked me in the eye, paused, and went on. "This was more important than what children these days learn in school," she added, something that I had already thought about when I met the village women journalists only a few weeks before.

Still new to India, I was recognizing the persistence of my urban Western-oriented perspective where diplomas and learning from books was the gauge of knowledge. I was beginning to love India, its land and its bursting exuberance, but my own culture kept intruding no matter how hard I tried to climb into the skins of others.

Under the careful guidance of Salome I got to know more extraordinary DDS women. In Humnapur village I met Lakshmi Begari, 35 and a famous multi-crop farmer and seedkeeper who distinguished herself as a land manager and supervisor of a 72-village seed bank program that was safeguarding traditional seeds.

But she was known far beyond her small Indian village. In April 2001, she had made newspaper headlines in Britain during a world conference on global agriculture when she had told farmers and researchers from all over the world about the harm she had seen hybrid and genetically modified seeds cause in her own village to farmers' health, to cattle, and to soil.

Lakshmi started life at the bottom of the heap, first as a child labourer who never went to school, and then as a child bride of barely 14, forced against her will to marry her mother's cousin who abandoned her six years later. She learned how to farm the traditional way from her grandmother.

On her own family farm of five acres, which expanded when Lakshmi and her mother acquired land through a land purchase program, she was growing 82 crop varieties a year — more than any other farmer in DDS.

She and her family, however, had had to learn the hard way that the traditional farming methods were best.

"In the 1980s, through government agricultural officers, multinational companies bribed us with seeds," she told 500 farmers from around the world at the conference. "They gave us hybrid seeds for single cash crop plantings along with a package of fertilizers and pesticides."

The yields, on the surface, looked good, but it cost the farmers more because every year they had to buy seeds from the company in addition to the required fertilizers and pesticides. "We didn't know that we wouldn't be able to take the seeds from the hybrids, and that from then on, we'd be stuck buying from the companies," she said.

Using traditional methods, the seeds, fertilizers, and pest repellents were free and came straight from the land. The diverse crops they grew fed the family, and any excess was sold at the market. "But with the single-crop hybrids, we found that all our food security from the land was gone, and we were forced to buy food, seeds, and fertilizers."

Where in the past the women controlled what happened to the harvest, with the cash crops, the men were in charge. Money from the harvest often went for drinking or gambling rather than to maintain the family, she commented.

Just when the women were questioning the worth of these highly touted cash crops, a farmer with wasteland rejuvenation experience blew into the village from the Deccan Development Society. A woman's sangham of 22 members sprung up in Lakshmi's village of Humnapur under her mother's leadership. A thrift and credit program that allowed members to borrow money at no interest got them started.

Lakshmi succeeded her mother as a leader in the mid 1990s when the DDS sanghams decided to create seed banks in their villages. For three years she was in charge of the seed bank in her village that built up more than 80 varieties of seed. "The village women insisted I keep the seedbank at my home because no men lived with us. Some of our members were afraid their husbands might steal the seeds and sell them in order to buy liquor," she explained.

Parallel to her work as a farmer and seedkeeper, Lakshmi had also learned how to make videos along with eight other women who were trained by DDS director P.V. Satheesh, who was also a filmmaker.

Because she became a leader in her community with something to say, she was invited to Canada, Cambodia, and London for various conferences that allowed her to show her videos about the accomplishments of Indian women doing organic agriculture. In the midst of all this she made sure her daughter was in school and doing well. Her daughter of 14 was in grade nine when I first visited. Four years later, in 2006, she was starting to work on a B.Sc. degree.

Raised as a child labourer and forced to marry at the age of 12, Anusuyamma is another example of a woman with no formal education whose hidden talents suddenly blossomed as a result of joining a DDS woman's village sangham.

Now a single Dalit woman in her late 30s who adopted a niece and put her through junior college, Anusuyamma supervises hundreds of acres of forestry plantations in 28 villages.

A self-learner who became literate by taking night classes, Anusuyamma's on-the-job training in forestry began when her sangham asked for a volunteer to create a tree nursery for their village.

A few years later, when 35 village sanghams held a meeting to discuss whether they wanted to create tree plantation collectives on government-owned wasteland areas, Anusuyamma was the most ardent advocate. In return for improving the 50 to 100 acres of scrub land around each village, members would get wages and the use of the land, she said.

She wanted to be the project leader, "but the men on the DDS staff and some sangham women said this was a job for a man." She tossed her head and smiled as she recalled their reaction. Ignoring their views, she showed such knowledge and enthusiasm that it was clear that no one could do the job more effectively, and she was hired to run the enterprise.

Anusuyamma oversaw the digging of pits for seedlings, established the proper mixture of mud and manure, helped in the selection of seedlings from all the different sangham nurseries, and ensured timely delivery. Her responsibilities started with five plantations and eventually expanded to 28.

Anusuyamma, a former child labourer, tends trees in her nursery for the village tree collectives she supervises under the Deccan Development Society.

A role model in the village for women who don't want to follow the traditional marriage path, Anusuyamma loves a challenge, and in her feisty manner, she usually finds a way to win. She most enjoyed inspiring women to form a sangham at Indoor, a village forced to relocate after the poorest people lost everything when the land was flooded in order to send drinking water from their district to Hyderabad.

One day while in the forest close to the Indoor tree plantation, she heard the brutal sounds of a tree being cut and was shocked to find six strapping men hacking away at a 100-year-old banyan tree.

"Come down from there," she ordered. "You can cut me, but not this tree." The men told her the village *sarpanch* (mayor) had sold it to them. When she wouldn't leave them alone, they tramped off to the village and dragged the sarpanch to the site.

"It's just an old tree," said the mayor when he arrived. "How can you object?"

"This tree," Anusuyamma declared, "was planted by our forefathers. One hundred people can sit in its shade, look at the honeycomb in the limbs, and the variety of birds taking shelter on the branches. You can get cash by cutting it down, but you can never replace what this tree is now giving." And with that, the sarpanch told the six men to stop cutting the tree. "After that," she said, "tree cutting in the land adjoining the Indoor plantation came to a halt."

Another favourite story concerned her fight to get the local administration to provide land to landless single Dalit women — including herself — in her village of Pastapur. A state government scheme helps landless Dalits acquire land and the district office told Anusuyamma they would assist her.

She got 12 women, most of them deserted by their husbands, to earmark land costing 20,000 rupees per acre and then negotiated with the landlord for the property transfer. This would happen when he received payment from the government under the program which provided a subsidy to the women of 35 percent and a loan of 65 percent to be paid with profits from the land's eventual produce.

"The officials said the transaction would take a month, but six months later we were still waiting," said Anusuyamma. "Suddenly the landlord threatened to sell the land to someone else. In desperation we went to the DDS director and he came up with an advance of 120,000 rupees against the total amount.

"The next day we all went to the district offices and said we weren't moving until he gave us the money. The following day," she smiled, "the cheque was ready."

Now, Anusuyamma, like Lakshmi, is also a world traveller. In Peru, for example, she helped small farmers organize community biodiversity registers to protect against the patenting of traditional seeds by agri-business.

Salome Yesudas served as my guide and translator working overtime and without pay during the several weeks I spent at DDS in what became my introduction to a virtual Garden of Eden in rural Andhra Pradesh. Now in her late 40s, she was an example of the dedicated women and men I met in India who worked with mission-like zeal for the empowerment of village women and the advancement of rural India. But like the grass-roots women, she too had to struggle for emancipation.

Her first job after she finished a master's degree from a Hyderabad university in nutrition, where she focused upon urban slums, was with the Deccan Development Society. But before she dared venture out, she spent eight years at home at the request of her husband. During this time she gave birth to daughter Sharon, now a special young friend on the way to becoming a journalist in India.

When her daughter was four, Salome saw an ad in the local paper for a nutritionist with DDS. Her interviewer for the job was Vithal Rajan, a man she continues to revere as a rural development visionary. Out of respect, she still refers to him as "Sir" or "Dr. Vithal" because of his British Ph.D. She remembered how pleased he was that she had been eight years outside the corridors of the university because he wanted her to be as untainted as possible by academic studies. Her job was to gather information on nutrition from the village women farmers themselves and then document it for the use of everyone.

She loved her experience at DDS, but after 10 years, and seeking the freedom to accept invitations from abroad to give papers and share her knowledge, she moved to an organization called the Andhra Pradesh Farmer Managed Groundwater Systems Project (APFAMGS). A UN Food and Agriculture supported organization, it worked in 650 villages in seven drought-prone districts of the state.

The project trained farmers in a scientific way how to monitor, store, and use available water. Salome's job was to guarantee that women were part of the village decision-making processes.

At international conferences in Japan, South Africa, and Canada, she disseminated her research around nutrition and traditional agriculture in south-eastern India.

In Montreal she worked under the Centre for Indigenous Peoples' Nutrition and Environment associated with McGill University's faculty of agriculture. With 11 other researchers from Third World countries she helped write a book that explored issues around nutrition and traditional ecological farming. Her focus naturally was the Dalit village women she had come to know so well in the Zaheerabad region of Andhra Pradesh.

On two different occasions she stayed at my home in Montreal and gave presentations to Montreal friends interested in women and development in India.

Over several visits I got to know Salome and her family and spent a little time with her mother-in-law Parama and father-in-law Keshapa who lived in the village of Alipur near Salome's place in Zaheerabad. Neither Parama nor Keshapa could speak English, so Salome's teenage daughter Sharon and I went together one day to visit them. Her grandparents lived in a four-room house, but they started off marriage in a joint family with nine other people in one long mud-and-dung floored room with a roof of logs and sticks.

Parama met Keshapa at the altar when she married him at the age of 10; he was 14. She was very much a child, and recalled that she got her period only seven months after her marriage. She immediately moved into that one long room with Keshapa's joint family. They all slept on the floor and there was no toilet. But a few months later Parama ran back to Pastapur because of all the back-breaking work she had to do toiling as a farm hand on landlords' land, grinding chilies, and making cow dung cakes. But her grandfather promptly returned her back to the joint family she'd married into.

At 13 she was pregnant, and at 14, after she had Yesudas, she kept working every day in the fields with him strapped to her back. She had two more sons plus two daughters that died of fevers. At 22, after five pregnancies, she had her tubes tied.

Working on landlords' land once they were married, Parama said that initially she made 5 rupees a day while her husband Keshapa worked for three litres of milk a day, but they diligently saved their money. After 18 years of marriage they were able to borrow 40,000 rupees in order to buy five acres of land for 50,000 rupees and paid it back in two years.

Keshapa said he and Parama didn't want their children to be coolies like them, so all their sons received some education. But Parama said that in order to send their children to school they sold their animals, which over the years included 10 cows, four bullocks, 10 goats, and 10 hens.

Yesudas earned an engineering degree, a second son with grade six learned on his own how to do electrical work and found a job at a Hyderabad country club, and a third son that finished grade 12 completed a diploma in electrical work.

I had met remarkable women in villages that were flourishing. Now it was time to feel the pulse of the village of Hoti where the women had been facing a crop crisis due to drought. I decided to live in Hoti for a few days.

In addition to my notebook, pen, and camera, I was armed with a shoulder bag containing a bottle of water, a toothbrush, soap, my trusty malaria pills that I took every day, and a small thin tea towel that dried quickly.

Tucked into my fanny pack were several rolled up pieces of toilet paper for visits to the fields since in the village even hole-in-the-ground toilets did not exist. Unwilling to eat runny curries with my fingers, I also had my trusty small plastic spoon. I knew I would be sleeping on the floor on a mat in a crowded hut and brought no change of clothes.

In 2002, while learning about the accomplishments of women associated with the Deccan Development Society I had a room at Krishi Vigyana Kendra (KVK), a farm science centre promoting organic agriculture run by the government and the Deccan Development Society in order to encourage traditional ecological farming. Staff worked with local farmers to learn as much as possible from them while also extending their knowledge as widely as possible to every farmer in the district.

For farmers coming in to take courses and exchange knowledge, KVK also provided dormitory-style accommodation with four to six sleeping mats on the floor.

In Indian villages people do not sleep alone, partly because there is not enough space, but also because they like to be together. Privacy is a Western value that is growing among the urban upper middle class but not yet entrenched.

Once, when invited to a middle class home in a town, I was given a room of my own which belonged to a teenage daughter. I had just settled down to sleep in a nice comfortable Western bed, when my host and daughter hauled in two floor mats, and lay down. They didn't want me to feel lonely.

In KVK, however, I'd been given my own room with a mat on the floor and a mosquito net plus a bathroom with a flush toilet and a shower. I had to make sure my mosquito net had no holes because the mosquitoes would buzz around all night in clouds over the net. At night when I was often alone, except for a security guard, I also had access to a small room with a computer where I could type my notes from the day's research. But I quickly learned not to count on anything.

India is a big bulging country with the stuffing pouring out and only a thin layer of modern infrastructure. Shortly after I arrived at KVK, a truck ran over the phone wires and for a week there was no phone or Internet. In the kitchen there was also no refrigeration. I ate what the cook had fried up an hour before, and that was it. Water was warmed by the sun in tanks, so 3:00 p.m. was good time for a bath.

Wake-up time was set at 6:30 a.m. Breakfast at 11:00 a.m. consisted of *upma*, a porridge of millets and nuts laced with garlic and chili that burnt a hole down my throat, but there was no alternative; it was that or starve.

From KVK I climbed, along with Salome, into a rattletrap three-wheeled autorickshaw that is rural India's favoured mode of village-to-village transport. Built like a large child's tricycle with a box on top, the sides were completely open with sagging front and back seats that could fit three passengers plus the driver. Usually, however, they were crammed to the roof with a whole family, along with maybe a stray goat and some fodder bursting out the sides.

Our rickshaw bumped over rocks on a thin dirt road that tossed up a torrent of red dust that pounded my face, but at least it kept the mosquitoes at bay. Even with insect repellent, usually the mosquitoes bit right through my Indian salwar pants so that my legs were now a mass of itchy red specks.

Hoti was already dark when we arrived in this hamlet of mostly mud and thatch huts. Here 300 families out of 1,000 households were landless,

100 people worked as bonded labourers, and almost half the children were working in the fields or looking after siblings.

All the children were in bed, and in the thatch shelters the milk buffaloes stirred. Indian music was playing softly in one of the huts. Off in the distance a dog barked.

The feeling of calm contrasted with a feeling of quiet urgency as women of all ages moved into a courtyard outside one of the sangham member's huts and sat down cross-legged in a circle on the ground for their meeting. I joined them at the back, also on the ground. My Indian salwar kameez, with an added zippered pocket, allowed me to sit anywhere in dignity, if not always in comfort.

At first glance the women looked as though the land had been good to them. All were clad in beautiful print and striped cotton saris that ranged from earth tones to tropical eye-catching colours. A necklace, earrings, bangles, and sometimes a nose drop completed the outfits.

No matter how hard life was, and even on their way to the fields or carrying a load of fodder on their heads, the rural women always looked as fresh as the sunflowers they sometimes grew.

"There won't be as many members as we had hoped for tonight," said Shammamma, a woman of 45, who had been group leader of her sangham of 60 members for eight years.

"Some of our people are out cutting cane," she explained. Cutting sugar cane as coolies for the richer farmers, who could afford to dig bore wells and irrigate, was what these villagers did when they needed money. "A husband and wife team working together could make 60 rupees a day if they cut a ton," she said.

That came to only 1 dollar Canadian each, in 2002, at 30 rupees to the Canadian dollar.

Earlier, en route to the meeting, I had stopped by a fruit and vegetable stand in Zaheerabad, and blew what would have been a half-day's earnings for a cane cutter on five oranges, two of which I had gobbled down without a thought. Fruit, I later discovered, was usually too costly for families to eat on a regular basis.

Normally, at this time of year (February), the women could afford the occasional fruit. Usually they were using up the last of the produce they had grown on their own few acres of land the previous summer, and combined that with earning money as daily agricultural labourers.

But, as I learned at the meeting, for the previous three years the summer crops they so carefully planted had dried up under the rainless skies and the hot sun.

"The monsoon rains didn't come," explained Shammamma, who had three grown-up daughters and became a sole-support parent 18 years before at the age of 26 when her husband died while digging a well that collapsed.

"All the nutritious millets, pulses, greens, and oil seeds the women so carefully planted resulted in almost no crops at all," said Salome.

Now they had to depend upon working for the richer farmers, who had better land in the valley where they could access water with bore wells, but there were often not enough jobs to go around. Some were talking of packing their babies on their backs and migrating to an area of Andhra Pradesh where richer farmers grew rice, or trying to find jobs as hotel maids or in construction in the capital city of Hyderabad.

Monthly costs of food alone for a family of four, according to a community worker, were 1,000 rupees. With a man making 40 rupees and his wife 20, and with only an average of 15 days a month of available work, those who could not depend upon their own crops were risking starvation by trying to survive as day labourers on around 900 rupees a month.

The crop failure had come just when the Hoti women decided it was worth it to stay on the land. In 1995 DDS provided funds for groups of women to upgrade their lands without chemicals and grow a range of diverse crops. Loans for this were to be paid back in the form of grain to stock a village public distribution system to supply subsidized grain to the poorest in the community.

Across India, among rural development researchers, this program, which covered 32 villages to start, had been singled out as an inspiring rival to the government's public rice distribution program that had run into difficulties and offered lower nutrition.

Hoti was one of the first villages to sign on to reclaim fallow lands for crops.

The first two years the women harvested enough crops to pay back their loans with grain, but for the following three years the pickings became thinner and thinner. At the meeting I learned that some women were buying grain from their friends in more prosperous villages in order to honour their loan commitments.

All this had the villagers wondering whether they should abandon the land, something that many small farmers had done across the Deccan Plateau in the late 1970s when there had been drought and then famine.

But over the previous three years not all the villages supported by DDS suffered from drought. "You can never tell what areas may be missed by the monsoons," said one of the KVK staff who pointed out that out of 32 villages, only 15 percent had gone through a bad period.

Shammamma was determined to hang in. "I've paid only half of what I owe," she said, "but when the rains are good I get six months of food security, and I can work as an agricultural labourer for the rest."

The sangham meeting ended at midnight, and Salome decided we should go back to KVK and return the next day. I was scheduled to stay at Shammamma's house with her daughter of 18 and two grandchildren who would now be asleep, but Shammamma looked as though she would be busy for a while.

In our autorickshaw on the way back we took on board one of the sangham members. This introduced me to the Shammamma's brilliant plan to help 30 sangham women avoid total dependence on the land. This took the form of a factory using neem seeds to extract neem oil that the women were selling as an efficient organic pest repellent. The residue that was left after the oil was squeezed from the pods went into neem cakes sold as a high-class organic fertilizer.

"Right now the most reliable time for electric power for our factory is in the middle of the night," said the woman just before she jumped off into some bushes. She ran down a trail to the factory to ensure the neem oil extracting machine worked until the sun came up. Normally the working hours of the factory were 12:00 p.m. to 6:00 p.m. and 3:00 a.m. to 6:00 a.m. when the power in the village was reliable. Shammamma was the leader and production manager of the enterprise even though she could neither read nor write.

The next day in the afternoon I was standing under a coconut tree at the entrance to Shammamma's courtyard. She was in her wine and gold-coloured sari waiting for me on the verandah of her house which was made of local stone and wood topped by a handsome slate roof.

She smiled and announced that from then on, all visitors were to stay at her place. This was because I insisted on giving her 30 rupees a day (only 1 dollar) so that I wouldn't cost her anything. I think she imagined I might be the thin edge of the wedge of a Hoti-style bed-and-breakfast business for Westerners eager to savour life in an Indian village. Because I loved spending time in India, I sometimes fantasized about helping her find the customers to get one going.

She jumped down to show me her small flower garden leading to a corridor at the side of the house holding a tall wood-pile-like stack of drying cow dung pats used for cooking.

On the other side of the house was a small walled-in area for cooking over an iron grate on the ground. Next to that was a bushel-sized pail with a smaller pitcher hanging from the side to be used for an India-style shower.

Facing this were two lolling milk buffaloes and a calf in a thatched shelter that Shammamma and her family had originally inhabited. She had been able to build a much more solid three-room house on the property four years before, thanks to a married daughter who provided the required 80,000 rupees.

We climbed up the stairs to her verandah that served as her living room and into her home. There was not a stick of furniture inside except for a clock that didn't work and two pale blue plastic chairs that were routinely offered to the infirm or Westerners such as myself.

Shammamma's main room included an area for kitchen utensils and another section for bags of Public Distribution System grain that also served as a sleeping area for her 18-year-old daughter Manjula, along with Maize, a grandson of six, and Ashvrini, a granddaughter of eight. Another small room was reserved for storage.

"Come on," she said, "I'm going to show you my land."

We walked two kilometres along a road in the valley area where landlords had the more fertile land. In a sugar cane field a small boy of 10 was weeding. The men get 40 rupees a day, the boys 30, and the women and children 20, she explained. In a second field, a bonded labourer was cutting cane. "He's the husband of a sangham member," said Shammamma. "He borrowed for his daughter's marriage and is now bonded for a year." Along with the other 100 bonded labourers in the village he was making a total of 12,000 rupees a year (about $400 Canadian) for a 10 to 12-hour day, every day of the year.

We walked up to higher ground to her three acres of rocky land that looked as parched as a moonscape. During normal monsoons the land would yield up to 500 kilograms of grain over two harvests — Kharif from June to October and Rabi from October to March. But the Rabi harvest had yielded only 10 kilograms of Bajra — enough for only 10 meals for the family.

As we walked back to the village, Shammamma told me how she had been married at 15, and for the first 10 years she and her husband worked as bonded labourers for a landlord because her husband had borrowed money to get married. They also owned three acres that they leased out for half the share of the crop and fodder.

Once they had paid off their debt, they began to work on their own land. Because of reliable monsoon rains, they received good crop yields along with milk from milk buffaloes. But two years later her husband died, and Shammamma was left alone on the land with three small daughters, the youngest just three months old.

She sent each of her daughters to school up to grade six so that they would learn to read, but always had one working with her on the land until each left to marry.

Her 18-year-old daughter Manjula went to grade four in the village government school, and to grade five in the DDS Green School. "I had to stop school because there was no money for notebooks," Manjula later told me. "I needed to cook for my mother, and also look after my nephew Maize and niece Ashvrini, both in school." Now she was training to become a tailor.

In the late afternoon I walked through the winding roads of the village filled with thatched huts made of stone or mud, all of them with shelters at the side for buffaloes, goats, and hens.

Children of all ages, dressed in beautiful colours, played in the courtyards or in the village square around the water pump. Young mothers lined up at the well for their water, one woman pumping while the others placed their tin or clay containers beneath. Children and mothers gathered around me, staring as though I were a creature from another planet. They talked at me, and I tried out my 25 words of Telugu.

Back at Shammamma's house, Maize and Ashvrini proudly showed me how they could count to 10 in English. After the sun set, we sat cross-legged on the floor outside on the verandah and had a dinner of rice, vegetable curry, dahl, and a chapatti with jaggery (like maple sugar) in it. From the house next door came Shammamma's sister-in-law, a widow who ate with her every night. In order to try to fit in I ate with my fingers and eschewed my plastic spoon.

After supper, women of all ages crammed onto the verandah for the purpose of viewing the white-faced visitor in Western-rigged Indian garb.

One woman tried to introduce me to her year-and-a-half old son, but at the sight of my pale face and my foreign look, he cried his head off. The next morning she came by again, and even from afar, he took one look and howled.

As with other village women I had met, they all wanted to know about my personal situation back in Canada. Who was my husband? What about my children? Were there any pictures? I stopped the questions by hauling out photos of my two grown-up and very handsome nephews, which the women winked at and eyed as possible marriage partners for their girls.

Later they wanted to know why I wasn't wearing a sari like them. There was no translator around, so using mime, I showed how I risked having the whole thing fall down, and they all laughed. A sari required expert winding around the waist and up over the shoulder with no room for pockets for a camera and notebook. Mind you, they had ways and means of carrying money and could easily balance themselves on motor scooters with a baby and even a load of firewood while keeping every fold of their outfit in place.

When bedtime rolled around (always early because the day in India starts at 6:00 a.m.) I lay down on a floor mat next to Manjula and the two grandkids. Shammamma slept outside on the verandah. My feet rubbed against large sacks of grain stored as part of the Public Distribution System for the village. It was like camping, but it was hot, the air was fragrant, a loving community surrounded me, and how much furniture did anyone need anyway?

In the middle of the night, I awoke with a need to take a visit to the fields. Very thirsty from the heat and the salty food, I had gulped down far too much water, some of it from the town pump. I grabbed my flashlight out of my zippered pocket, and crept outside past Shammamma on the verandah. Rather than taking off to the unknown scrub of the fields where my friend Vithal had warned of snakes, I crouched down behind the cow pat pile at the side of the house.

At 6:00 a.m., at the sound of cocks crowing and milk buffaloes mooing, Manjula was up cooking rice on the wood stove grill next to the animals. Shammamma had already milked her buffaloes and taken off to get water for washing.

Manjula gave me a cup of hot sweetened tea. Hidden from everyone except the buffaloes, I stripped naked and threw a few pitchers of coldish water over myself for a typical Indian shower. With my trusty tea towel that took no space and dried quickly in the sun, I whisked off the water that had not evaporated and climbed back into my clothes. Whew! I hung my tea towel on a small nail.

Newly refreshed, and knowing there would be no breakfast for a few hours, I decided to take a walk on the paved road that went past the village. Soon a tractor lumbered up followed by a large truck filled with what appeared to be 50 eager and cute grade-school children peering out over the side. Where we they off to? To badi? I asked, meaning school in Telugu. No, a villager said. They were off, I knew, to a landlord's sugar cane fields.

Back at the house, Manjula was now raking cow dung out into the centre of the courtyard where she dumped it into a pail of water and then made cow pats that she placed to dry on the thatch shelter. Later they would be lifted off to use as fuel or to add to her vermiculture compost strip.

Getting the grandkids ready for school, Shammamma braided Ashvrini's hair and slipped her into a bright orange jumper and then helped Maize pull on fresh beige pants. Each wore matching striped orange belts. Shammamma spooned rice, vegetable curry, and dahl into a neat stack of tins with a handle on top for their lunch and the pair set off hand-in-hand for school.

Later, over a breakfast of curry with chili, I was amazed to suddenly see two men in suits in the courtyard. More people who spoke English, I figured, so I went out and quickly introduced myself.

Without any prompting I was treated to an enthusiastic oration in favour of Shammamma from two Zaheerabad bankers who were lending the neem factory money. The men waxed on about the talents of Shammamma who, they said, had a great mind for figures, administration, and production, and knew how to turn a profit. "Who cares that she can't read," one of them said. "That's something her daughter can help with. What counts is that Shammamma knows how to run a successful business."

The enterprise, the bankers said, had been going for six months, the women were paying back a loan of 200,000 rupees very promptly, and each woman was making more a day from the factory than they were as coolies in the field. Thirty sangham women — most of them landless — were involved, each working one week out of three, so the earnings could be spread around.

The bankers said that the business was so successful they were planning to loan the women more money for a second vermiculture compost enterprise.

When I returned to Hoti village in 2006, the loans of 100,000 rupees from DDS at no interest, and 200,000 rupees at 11 percent from the bank had all been paid up and all the profits were now going completely to the women.

They would each receive a salary of 25 rupees a day, and share a profit of 60,000 rupees, said Shammamma. Divided among the women this would come to 2,222 rupees each. Since they each worked about 120 days a year that meant they would make a total 44 rupees a day, way more than their earnings as coolies in the fields.

Their sales per year, she said, were 500 litres of oil for organic pesticide, plus 10 tons of neem cake for fertilizer. Though helped initially by DDS, the women had started their own enterprise that was now owned and run by them.

Shammamma's family was doing well too. Manjula, now 22, was married with a daughter two years old, and lived in a village 20 kilometres away with her lorry-driver husband. The pair had a half-acre of land where she was growing sugar cane and sharing a borewell with three of her husband's brothers.

The two grandchildren I first met were still with her. The boy, 10, was in grade one in a residential English school, because all he had completed was grade two in Telugu in the village school, and the girl of 12 was in grade five in Zaheerabad.

In the past, the families of the women I met had been landless day labourers working for landlords. Through a government policy in the mid-1970s that gave land to lower-caste people, and through a current policy whereby Dalits could buy land, women had up to three acres and sometimes more. In addition — in sangham collectives — they were leasing fallow lands belonging to other farmers.

And now, in a strange reversal of roles, the landlords in the area were starting to curry favour with the Deccan Development Society farmer women.

During my visit, about 100 landlords came to KVK to open discussions with sangham women from some 70 villages. The topic: how they might work with them to grow traditional crops using "non-pesticide management" rather than crops from hybrid seeds that required pesticides and chemical fertilizers that were burning up the land.

The higher-caste farmers with more land recognized the power and knowledge of the women and wanted to join with the women to form special village agricultural committees.

Many of the farmers saw that chemicals weren't good for the dryland they farmed and that traditional crops could be grown more cheaply.

The problem they saw was getting a market for the traditional crops of millets, pulses, and oil seeds. Rice, which wasn't as nutritious, and came from the coast, was peddled by the central government at subsidized rates and was taking over. The traditional crops were seen as "low-caste" crops.

The women were willing to work with the farmers to develop this market. Already people in nearby Zaheerabad, a town of 40,000, were interested in buying from a produce shop opened by the sangham women.

This recognition of the knowledge and power of the Dalit women represented an astonishing change in attitudes across the country. And now, organic farming, which suited dryland agriculture in the Deccan plateau, was receiving some support from the Andhra Pradesh government. Off in the future was a market for consumers in the West in support of the Slow Food Movement, and people willing to pay top dollar for organic produce.

The creation of village sanghams was perhaps the most vital instrument for the women who turned out to be creative and knowledgeable entrepreneurs. By 2006, some of these collectives had capital funds that gave them economic power. Individually the women had become self-sufficient, but community values backed by women's solidarity were still flourishing. As one of the Dalit women had told Vithal so many years ago: "When 10 of us are together, God is with us."

6
HYDERABAD VILLAGE CITY

After several weeks in the villages, I moved back to the city of Hyderabad with its minarets and temples crowned by the majestic ruins of Golconda Fort, famous for its diamond market during the Qutub Shah dynasty in the 16th century. Vithal's house in the elegant villa-suburb of Habsiguda was full, so I settled into a small modern hotel called Minerva that became a home away from home. My purpose was to type up my notes and send emails. In contrast to the villages, I was back to a regular bed with a mattress, a flush toilet, an elevator, and air conditioning.

I was now in the centre of the city, close to the world's tallest Buddha statue that rose out of Hussain Sagar Lake and within rickshaw distance of scenes from the Ramayana and Mahabharata epics in a Hindu pilgrimage temple. But I was also in an information technology centre. Hotel Minerva sat on bustling Himayathnagar Road, an artery that at first glance typified the India of the Western news magazines with its banks, stock broking agencies, cell phone outlets, and signs blaring opportunities for overseas careers.

Nearby were high-end clothing stores with names like Arrow and Nike along with silk-festooned sari shops next to beauty salons and modelling schools.

Internet Cafés thrived. My favourite was part of a chain called Reliance WebWorld, where I could enjoy a steaming cappuccino and a veggie wrap along with a hefty piece of chocolate cake. This one was also popular with the Bank of America and the state education department.

When men in pinstripes from these outfits took over the cyber shop to run workshops for special groups, I would weave down a dark alley and up some twisting outdoor stairs to a hole-in-the-wall spot in a musty building with floors so cracked you could see down to the floor below. Open until midnight, this Dickensian place scattered with dubious characters was a far cry from the landmark Cyber Towers of Hitech City that were housing software development corporations a few kilometers away.

In amongst all this were fancy restaurants like The Blue Fox, known for chili, along with a Chinese restaurant that played Christmas music all year long. At a takeout place called Hyderabad House I could chat with the locals and eat scrumptious Tandoori chicken or Hyderabad's celebrated mutton biryani for only $2. The Almond House, showcasing hundreds of inch-square, high-quality Indian sweets, would sell me five or six favourites before I turned in at night to watch BBC World.

But this was just the consumer side of Himayathnagar Road — the "shining India" of software and the stock market and high living.

There were also the itinerant sellers of bananas, mangos, and fresh juices as well as hot samosas fried up on the spot. I bought at these places regularly and became friendly with the sellers.

The great range of characters that filled the streets along with the occasional wandering cow or bullock made Himayathnagar Road sing like a village. A block from Hotel Minerva, against a wall leading into a sumptuous villa, a man sat cross-legged on the ground under a large blue plastic sheet where he ran a popular barber and shaving shop. Next to him a lady in a lime green sari with a four-year-old girl at her feet peddled exquisite bouquets of pale pink roses, orange mums, and red carnations arranged in triangular shapes.

A few feet away a small-boned man in bare feet encouraged me to admire his outdoor gallery of paintings hanging on the villa wall. Specially featured were multi-coloured icons of the goddess Durga in a bejewelled gold headdress, with several arms carrying swords and tridents, ready to slay demons from her mount on a fierce-looking tiger.

When I tore a hole in the sleeve of my tunic kameez, I walked down a side street to an open-air shop and the tailor repaired it while I stood there with it still on. He became a neighbourhood friend that I talked to whenever I went by.

Right outside the hotel a grizzled man in a dhoti sold pencils, key rings, small knives, and cheap jewellery off a rickety table at the side of the road. "Every day you look and you never buy," he'd say. I finally obliged by stocking up on pens.

A young man in a suit tried to sell me a heavy Oxford dictionary and a Roget's Thesaurus on a regular basis. He always chose to make an impassioned sales pitch just as I was negotiating the lunatic traffic of Himayathnagar Road. "Very cheap dictionary, will give at very good price," he'd yell at me as I was leaping between a rickshaw and a motor scooter coming straight for me.

Every one of these people, I felt, had a story to tell. I was reading *Malgudi Days* by the celebrated Indian novelist R.K. Narayan who wrote about people in a south Indian village. In his introduction he said that in India, the writer had to only look out the window to pick up a character, and thereby a story.

One day during my wanderings in the neighbourhood, I sat down to rest on a step under a shady tree outside the Almond House on Himayathnagar Road, which was teeming with every kind of honking vehicle flying by like whirling dervishes with all the parts falling off. Only the odd bullock would take its time, sometimes all on its own, unhitched from some stone-filled cart that had careened down a hill and smashed into some poor guy's travelling vegetable stand.

Suddenly a tattered bus crammed with people hanging out the side tried to pass a motor scooter carrying a boy and girl in their late teens. It veered too close and the motor scooter wavered and then fell to the ground.

The girl, a gorgeous beauty in an orange chiffon salwar kameez, lay lifeless on the street. Horrified, we all gathered around.

The boy insisted she would be all right. The girl opened her eyes, smiled as though everything was normal, and the boy gathered her in his arms and put her on a white plastic chair outside the Almond House while a worried crowd pressed in, and in Telugu an older man asked questions.

"Her husband?" I asked a man next to me who spoke English. I saw she had rings on her left hand. "No," he said. Noticing a slight protrusion through her tunic, I wondered if perhaps she was pregnant. She leaned over the side of the chair as if to be sick but was able to hold back.

Her boyfriend, who was carrying a backpack, held her hand and gently stroked her face. I thought of a story from a village I had visited, where a young couple from different castes wanted to marry and couldn't, so they eloped.

The owner of the sweets store hailed down an autorickshaw taxi. I picked up her battered sandals lying on the street, she struggled to put them on, and the pair disappeared into the raging traffic.

It was time to eat, and with my eye on Hyderabad House, I stepped out into the road in between several motor scooters that treated me like a post on a slalom ski trail. A lurching autorickshaw was coming straight for me, and I have never, I say never, seen any such vehicle put on the brakes. If they even have any, they're probably in shreds, because this country uses equipment until it collapses.

Crossing the street was always a terrifying experience. In a big Indian city it helped if you were a gymnast or an Olympic runner if you wanted to use your legs to move around. There were no crosswalks and the red lights were completely ignored, where there were red lights.

I stood there like a freak, suddenly smack in the middle of the road with all these misshapen carcasses attached to wheels zigzagging around and told myself it was a good idea I made out my will before I left Montreal. Look left, look right, everyone was wrong.

"Oh Lord Shiva!" That's the god of destruction in this country. "Help!" A car nearly ran over my feet. And here was this kid coming at me pawing my arm for coins.

How did this kid get into the centre of the road? He looked about five, although I knew he was probably seven. Maybe I should pick him up and take him to the side of the road.

No, maybe he should take me to the other side of the road. I had a 100-rupee bill in my pocket.

Elegant fashion stores around Panjagutta Square in high-tech Hyderabad serve India's expanding middle class.

Here kid. And I shoved this bill at him. He seemed small and innocent but he knew a 100-rupee bill when he saw one. It was only three bucks Canadian, but it was five days work if you were a child labourer in the fields.

He smiled up at me. Enough to melt anyone, except the zoo on wheels was about to melt us both if we didn't do something. I grabbed his hand hoping he was better at running at the right time than I was.

We were sprinting together to the other side of the road, and his bedraggled mother was on the other side holding a baby. And there was this big crowd standing there watching. What was this funny look-ing lady with an overheated face and faded brown hair in semi-Indian clothes doing in the middle of the road with this kid?

We made it! I looked up to see a favourite café called Croquette which sold fat pieces of chocolate cake with a lot of icing and fresh fruit drinks. I let go of the kid's hand, even though I felt he was some kind of saviour. In this crazy place I needed a friend, and he could be it. Maybe he would like a drink, or a piece of that chocolate cake, but he had scam-pered off to his mother.

I had definitely lost it. I struggled up the steps to the coffee shop. There was a guard at the door to keep out thieves and weirdos. I hoped I wouldn't pass for one. I stepped inside and slumped into a chair.

I was spending lots of time alone between assignments to villages and I looked forward to daily encounters on the street, but I was also becoming aware of the poverty. Across India more and more landless villagers were flooding into cities, swelling the total numbers of urban poor to over 75 million.

In all the time I stayed at the Minerva Hotel, I was the only Westerner around, and I became not only a curiosity but also a target for people with various pitches designed to shake me down for rupees.

My Indian friends told me never to give to beggars. "These are just the front line for mothers who are young enough to work and in some cases nasty guys in their 20s milking them for money in return for promises that are never kept."

But when they clawed at my arms, I would dig into my pockets and give them whatever change I had. After a while, out of guilt, and also wanting to be part of the scene, I gave them 10 rupee notes, which was only about 30 cents.

Finally every morning, as soon as I came out of the hotel en route to my Internet Café, some tough looking old ladies were waiting for me. They were the vanguard of a posse of beggars that was growing by the day after they discovered that a white lady in a beige sun hat gave out money every morning outside the Minerva Hotel.

"Ten rupees," the ladies would shriek, pulling at my arms and patting the sides of my pants.

"Never give money to beggars in the area where you live," said Eleazar, my 20-something advisor at the internet café, but it was too late.

Now, also on the advice of my Indian friends, I had a policy. No money, only food. "The pimps aren't interested in food," they said.

I couldn't resist responding to three nimble-footed girls of about eight years old that wore the same tattered clothes every day. They were bright and eager, and after a while everyone realized that I gave only to them.

Every morning I would meet the little trio of beggarettes and we would traipse down to the banana man where from his travelling cart I would order 5 rupees of bananas for each girl. They would hold out their skirts and smile, like it was a game, and because they didn't ask for money I knew they were happy with the food.

The first day, as soon as I gave them the bananas, they sat on the pavement, ripped off the skins, and wolfed them down as though they hadn't eaten for a while. I couldn't help thinking that they were probably among the 40 to 60 percent of children in the country that Indian Nobel economist Amartya Sen claimed were undernourished.

The banana man also carried oranges, so I gave each girl one of those. Then I dragged them down to the juice squeezer who pressed out a pine-apple juice that they also tossed down in a hurry.

I said to myself that one day I would get a translator and find out what was happening to these little girls, but I never did. My excuse was that I was busy typing up my research from the villages, and my next stop would be the Muslim-dominated old city where an NGO called Confederation of Voluntary Associations (COVA) worked with poor Muslim and Hindu women and children maybe a little like these girls.

I felt overwhelmed by beggars in the city, particularly the children. In the villages, despite their low incomes, women and their families that had linked together under NGOs were flourishing, and some-times I felt even a little envious of the rich spirit that infused their communities.

But here in the city, alongside the burgeoning middle class working in Hi-Tech City a few kilometers away, were runaways from villages who thought they might fare better in the cities. But without literacy and a trade they were doomed to swell the slums.

At my internet café I met a woman who told me that in her vil-lage, which had suffered several years of drought, 300 people had left for Hyderabad with the hope of finding work in construction or road building, but some were resorting to begging. She was part of a Dalit women's organization of cooperatives that I would later investigate called

Ankuram Sangamam Poram (ASP) composed of 80,000 women working in self-help groups in half the districts of Andhra Pradesh.

Sometimes a family disaster or illness pushed the children to the city. AIDS orphans were growing in India partly because of men migrating to cities or other parts of the country where they consorted with AIDS-infected prostitutes. The men would return and pass the disease to their unsuspecting wives.

AIDS was also being passed to young, sexually inexperienced men on the eve of their marriages. I discovered they were being initiated into sex by "aunties" or older women whose husbands were frequently away. Many of these "aunties" were HIV-positive or suffered from AIDS because of their itinerant husbands, and this was being passed on to unwary and naïve young men.

One morning, again en route to the internet café, I encountered a boy of seven and a girl of five. They looked sturdy and wise but they were just kids alone and barefoot on the street. As I tried to cross the road they held out their tiny hands.

Following my rule of not giving money I dragged them to the Croquette bake shop and sat them down at an outside table and ordered them two chicken and veggie wraps and a couple of drinks. They ate voraciously and were very happy to talk.

The young waiter served as the translator from English to Telugu. In their village their mother had died and their father had disappeared, so they were staying with their grandmother outside Hyderabad, but were not going to school.

They were very small, and obviously far from home, but they seemed to have the street smarts of teen urchins. When they finished eating, they ran down the steps, looked up and smiled and waved. The boy put his arm protectively around his sister and they took off.

7
BURQAS FOR PEACE

After working in the villages, Vithal Rajan had turned his sights to the old city which had a history of Hindu-Muslim conflict dating back to Indian independence when the Nizam initially refused to join India and the Indian army marched in. Over the years, prodded by scheming local politicians seeking power, Hindus and Muslims in the old city were sometimes led to blows. With the goal of creating communal harmony by helping the poor of both groups work together against poverty and local provocateurs, Vithal started the Confederation of Voluntary Associations, or COVA, an organization that would eventually work across Andhra Pradesh and in other states. The focus once again was upon women, children, and youth.

But now the federal government, under the Hindu nationalist Bharatiya Janata Party (BJP), was stirring up trouble. With an agenda of ethnic cleansing, it was persecuting the Muslim minority that accounted for 138 million people representing 12 percent of the overall Indian population.

In February and March 2002 across India, all eyes were pinned to the city of Ayodhya in the northern state of Uttar Pradesh, where Hindus in 1992 had destroyed a 16th century mosque, claiming it stood on the birth place of one of their gods, Lord Ram. In defiance of a Supreme Court ruling, Hindu pilgrims were boarding trains to plan construction of a Hindu temple at the site. Muslims in the country, including those in the old city in Hyderabad, were fuming.

Andhra Pradesh is 95 percent Hindu and most of the people I had met in the villages had Hindu roots, even though many Dalits had turned to Christianity, Buddhism, and even Islam to escape caste discrimination. But in this metropolis born out of the love of a Muslim prince for his Hindu wife, I was now en route to the old city of a half a million people, 75 percent of them Muslim and most of them poor.

In a fire-breathing, mechanized three-wheeler that rattled and shuddered its way over bumps and gapping manholes, my cowboy rickshaw driver merrily zipped around buses, burqas, bicycles, and buffaloes by leaning perpetually on his blood-curdling horn. On narrow streets, when I feared I was about to slide off the slippery seat of the rickshaw straight into a mound of bullock dung or hurtle into a tree, I seized a thin bar that held the contraption together.

We passed out of the boulevards of Himayathnagar and into the tourist-oriented Abids area and finally across the river towards the old city.

Slowing down to a more reverential pace, we entered the old city through the spectacular four-columned Indian Arc de Triomphe with minarets on top. Called the Charminar, it was built in the 16th century by the Qutub Shah dynasty whose reign marked a golden age of architecture and art in Andhra Pradesh. Inside stood the dynasty's majestic Mecca Masjid, one of the world's largest mosques, its gates embedded with bricks containing soil from Mecca.

Taking our time so I could enjoy the sights, we wove through lanes exhibiting fabrics, perfumes, large pots, musical instruments, and jewellery, including Hyderabad's famous pearls and its multi-coloured glass bangles.

Soon we were bumping through dusty slum neighbourhoods lined with one-room concrete houses in pale colours streaked with rust and fungus. As in the villages, families here lived without furniture. Houses were mostly a repository for cooking utensils and tins along with bags of rice and maybe a second set of clothes. At night everyone slept close together on the floor. Outside of working hours, women gathered to gossip and eat on a two-foot-wide ledge in front of the door that served as a verandah.

I was smack in the middle of Hyderabad but it felt like a village. Goats and cows wandered around as naturally as dogs in a park. Bullocks tied to carts hauled bulging gunnysacks, stones for construction, and fodder for animals. The narrow streets smelled strongly of urine. Toilet facilities were communal and sometimes maybe a little too far away to bother with. Junk lay everywhere because there was no garbage pickup. Water came from communal water pumps.

Despite the poverty, the streets were bursting with energy. Laughing children, barefoot and in colourful clothes, contrasted with women in burqas sweating in the heat.

Shops the size of cupboards lined the streets selling tin, bicycle parts, piles of wood, fans, saris, kerosene, autorickshaws, Indian spices, chickpeas, lentils, teas, and basic groceries. Hunks of red beef, mutton, and chicken swung from ropes in front of meat chops catering to non-vegetarian Muslims. Roving vegetable and fruit carts were everywhere.

Mini hair "saloons" and parlours advertising face bleaching beckoned. On every second street, small mosques were interspersed with white Hindu temples the size of small dog houses. Tea stalls that offered piping hot, highly sweetened tea with milk along with Indian sweets were doing a brisk trade.

We arrived at our destination — a small room right off the street — to find sleeping children packed in so tight there wasn't an inch between them. The preschool (one of 15 run by COVA, serving 600 children) was having its nap. The teacher woke up the children who grabbed little bags and tins holding lunch, and they were off.

Soon the place filled up with 10 women from a woman's thrift and credit group called Zareen Mahila Mandali from the surrounding neighbourhood of Tadla Kunta — home to about 325 families, most of them Muslim.

The group was one of 200 under the Roshan Vikas Thrift Cooperative covering nearly 5,000 members with savings of nearly 2 million rupees (about $66,000 Canadian) used to take loans for education and health, and most important, to kick off small businesses. By August 2008, the cooperative had grown to 15,000 members with savings of nearly 7 million rupees and about $175,000 Canadian.

When I visited in 2002, some of the women I met were wearing coal black burqas, which they kept on since the translator I had with me from COVA was a man, but underneath around their ankles, colourful clothing beamed.

Of these women, three worked as Link Volunteers, each in charge of about 20 families, helping them get services and listening to their problems.

Across 125 poor slum neighbourhoods in the old city, every week about 1,000 Link Volunteers visited a total of 22,000 homes under their purview and made sure that health services were delivered. Once a month, in each slum area, savings and loans would be collected and local issues and problems discussed.

Meet Gori Bee, a grandmother, not in a burqa, who ran a small grocery that carried eggs, dry fish, as well as sweets like biscuits and chocolates.

Once a month she took a nurse from the local health centre to visit 20 families to line up vaccinations for the children and doctor's appointments for the pregnant women, as well as anyone else who might need it.

Later in discussions, she and two others highlighted one of the biggest problems facing people in the community — total lack of confidence in the government school system.

"My grandchildren go to private schools," she said. "The government school is too far away — two or three kilometres. Besides, they get a better education going to private school. There are not enough teachers in government schools, and sometimes there are no toilets or drinking water. Only very poor people send their children there."

One of the women who worked as a housemaid had two children aged eight and 10, and she admitted that the government school was all she could afford.

A second Link Volunteer, Afiya Parveen, a 35-year-old housewife whose husband was an electrician, had enrolled her daughter of 11 in a Christian missionary school, not because she was Christian herself, but because it was a good school.

"I'm working with four groups representing up to 200 people. We are asking the government to give us a local school with enough teachers. We're hoping that in two months when the new school year starts we'll have it," she said.

A girl of 14 who was not part of the group but whose grandmother was a Link Volunteer drifted in and sat down. I asked her why she wasn't in school.

"I was in grade seven at the local government school," she said, "but there were only four teachers for 150 students. We would come to school at nine and expect to leave at 3:30, but quite often the teachers sent us home at noon. My parents can't afford to send me to a private school, but if we get a new school here, I'll go to it."

Her grandmother, Yasanna Bee, 55, whose husband was an imam, had three boys and a girl. Her youngest son, then in grade 10 and finishing high school, was the only one of her children who had gone to school.

She agreed that education was an important issue for residents, but said people should also mobilize for garbage collection and more water from the corner borewell taps. "Right now," she said, "water is available only one and a half hours a day."

A few days before I had talked with Smarajit Ray, the top civil servant in charge of rural development and the District Poverty Initiatives Program (DPIP) in Andhra Pradesh. The state, which was making headway in terms of literacy and family planning, was putting all its hopes for development in the hands of women's thrift and credit groups like the one that was gathered in this cubby-hole room.

But the most important thing these women were doing was to discuss what was happening in their communities and in their own small ways to work for social change, though they would never call it that.

Recognizing that education was so important, COVA, at the request of thrift and credit groups, had started adult literacy classes as well as schools where child labourers could learn to read and write and eventually finish grade seven. The children attended classes early in the morning before they went to work.

Certain kinds of child labour were illegal but hard to stamp out so the goal was to make sure that, no matter what, youngsters had access to education. There were also bridge schools where children who had fallen behind or dropped out could take concentrated classes that would allow them to enter a regular class in a government school.

But government schools were so notoriously inadequate that by 2008 the cooperative had created a school education loan program. Four thousand poor children, half of them girls, were as a result benefitting from education in better-run private schools known for solid English-language instruction.

COVA was also providing vocational training for adolescent girls wanting to become tailors, beauticians, secretaries, computer operators, and phone operators. Young men were making a living after taking courses in bookbinding, card printing, and making videos for special events and family gatherings.

But the core of COVA's work involved the creation of micro-enterprises making garments, home accessories, food, and doing catering. Later that day I went to three micro-enterprises, each headed by a woman entrepreneur giving daily work to groups of women in these slum areas.

At the first two everyone was dressed from head to toe in black, and their faces would have been covered too if they were outside. The last group I visited was completely Muslim, but the women were all in colours.

The groups were part of the Mahila Sanatkar Mutually Aided Cooperative Society with 40 entrepreneurs and 120 Muslim and Hindu women often working together.

For blouses and dresses, the women worked on pedal sewing machines my mother had used. "We have orders to fill," said Asiya Khatoom, director of the Mahila Sanatkar, "and there are too many power outages for us to rely on electric sewing machines."

The clothes I saw were beautiful — all of them designed by a group at the COVA office that handled training, ordering raw materials, quality control, and sales. Over the years that I came to Hyderabad I always visited and usually bought something from their shop in the old city.

A warm atmosphere prevailed in the houses or centres where the women were working. In between concentrated work on beading and

A Hindu and Muslim woman work together to create colourful garments for sale.
Photo courtesy of the Confederation of Voluntary Associations.

embroidery, the women talked and joked. But they all worked hard. By 2008 sales had topped 2.5 million rupees (about $62,000 Canadian) with 162 artisans.

The next evening I accompanied a COVA organizer to a mixed Hindu and Muslim "sensitive neighbourhood" where we saw where a Hindu mob had broken down the doors of some Muslim houses. But on the street where women were waiting to talk to us, Hindu and Muslim families were peacefully living together. A small Hindu temple stood on one side of the street facing a Muslim graveyard on the other.

On a front porch ledge, Hindu and Muslim women were sitting close together and the friendly gab revealed that the neighbourhood had no school, but they wanted one. And wouldn't it be nice if the padlock could come off the community hall the government built? Maybe they could have some vocational training there, they said. A Link Volunteer, the COVA organizer decided, would be selected from the neighbourhood to start working with them.

The next day I was at a peace gathering set up by COVA designed to emphasize communal harmony in the wake of the troubles unfolding in the northern state of Uttar Pradesh that had unleashed conflicts elsewhere in the country.

I sat in the front row in the shade of the 400-year-old Mecca Masjid with space for 10,000 worshippers at the entrance to the old city and listened to imams, Christian ministers, and Buddhists — all of them men — intone about the evils of intolerance.

Far more important, in terms of the future of the community, were three women that hadn't spoken after about two hours of long speeches. I had already met COVA's Asiya Khatoom in charge of women's economic empowerment. Next to her was Ismat Memdi with a Gandhian movement called Sarvodaya. A third was Amrita Ahluwalia, a volunteer social worker who worked with women but made her living as an air hostess.

These women, in their quiet, task-oriented ways — just like the thrift and credit members — were concerned not about where the next temple or mosque would be built, but rather how to have better schools, good health services, enough water, and regular garbage collection. And of course jobs so that children received enough to eat.

International Women's Day was coming up and there would be a meeting of Muslim and Hindu women who had acted as "saviours" or had been "victims" during recent troubles in the old city and they would meet in solidarity to tell their stories and to work for peace.

The atmosphere in these heady days of February and March of 2002 continued to be charged. The country was reeling after 57 Hindu pilgrims bound for Ahmedabad from Ayodhya had died in a fire on the train. Police (all of them Hindus) claimed the fire had resulted when Muslim agitators hurled fire bombs into one of the cars.

Three years later an exhaustive forensic investigation established that the fire had been caused by an accident possibly caused by travellers cooking within the train car and not by external troublemakers. But everyone at the time — though not my friend Vithal, who did not believe the official story — was blaming Muslims.

In the old city I too was swept up by events. One Friday in an internet café near the Mecca Masjid mosque I heard some deep rumbling when the owner, who was Muslim, suddenly pulled down the roll-down black steel doors and locked us all in. Prayers had come to an end, the police were waiting for the men coming out, and some Muslim youth were taking them on. The internet owner wanted to protect his business.

That morning I had arrived at the nearby COVA offices to go out to a neighbourhood with a Link Volunteer and I was told we would go out only if there had been no disturbances after Friday prayers. Once the internet café was unlocked, I went to COVA and found out that although the "riot" was over near the mosque, tension was possible in the neighbourhoods, so any visits with a Link Volunteer were out.

The following week Hyderabad was warming up again for possible riots. The day was approaching when Hindu pilgrims in Uttar Pradesh were to start symbolic construction of the Hindu temple.

At the COVA offices I sat in on some on-the-floor meetings where Hindu and Muslim staff set up teams that would guard against possible violence with volunteers in the neighbourhoods. The teams decided that throughout the old city's slums Hindus would protect the mosques while Muslims would protect the temples.

The woman who was responsible for the operation was Noor Jehan, a Muslim peace activist who had been working with COVA for six years. To calm any situation that might arise between police and men emerging from the Mecca Masjid after Friday prayers, she suggested that women be ready to form a human chain.

After the planning meetings I accompanied COVA organizers to a special meeting with the police commissioner in charge of the old city. The idea was to inform him that teams of Hindus and Muslims had been organized to guard against any violence that might erupt.

I don't know what possessed me but I ended up giving an affirmative action lecture to the Hindu police commissioner. He was in charge of 1,500 officers with almost no Muslim police constables for a population of half a million people, 75 percent of them Muslim.

A plaque on the wall listed all the commissioners for the old city since 1959, but there was not one Muslim name.

"Why," I asked?

"The centre," he said, meaning the federal government, "appoints the top people."

Despite COVA's attempt to work with police to guarantee communal harmony, a few days later a phalanx of Hindu police was standing outside the Mecca Masjid. In outright provocation they were waiting with raised batons for the young Muslim men to emerge from the mosque after prayers.

The police were barely in place when a large group of women clad in black burqas formed a tight human chain between the police and the men emerging from the mosque. As the police with batons tried to break the human chain and the youth began to throw stones, Noor Jehan pleaded with the police to show restraint, cautioning that the situation would flare into real violence if they lost their tempers.

When policemen forced their way close to the youth, several older Muslim women went into the pack and talked quietly with the young men while the cord of women kept the police at bay. Eventually the youth disbanded. The women in burqas had saved the day and I quickly fired off a piece about them for the *Montreal Gazette* in my home city.

I was now packed and ready to fly to the city of Ahmedabad in the state of Gujarat. The goal was to spend time at the flagship Self Employed Women's Association (SEWA) where poor rag pickers and street vendors — under the auspices of an incredible woman called Ela Bhatt — had started their own bank.

There had been extensive violence against Muslims in Gujarat where the Hindu fundamentalist BJP party was in power at the state level. But it was also a state where Mahatma Gandhi had worked and lived in a

To prevent a riot, Muslim women form a human chain in front of the Charminar leading to Hyderabad's largest mosque. Photo courtesy of the Confederation of Voluntary Associations.

famous ashram and I was anxious to go. Vithal assured me "the blood-bath there was over."

After four months in Andhra Pradesh, I had fallen in love with the India of villages and farms. I had met extraordinary women that had banded together to make the deserts bloom and their communities thrive. The courage of the women in burqas who had kept the peace in the old city was still fresh in my mind. But now I was to step into a Dante's Inferno and another side of this incredible country. Unfortunately the battles were still raging, and I found myself in the middle of it.

8
THE STREET VENDORS' BANK

Upon arriving in Ahmedabad, I was reminded of the October Crisis that I had lived through while reporting at the *Montreal Star* when the War Measures Act was invoked and the army marched into Quebec. Army trucks packed with guys were moving around the streets, but the Montreal and Ahmedabad situations were hardly comparable; in Quebec, only four people died as a result of the nationalist crisis, and that was over a period of years.

In Ahmedabad, according to the morning's paper I picked up, thousands were in refugee camps as a result of Hindu mob violence. The eventual confirmed Muslim death count would reach 2,000 with 200,000 homeless. I would later hear from the people in the refugee camps that police had facilitated, and even initiated, many assaults. I personally witnessed police beating up television reporters who were covering a peace conference at the Mahatma Gandhi ashram.

I had come to Ahmedabad to meet street vendors and paper pickers with the Self Employed Women's Association (SEWA) who had started their own bank and organized themselves into unions and cooperatives. In Ahmedabad, a friend of Vithal's at Friends of Women's World Banking was my main contact. Friends of Women's World Banking was affiliated with the New York-based Women's World Banking, which supported women and microcredit. She had agreed to book me into a hotel with an internet connection close to the old city where SEWA was most active.

I was met at the airport by a representative of the Park Plaza hotel and told I would be paying $100 a night. Compared to the $5 a night (with food) that I paid at the farm centre of the Deccan Development Society, or even the rate at the very comfortable Minerva in Hyderabad, it was a fortune. The hotel representative told me it was very low compared to the rate paid by the last hotel guest from the West. She was an American woman, he said, working for an organization dealing with hunger in India and she stayed a month and paid $1,000 U.S. a night for a suite, though she was only one person.

I was the only guest because of a strict curfew in the old city around the hotel; everyone else was staying away. In the old city very poor Muslims had been burned out and lost housing along with businesses such as rickshaw shops, bakeries, and cycle repair stores. And the violence wasn't over. I found myself virtually locked in. The hotel staff was happy to have me, but a young M.B.A. graduate at the front desk advised me the next morning to move into the safer business centre of the city, which I did.

Over the next few days, determined to do my research, I met a range of people from the Self Employed Women's Association that had organized thousands of rag pickers, clothes recyclers, waste paper foragers, head loaders, and vegetable vendors, along with women who worked inside their flimsy huts making indigenous cigarettes called bidis, incense sticks, garments, and rag quilts.

Under British rule, Ahmedabad had flourished as the Manchester of Asia. But when the textile factories started closing down in the 1970s, more than 100,000 men became unemployed. Families in the slums soon began to depend upon the starvation wages that women made after middlemen and moneylenders charging as much as 10 percent a day had taken their hefty cuts.

Life for working women at the bottom of the heap began to improve in 1972 when Ela Bhatt, a fearless and energetic lawyer — then in charge of the women's wing of the Textile Labor Association started in the 1920s by Mahatma Gandhi — decided to organize self-employed women in the slums.

In India, over 90 percent of women work in the informal sector of the labour force without security or benefits. To give them a voice, and the power to stop the kind of exploitation that was keeping them in poverty, Ela Bhatt decided to help women band together in unions and cooperatives.

As she later described in her book, *We Are Poor But So Many*, she began her work by befriending Soopa, a head loader who carried bulks of cloth on her head from wholesalers to retailers during the day but who slept on the sidewalk at night. A migrant from another state, this head loader made 20 trips a day at 2 rupees per trip for a total of about $5 Canadian, but half of this income went from her employer to the contractors that had brought her from her village to the city, so she made barely $2.50 a day.

Chandaben, who went to wealthy neighbourhoods and bartered stainless steel utensils for hand-me-down clothes of the rich, became her entry point into the world of clothes recyclers. Along with seven family members working around the clock at two sewing machines in their hut, Chandaben repaired the clothes and sold them in a recycled clothes market.

In Ahmedabad, 80,000 street vendors were selling fruits, vegetables, fish, and other items in handcarts or in baskets on the ground beside them. Lakshmi Teta was a vegetable vendor whose family had been selling on the pavement for several generations. A woman who had actually given birth to one of her children at her work station on the street, Laskshmi ushered Ela into the hand-to-mouth world of street vendors.

With Ela Bhatt, these three women became comrades-in-arms, and as a team they began to organize women labouring at different jobs in the slums.

Over time, with hard work, and what Ela Bhatt called "dumb luck," the piece work rate for head loaders jumped by 30 percent.

Through strikes and court actions, eventually bidi workers increased their earnings from 5 rupees to 28 rupees for 1,000 bidis.

Right from the beginning SEWA tried to work with local banks, but the middle class men at the banks couldn't deal with illiterate women who sometimes arrived in dirty clothes with children in tow. It was difficult for the women to get to out-of-the-way banks open only during regular office hours, and when they did show up to try to open accounts they were so insulted by bank staff that they didn't want to persevere.

In 1974, discussing what they should do, Chandeben said, "Why can't we have our own bank?" By this time they had formed unions and cooperatives, why not a bank?

"Because we have no money," said Ela, pointing out that a large amount of capital was needed to start a bank.

Chandeben replied, "We may be poor but we are so many," which became the title of Ela Bhatt's book about SEWA, published in 2006.

Refusing to let go of their dream of setting up their own bank, the women conducted a survey of the bank's potential clientele and discovered that large numbers of women rented equipment, average debt was 700 rupees (at the time $87 Canadian), and the women's economic contribution was crucial to family survival.

With bank shares set at 10 rupees each, the equivalent of about $1.25 Canadian, the women set out to form their own bank. Within six months, 71,320 rupees (nearly $9,000 Canadian) had been collected from more than 6,000 members. Nevertheless, the registrar of cooperatives refused to register the bank, saying to Ela, "How can you ever do banking with illiterates?"

Promoters had to sign registration papers, and not even one of the 15 promoters of the bank could write her name, so over a long night Ela worked painstakingly until each one could successfully sign her name. After Ela proposed that illiterate SEWA depositors use a photograph on their passbooks, and it was agreed that members could sign with a thumb print, the registrar finally consented to register the SEWA Women's Cooperative Bank.

Always practical, the grassroots SEWA women, who formed the majority on the bank's board of directors, decided the interest would be similar to commercial banks. Since so many SEWA members lived from hand to mouth, this was to make sure that members weren't tempted to borrow money and then lend it out at higher rates.

The required interest on money borrowed from its own depositors credit fund became 17 percent, but interest on housing finance institution

Vegetable vendor Rajiben collected 10 rupees from hundreds of vendors to help 6,000 women launch their own bank and avoid gouging money lenders.

loans was set at 14 percent. The women's savings yielded a yearly dividend for them of 15 percent.

To make sure women could deposit money on a daily basis and easily repay loans, doorstep banking was pioneered through mobile vans, and banksathis or hand holders provided financial counselling.

These frontline workers lived in the same neighbourhoods as the customers and laboured in similar trades. No collateral was required for loans but women had to save for at least a year before they were eligible to apply for a loan. Eager to keep the extent of their savings secret from husbands, many women kept their passbooks at the bank for safekeeping and made sure no bank statements were ever sent to their homes. Later, in the 1990s, SEWA began banking activities in rural districts through the formation of self-help groups that collected and deposited savings from members at the bank.

Thirty years after she first began to organize, Ela Bhatt, a wiry woman now in her 70s, was still the brains and inspiration behind one of most important grassroots women's organizations in India with over 500,000 members in Gujarat and another 160,000 in six other Indian states.

Consisting of a blend of gutsy young college-educated women organizers along with steadfast grassroots women leaders from slums and villages, SEWA was responsible for the formation of a range of unions covering incense-stick rollers, street vendors, home garment workers, headload workers, construction workers, paper pickers, bidi-rollers, and more.

In addition, 85 autonomous cooperatives had been created for several occupational groups. This included scrap paper pickers who were turning out office stationery, office cleaners who organized to take contracts to clean government buildings, and even service providers such as health and child care workers, as well as midwives.

In rural areas, dairy cow owners, tree gum collectors, and salt farmers had formed cooperatives along with embroiderers who had formed artisan groups that were selling to upscale Indians, and even Western markets, mainly through exhibitions. Farmers were organized into producer groups. All were selling through marketing organizations set up by SEWA to avoid middlemen.

At various times men wanted to join SEWA partly because many worked alongside women in the same occupations. Although Ela Bhatt was open to the idea, the SEWA women always refused because they felt that the men would dominate. In addition, they firmly believed that their community values and concern for their families were very different from those of the men who sometimes wasted money on alcohol and favoured greater spending on consumer items.

Keenly aware of the range of needs through the whole cycle of life, SEWA members have made health care, child care, housing, and insurance top priorities.

Health care was provided through SEWA's health workers cooperatives working in coordination with government health services.

Child care centres funded by a combination of SEWA members, the government, employers, and private trusts provided children with regular health checkups, good nutrition, and child development activities.

Since many women worked out of their homes, solid weather-proof homes were essential. Through the SEWA bank, a housing trust offered financial and technical aid and worked with the Ahmedabad municipal authorities for improved infrastructure services such as electricity, water, and sanitation.

Also through the bank, SEWA offered an integrated health, accident, life, and disaster insurance scheme that women could buy into to cover them in times of crisis.

Under Ela's leadership, SEWA had also used the courts, demonstrations of various kinds, and political pressure to entrench the rights of self-employed workers.

But perhaps most important, thanks to her determination, slum-dwelling women supported by savvy financial professionals were running a flourishing poor people's bank.

At the Shri Mahila SEWA Sahakari Bank 200,000 poor women had savings of more than $15 million Canadian and had taken loans totalling over $3 million to develop businesses and pay off old debts.

A SEWA Academy had been set up to train women for leadership, and women were turning out videos promoting income generation and education. Literacy programs were available to those that wanted them.

I wanted to meet grassroots SEWA women in the slums, but the recurring violence in the city made this difficult. Half of SEWA members were Muslims, and 40,000 were now in refugee camps in the wake of the violence by Hindu mobs.

Because of the riots, SEWA staff who spoke English and could translate continued to be reluctant to take me into the old city to meet grassroots women and told me to "come back in two weeks."

I thought of leaving town because I had not come to India to write about violence, but the longer I stayed the more horror-struck I became at the organized lynching of Muslims. My friends from back home couldn't understand why I was sticking around where violence was taking place, but I could not turn my back on it.

9
INTO THE INFERNO

My new hotel was in a safe part of Ahmedabad where no violence was taking place, but one evening I saw clear evidence of the state-led assault against Muslims when a young front desk employee at my hotel offered me a lift on his motor scooter to a late-night internet café. As we wove through the city, he pointed out all the burned out Muslim-owned restaurants, businesses, factories, and hotels that had been systematically torched by vigilantes. In preparation for this, a survey pinpointing Muslim houses and establishments had apparently been carried out by the state government.

At the internet café, a Hindu icon outside made sure no one would think the place was owned by a Muslim. This was a city where it was plainly dangerous to be a Muslim. Groups supported by the Hindu fundamentalist BJP government in power in Gujarat and at the federal level were systematically targeting everything Muslim. But emails from friends in far-flung parts of the world, including Montreal, revealed that this important story was getting little coverage.

Upon the suggestion of Vijayalakshmi Das at Friends of Women's World Banking, I went off to meet a group of Hindu, Muslim, and Christian community organizers and peace activists working out of a Jesuit social service centre. Called the Citizens Initiative, the goal of these dedicated people from a range of non-government organizations was to stop the violence and help the refugees in the camps where the government had been sending in rotten rice.

Composed mostly of Hindus with a history of working in the fields of poverty, human rights, minorities, and women's empowerment, it was supporting the refugees with food, health services, legal counselling and activities for the thousands of children who were not attending school.

Every day members gathered at the St. Xavier Social Service Society, an agency run by Father Victor Moses, a Jesuit dedicated to communal harmony and the eradication of poverty.

An important member of the coalition was Wilfred D'costa, the general secretary of the Indian Social Action Forum (INSAF), a federation of 400 social action groups from across India. He said the BJP government in Gujarat drew its support from several Hindu fundamentalist organizations inspired by the Nazi model. "Their goal," he said, "is to obliterate the Muslims."

He said the chief minister of the state, Narendra Modi, was shaped by the Rashtriya Swayamsevak Sangh (RSS), a Hindu organization of more than 100,000 members "with a fascist military orientation." He particularly deplored the behavior of the Bajrang Dal, composed of thousands of young men that were being trained to act as hoodlums.

Across the city and the state, thousands of Muslim establishments had been systematically destroyed, he said. Before the riots, there had been a chain of 1,100 Muslim-owned vegetarian restaurants. Now only 100 were left.

Losses in houses, assets, and vehicles were estimated at $100 million Canadian and economic damage at $1 billion Canadian.

A university professor, who did not want to be named, said that Dalits and lower-caste Hindus, who had always been treated badly, were given the mission of carrying the torch of Hinduism and were being used by upper-caste Hindus in the fundamentalist organizations and the government to perform their dirty work.

I felt the heart-breaking effects of this inferno that had descended upon innocent people when I visited the refugee camps with a young man from the Citizens Initiative who specialized in trauma counselling.

Thousands of lost and sad homeless people, many of whom had witnessed the killing of their husbands and families, were crammed into the courtyards of mosques or on abandoned lots. Children were silent and hollow-eyed. If they were lucky, they had rags to sit on and a tent over their heads to protect them from the brutal rays of the sun.

Across Ahmedabad about 75,000 refugees were in camps. The worst of the attacks seemed to be over, but calls to arms were not. During a Hindu holiday a few days before my visit to the camps, pamphlets had been dropped all over Hindu neighbourhoods entreating people to use the holiday to continue to attack the Muslims.

At the first camp I visited, 10,000 people were tightly packed into the courtyards around a mosque in the old city where temperatures were more than 40 degrees.

A woman of 32 with six children told me how her husband had been burned to death when a mob of thousands moved into Naroda-Patia on the outskirts of the city. "They grabbed my husband's rickshaw and threw kerosene on it and burned it. Then they threw him on top of it," she said.

When the mob set fire to her house, she and her children escaped with the help of some Christians who were later attacked. "I can never go back to my neighbourhood," she said. "I'd be too afraid."

A barefoot woman of 22, with two restless preschool sons sitting next to her on the bare ground under the blazing sun, described how five members of her extended family died in the same area after her mother pleaded with police to protect them.

"Police told my mother they had a vehicle that would take them to safety and were told to walk down a road," she said. "When they got to the end, they faced an open field where a mob threw kerosene over them and burned them to death." The woman said an NGO had brought her to the camp. "I was lucky. Many of the women here at the camp were raped."

Harsh Mander, a senior federal government civil servant, on leave and directing an NGO called ActionAid India, told me that he had never seen sexual crimes against women used so widely by mobs.

"There are reports everywhere of gang rapes of young girls and women, followed by their murder by burning alive or bludgeoning with a hammer.

What can you say about a woman eight months pregnant who begged to be spared? Her assailants instead slit open her stomach, pulled out her fetus, and slaughtered it before her eyes," he wrote in the *India Times*, a major English-language daily in India which was covering the story.

Munir Shaikh, the administrator of the Shah-e-Alam camp where I conducted many interviews, said the future for Muslims in the state was bleak.

With about 138 million Muslims in India as a whole, they were an integral part of the country with deep cultural roots, and couldn't just be flushed away. Ahmedabad alone had 600,000 Muslims, while Gujarat had five million out of a total population of 50 million.

Over a four-week period, an estimated 1,300 Ahmedabad people had died in addition to another 700 in villages across Gujarat. These figures came from Ahmedabad Jesuits who monitored human rights and were reliable, but the police were telling reporters that only 800 had died and at least one American wire service used that figure.

I had become an almost ex officio member of the Citizens Initiative which met at the Jesuit social service centre and, for the sake of my new Muslim friends, I felt I had to contribute and not just observe. So I filed a story about the refugee camps which appeared in the *Montreal Gazette*.

The genocidal violence had surged in the wake of the train-car fire that killed Hindu pilgrims returning from Ayodaya. The official explanation, which turned out to be a lie — pinning the blame on Muslim extremists — suited the political goals of the Hindu nationalist Bharatiya Janata Party (BJP) and was fed to an unquestioning population.

Unfortunately, with the article I ended up writing for the *Montreal Gazette*, I was guilty along with many others of circulating this erroneous background information blaming Muslims for the fire. In the months after 9/11 such stories fuelled a Western press eager to demonize Muslims across the world.

At the Citizens Initiative, which I visited each day, disturbing news kept streaming in. A research team reported that Hindu fundamentalist groups were using intimidation to recruit marginalized Tribal people to drive more than 10,000 Muslims out of their homes in an eastern corridor of the state.

If there was one sanctuary where peace activists felt they could meet in tranquility, that was the Sabarmati Ashram, Gandhi's headquarters during the long struggle for Indian independence. But even that came under attack.

A peace conference gathering people from all over India was organized by Indian dancer and actress Mallika Sarabhai, well-known for her support for women's organizations and communal harmony. One of the participants was Medha Patkar, known for her opposition to a large dam project in Gujarat.

Three hours into the conference, a mob of young men that organizers recognized as being part of the BJP party burst into the quiet serenity of the ashram calling for the expulsion of Patkar.

To protect her, peace activists spirited Patkar away into a backroom while police suddenly flooded the ashram and began beating up six journalists.

While this was going on, I hastily put away my notebook and pen, donned a sun hat mashed into the bottom of my shoulder bag, and pretended to be a British tourist. But the police still wanted to know who I was. "Just interested in Gandhi," I said as airily as I could muster.

Eventually the peace activists agreed to allow Patkar to be escorted from the ashram, after insisting some women police officers be called in to accompany her. The male police officers finally steered the mob out of the building, but then they surrounded the open meeting place of the peace activists. Refusing to continue their meeting under hostile eyes of the police, they spontaneously joined hands and sang "We Shall Overcome," after which they sang the Indian national anthem and dispersed.

The next morning while walking down the street from my downtown hotel to the internet café, what should I see but an elephant! In the midst of the brutality that had gripped the city, the sight of this friendly gray elephant was almost comforting. The email café down from my hotel was on a residential road marked by villas with high gates. This slow-moving elephant lifted his trunk over an imposing entry way and accepted from a maid a 10-rupee note that he lifted up every so casually to a young man sitting on his back.

I tried to get someone to tell me in English what this elephant with the painted ears was doing wandering around the neighbourhood soliciting rupees, but the residents all spoke only Gujarati or Hindi. The best thing about the elephant, I thought, was that he wasn't Muslim or Hindu or Christian. He was just an ordinary secular elephant out begging with a cheerful-looking young man on his back.

But later that day at the Jesuit social service centre, I learned that my treasured secular elephant was in fact a card-carrying Hindu.

A famous temple in the city kept 50 elephants that were expected to beg for their food and also toil as temple fund-raisers. The temple was the starting point for riots reminiscent of Northern Ireland. On special days, religious processions led by elephants wound through the city. When the parade passed by mosques, the Hindus would yell abusive slogans and confrontations would follow.

The following day, back on the on the beat, so to speak, I went off with members of the Citizens Initiative to Babunagar, a poor, working-class village on the edge of the city that had experienced mob violence. Community organizers wanted to start a Peace Collective composed of young Hindus and Muslims who would work together on projects to establish harmony between the two communities.

The Muslim side of the village, separated from the Hindu part by a wide road, had experienced 25 deaths and the destruction of 1,700 homes and 900 shops, 200 of them along the dividing road.

A key member of the Citizens Initiative was Hausla Prasad Mishra who ran a workers movement for occupational safety with members from both sides of the village. Mishra was himself of Hindu background, but the headquarters of his movement was in the Muslim quarter, which was where we were headed.

The right-wing fundamentalist Hindus on the other side of the village had wanted to stop him from serving Muslims, but the Hindu members involved in the workers movement had fully supported him. It was because of his leadership capacity and his proven ability to work with grassroots people from both groups that Babunagar had been chosen as the starting point for setting up peace collectives.

We climbed out of our rickshaws on the Muslim side and into what looked like a war zone with cratered houses, piles of bricks, twisted, up-ended rickshaws, and row after row of black holes where shops and houses had been torched.

For about an hour we listened to Muslim men talk about the violence their neighbourhood had endured. Some of the participants came from a refugee camp in the interior of the village where 10,000 people, belonging to 1,800 families from several Muslim communities, were crammed in together on the ground under rag roofs. Of these families, 1,300 came from Bapunagar and were now homeless. At the meeting, there seemed to be only one cry: "Tell them not to attack us!"

After the initial meeting I decided to come back on my own with a young woman who had volunteered in the camps.

Sitting on the floor the next day in one of their huts, a group of Muslims told me that the day after the Hindu pilgrims died in the train car on the way back from Ayodhya, they started hearing the rising sound of rhythmic drumbeats coming from the Hindu side of the village.

Eventually a mob of thousands led by goons with rifles and kerosene cylinders moved in on them. In addition to those who had lost their homes, hundreds more were now hiding away in three refugee camps because they were too afraid to be in their houses.

On the Hindu side, the Hindu militarist organizations tied to the Hindu nationalist government in power in Gujarat had been running fascist-style indoctrination camps for youth for several years. They would meet at 6:00 a.m. and start with Hindu prayers, and then sing chants invoking the Hindu homeland. Training in how to use various kinds of weapons, including tools for arson, came next, with the eventual goal of obliterating the enemy within, namely their fellow Muslim citizens.

When the goons arrived on the Hindu side on February 28, they told the residents that if they refused to join the mob and attack the Muslims, their own homes would be burned and looted.

Some Muslim families I spoke to were still too scared to stay at home, but didn't want to move to camps. So, for security and solace, a few families huddled together at night in a single hut with all the lights out, lying awake, hoping that they wouldn't be attacked.

SARIS ON SCOOTERS

On my last day in Babunagar, I went to several homes and talked to families that had lost members in the violence. The worst story came from a woman whose 12-year-old son had been playing cricket in a field close to her house with his friends. He had been killed by a sniper using a rifle.

I had plans to talk to residents on the Hindu side of the village but it was not to be.

The violence that I had tried to live with as a reporter covering a story was beginning to make me sick. Also, I had been in Harbin in the north of China the summer before where I had contracted pneumonia from the pollution, and Ahmedabad was a severely polluted place. I was experiencing the same wheeze I had had in Harbin.

I had wanted to stay in the city until I could do interviews in the old city with grassroots SEWA women, but I had lost all my energy. It was time to leave. I would eventually return to Ahmedabad six years later to spend time with SEWA embroiderers who were selling in the global market. But now, in April of 2002, I had to pack up and go. Always looking out for me, Vithal Rajan had arranged for me to go to Chennai on the Bay of Bengal and fend off pneumonia at the home of a delightful sugar heiress who had been a fellow student of his while he was completing a doctorate at the London School of Economics.

When I returned to Ahmedabad in January 2008, the situation was a lot more stable, although thousands of Muslims who had not been resettled were living in ramshackle relief colonies. Then in July 2008, 40 Ahmedabadis died when a little-known group calling itself the Indian Mujahedeen set off blasts, in revenge, they said, for the carnage inflicted on Muslims in 2002.

But the political situation at the federal level by 2008 was much different, although in Gujarat at the state level the Hindu fundamentalist BJP was still in power. Seeking to keep the peace between local Hindus and Muslims in Ahmedabad, Prime Minister Manmohan Singh and Congress party leader Sonia Gandhi visited the city to comfort the wounded and, most important, to call for calm.

10
IN THE PRESENCE OF THE SEEDKEEPER

More than two years went by and in late November of 2004 I was back in India, this time to explore the work of Vandana Shiva, a fireball of a woman with a physics degree from the University of Western Ontario who was promoting organic agriculture, especially among women farmers. Through her organization, Navdanya, in the Himalayan state of Uttaranchal in the north of the country, this physicist turned environmentalist and activist was bent on rescuing Indian agriculture from the jaws of western agribusiness. She was also making waves on the international stage.

The Slow Food Movement which endorsed traditional foods and crops had taken off in the West and it was giving top awards to women in the developing world. One of them was Bija Devi, a brilliant non-literate woman from the Himalayan hills who ran Navdanya's model farm in the foothills near the capital Dehradun and served as its seedkeeper.

To ease my way in, I had decided to take a two-week course called "Gandhi, Cultures of Non-violence and Globalization," given at the farm centre by Vandana Shiva and Satish Kumar, a former child monk and peace pilgrim who ran a college for ecological studies in England.

I flew first to Delhi, and thanks to a Toronto friend, found myself renting a room for $50 U.S. a night (definitely not cheap by Indian standards) in a private home. After a few days I would take a train to Dehradun.

I was back in the swing of India with all the swirling sights, smells, and sounds along with its captivating characters.

In Delhi I was for a short while in an upper-class setting, this time Muslim, with the "daughter of the last advisor to the last Nizam of Hyderabad." My bed and breakfast host had grown up "in a royal family," she said, "with servants who knew how to do things," a commentary, I assumed, on what she had to endure in her present situation. She had one full-time servant and a few others that appeared at various times and she complained about the burden of having to deal with their "sordid tales."

Hajira, her full-time cook and general maid, lived on the top floor separate from the rest of the house. Abandoned by her husband who had disappeared to Kashmir with her children, Hajira had become romantically interested in a security guard from the neighbourhood. My hostess, who lived alone, didn't allow him in the door, so they sat on the outside steps and scandalized the neighbours just by talking to one another.

I felt sorry for Hajira who was engaging and sensitive. In this country, having a boyfriend, let alone a lover, required secrecy. In its food, dancing, music, and mythologies, India explodes with sensuality, but it also wears a veil of Victorian Puritanism.

I encountered many illustrations of this. In Hyderabad, a Toronto Indian friend who sat on a bench in a park with her Indian boyfriend was surprised when a total stranger announced that they were sitting too close together. And an Indian woman in her 20s told me she could not take a holiday with her fiancé because hotels would refuse to rent them a room together.

Hajira was a fantastic cook and eager to please. She warmed to me because I enjoyed her curries and complimented her upon her clothes via translation, since she did not speak English. She reminded me of the women I had met in the villages and I felt we could have become friends.

The first night, my host invited me to go to an outdoor play along with a friend who worked in the IT business and had three daughters in the U.S. holding down big jobs.

Mounted by a Tribal group, the play featured Sikhs, Muslims, and Hindus in a marketplace fighting with one another but then coming together. The neighbour, Ram, who provided a running translation, said it was about national unity. But according to my host, "Ram had no culture and didn't understand the play," which she claimed "was about Urdu poetry." We left before the play ended because she became offended by the hum of Ram whispering a translation of the play's dialogue into my ear.

That day in Delhi had seen many weddings — apparently 14,000 — because of the day being auspicious and with a full moon, said Ram. The air was heavy with the sweetness of tropical flowers. En route back from the theatre, Ram pointed out overflowing colourful wedding tents pealing with music and cars draped with garlands.

No matter what time of the day or night, life was astir in this big city. In the middle of the night I looked outside to see a small calf curled up in the centre of the road. The dogs started barking early along with various hawkers peddling wares. My hostess took me for a walk at 8:00 a.m. when the streets around her were filled with sweepers, sellers of fruits and vegetables, and desperate-looking women carrying huge loads of rags. The two-storey housing we walked through felt upper class, but my hostess said the place was teeming with a population of servants living in nominal shelter along back lanes.

After a few days recovering from jet lag, I headed off in an autorickshaw to the Delhi station with a cast-off sweater around my neck, provided by my hostess who said I was not equipped for the cold weather I would encounter in the Himalayan foothills and mountains. My policy was always to travel light and buy extra clothes where necessary.

My rickshaw journey through the Delhi streets was a nightmare because there were two major stations, and we were part way to one station before the driver realized he should be heading to the other.

Once in the station, I figured it was just a question of looking at a notice board for the train for Dehradun and then boarding it the way I would in Montreal. I was after all in the capital city of the country.

There was a notice board all right, and I found Dehradun on it with a track number, but I should have known to check the information. Along with a surging mass of humanity carrying babies, chickens, and heaps of worldly possessions, I proceeded to weave my way up and down stairs and across overpasses. Thoroughly whacked out, I finally arrived at the indicated track with a train about to pull out.

It had taken me so long I thought that maybe this was my train and yelled "To Dehradun?" into a crowd boarding. No one replied. The train pulled away and I frantically searched the people waiting by the tracks for someone official. Eventually I found what looked like a porter who actually spoke English. He told me this was definitely not the track for the Dehradun train, and that I was supposed to wait in line at an information desk inside the station to get the track number. The board, he said, was never right. Taking pity, he consulted someone and came up with the correct track number for Dehradun.

"Run," he said with a smile, "the train leaves in 15 minutes." Carrying my duffle bag with enough clothes for six months, a shoulder bag with a computer, a water bottle swinging from my wrist, and my fanny pack around my waist, I became so hot I flung my host's bulky sweater into the crowd like a bride hurling her wedding bouquet. With only a minute to spare, I climbed onto the last car just before this elusive train to the foothills of the Himalayas pulled out.

I was met in Dehradun, and along with some Ugandans also enrolled in the course, we rattled for 16 kilometres in a jeep past small villages and farm land glowing green until a sign reading Navdanya appeared. The road in meandered past one-room farm huts filled with welcoming children until it reached a series of handsome red brick buildings surrounded by an expanse of farm land.

This was the home of Navdanya's 24 acre model organic farm with its rice, millets, wheat, mango, and every kind of vegetable. A small office run by Rashid, who also ran a soil lab, welcomed us. Walls plastered with information about Navdanya's organic farming campaigns and the merits of traditional seeds as opposed to hybrid seeds told us right away that this was also a centre for activism.

I took a few minutes to read that land throughout India, which had traditionally served as a village commons for farmers to use for grazing, was being parcelled off to rich landlords and corporations. There was a call for villagers to rejuvenate the commons and contest cases of private appropriation.

In addition to the model organic farm, this was also the campus of Bija Vidyapeeth, an international learning centre for sustainable development. From time to time it offered a range of courses for students who stayed in rooms and dormitories along a monastery-like walk looking into flower gardens.

For our course we would be about 25 students from India, Latin America, Africa, Europe, the U.S., and Canada, among them two Canadians of Punjabi background and a British Indian studying in Guelph, Ontario. Off facing the fields under a thatched roof was an outdoor space with chairs for our course where we would listen and exchange.

The centre also served as a meeting ground for Indian organic farmers to learn more about crops and unite to protect their biodiversity heritage against the onslaught of chemically-based agriculture and companies wanting to patent the farmers' traditional seeds.

The heady aroma of curried vegetables floated from the kitchen which was presided over by Bujan, who in deference to the Westerners did his best not to inject too much chili into his meals. Everything cooking in the kitchen had been raised on Navdanya's farm which stretched off into the distance.

During the course, we would take turns in the kitchen, peeling and cutting produce; on the land, weeding; and at the seedbank, picking out stones from the rice. Study as well as chores, including cleaning toilets and sweeping the floors, were part of the Gandhi-inspired ashram experience. The day began at sunrise, after a cup of sweet milky tea, with meditation and body-stretching yoga. For intellectual reflection, a small library was available with books on water, ecology, organic farming, and the perils of industrial agriculture.

I settled into my room and met my roommate who was an Indian university student from Pune in the state of Maharashtra.

But I knew that the heart of the Navdanya biodiversity farm and learning centre was the seedbank. I went down a path behind the kitchen through tendrils of wheat and mustard to a rough road next to simple thatched huts belonging to nearby villagers.

At the end of the road, seedkeeper Bija Devi, who ran the farm and knew every plant on the place, reigned supreme over a colourful brick red and pale yellow seedbank centre.

Wrapped up in heavy purple, blue, and pink cotton against the chilly weather, Bija sat cross-legged on a concrete deck, meticulously separating chickpeas from weed seeds, bouncing them up in the air into a straw basket with a wire mesh bottom. Next to her, other women farmers were sorting seeds. Similar activity took place on the roof deck where as a farm volunteer I later banged rice out of sheaves after the rice harvest.

Seedkeeper Bija Devi oversees the seedbank and model farm for Navdanya, which helps small farmers expand organic agriculture.

Next door was a small barn littered with sweet-smelling hay which sheltered the bullocks that ploughed the fields. A stone's throw away a compost house with rows of vermiculture, and a large bin for regular green manure, guaranteed that the land was moist and fertile.

Over a fence from the seedbank was Ramgarh village. In the early morning, I would wake up to the keening of an imam calling the villagers to prayer, the tones resonating across the countryside. From the Hindu side of the village gongs rang throughout the day, heralding Hindu ceremonies.

These sounds from India's two main cultures punctuated the hours from dawn to dusk and reflected how Hindus and Muslims in Ramgarh village cooperated. At harvest time, the fields of the model farm were filled with women from both groups. For the joy of celebrating the arrival of the crops, they would give their time to support an organization that was helping them maintain sustainable agriculture practices that were centuries old.

Until Bija Devi came along 10 years before and persuaded them to practice organic agriculture, most farmers in both sections of the village were using chemicals promoted by Western agri-businesses. After the land began to deteriorate with lower crop yields and depleted water, they were willing to listen to Bija tell them how best to shift back to traditional methods. Gifts of indigenous seed, requiring only dung and green manure fertilizer from their own land, were in Bija Devi's hands waiting to be put into their ground.

The course I had enrolled in was illuminating, but much more so, for me, was getting to know Bija Devi, the guiding spirit and soul behind Navdanya. I did this by doing volunteer farm work for her. Under her guidance, I sat on the verandah of the seedbank and selected sticks of turmeric and ginger for use as seeds, and picked stones out of barrels of chickpeas and sacks of rice.

Surrounding us, in fields of resplendent green, were a diversity of crops of different shapes and heights, among them wheat, mustard, green vegetables, eggplant, carrots, onions, radish, gram, broad bean, coriander, garlic, spinach, turmeric, ginger, canola, cabbage, and salad greens. On other sites, inch-high seedlings were poking through rich brown soil still pungent with the smell of fresh compost threaded with cow dung. Among the flowering medicinal plants, daisy-like chamomile stalks nodded gently in the wind. It was now December, so the rice had already been harvested, and inside the seedbank sheaves wrapped in newspaper were waiting to be shaken out.

Biodiversity was the overriding theme at this farm where crops in most fields grew in pairs or trios — wheat with mustard, lemon trees with wild vegetable greens, rice and millets, cucumber with maize, sugarcane with potatoes — all for the purpose of nurturing the soil and confusing the pest population. For demonstration purposes, Bija also scattered seed for 12 crops (known as *baranaja* in Hindi) to preserve nutrients in dryland soils typical of the hill farming areas in the Garhwal area of the Himalayas where she was born.

Another day I picked lemons from the lemon orchard among mustard and wild greens growing together. Later on, in another field, I pulled clumps of grass and weeds from patches that had already been seeded with vegetables. I worried about dislodging the seeds but she told me that as long as I dusted the earth off the clumps the seeds would be fine.

Sitting around in dirt while weeding or heaving out patches of grass was something I had to get used to. Unlike Indian women who always looked so clean and pristine, I could not balance on my haunches nicely off the ground the way they could. The only problem was that to keep warm at night I sometimes slept in the clothes I worked in. Because I believed in travelling light I had only one pair of pants and at night I usually washed them. There was no heating and our room was as cold as a Canadian camp site in November.

Climbing into a freezing bed, I was usually wrapped up in warm pants that had been sitting around on composted soil, a sweater infused with dust, and a thick Tibetan coat. And I was still colder than I'd ever been in Montreal with its occasional 40-below-zero winter temperatures. At night in these Himalayan foothills, a damp cold chilled the bones, though under the sun in the middle of the day I could weed out in Bija's fields in a cotton shirt.

I got to know Bija over several meetings, always with a translator, first at the seedbank and then at her house where I was invited to spend the night and to meet her daughter Rajni.

At 57, Bija (which means seed in Hindi) was strong and lean, her sun-tanned face a smooth chocolate brown. She wore glasses that gave her a no-nonsense look, but she had a sense of humour and brought a quick intelligence to every question.

She had a daughter of 28 who taught school, a married son of 30 working as a technician in a battery factory near Delhi, and she was about to become a grandmother. Her husband had died four years before.

Her experience as a farmer, I knew, started at the age of seven. I asked her to tell me about her early years. "I didn't go to school," she said. "I helped my parents on the farm in the small village of Badiargard of only 40 families in the Tehri Garhwal District." Life, she recalled, was tough. Even though there was sometimes snow on the ground, she never wore socks and shoes and the women in the family owned only two saris.

She couldn't read, but she was clearly the principal teacher and prevailing Earth Mother at the Navdanya farm where women farmers gathered to seek her counsel and a male staff member with an agriculture degree recognized her enormous practical knowledge and wisdom.

Right from the beginning, sometimes with Vandana Shiva, Bija was meeting farmers, collecting indigenous seed in danger of disappearing, and encouraging growers using chemical fertilizers and pesticides to change to traditional organic methods. Along the way she picked up information about soil conditions and new plant types that she stored in her head for use whenever needed.

"She does the seedkeeping, and we mark the names on containers," said Indu Negi, one of the Navdanya community organizers. But Bija knew her seeds and didn't need a name on a jar to remind her of the contents. Under her leadership, hundreds of types of vegetables, including 250 varieties of rice, were grown, and she monitored the state of the seeds at the seedbank for all of them.

Returning to talk about her early days as a child farmer, she said, "There were four sisters and four brothers, nine in the family with me in the middle." The family possessed fields scattered in different places in the hills and practiced organic dryland agriculture, which meant they depended upon rain water and used heritage seeds that didn't need a lot of moisture. With labour from several of the children, they were able feed 11 people from it.

She learned about the crops by helping her parents sow and harvest pulses, soybean, four kinds of millet, sesame seed, and vegetables. Since her mother was the seedkeeper, she learned about that too.

At the age of 12, her parents decided it was time to marry her off. "My husband's parents came to my house to speak to my parents." Before she knew it she was married to a 28-year-old man, and found herself living four hours away from her home in the unfamiliar village of Reegoli.

What made it especially difficult was that her husband was working in Dehradun as a cook, and arrived at the village of his parents simply to get married. Prior to that, in order to bring in cash to the family, he had been working at a lawn tennis facility in Mussoori, known for its holiday hotels.

After the marriage he went back to Dehradun, leaving his bride alone with her newly acquired family of in-laws. "I didn't know anyone, and I was crying sometimes," she said.

Bija's husband visited, but when she did not become pregnant, she was taken to a doctor in Dehradun and discovered that she was suffering from a form of TB that was preventing conception. She received treatment but remained in Reegoli. By this time her father-in-law had died, and even though there were other family members, "it was the tradition," said her daughter Rajni, "for the daughter-in-law to stay with the extended family of her husband." Once her mother-in-law died, however, she left Reegoli and went to live with her husband in Dehradun where she gave birth to two children.

"But I missed growing things," she said. When her children were in grades 11 and 12, and she was 40, she bought one *bigha* of land (about one-fifth of an acre) 10 kilometres away from Dehradun. She built herself a one-room shack where she could sometimes stay and grew pulses, ginger, turmeric, rice, and wheat. In 2004 when I spoke to her, she was growing mostly turmeric on her land.

Then she met Vandana Shiva with her mission to save small Indian farmers, most of them women. At the time Vandana was giving a course to children on organic farming and asked Bija to make some food for the students. Two years later she recruited Bija to grow a vegetable garden at her house. After Vandana selected land near Ramgarh village for a model organic farm including a seedbank, Bija was a natural to be in charge.

Under Bija's lively leadership, the farm was run as a collective composed of a group of farmers who had grown crops in the hill area. Five of them were still involved. Vandana, who had never farmed, came in and out, and together they transformed a land made into desert by eucalyptus trees into a habitat of organic agriculture where over 650 varieties of plants flourish.

When they arrived, the land was riddled with stones and they had to dig up eucalyptus roots that drink a lot of water and nutrients, said Bija. Soil improvement was the first big challenge. Water was the second. There was no irrigation in the fields. The neighbouring village of Ramgarh gave them drinking water, and they hauled water from a government well that served just half a field.

For the first year they depended almost completely on rainwater. But eventually they dug a well and now the fields are regularly flooded with water from a spring. "Right from the beginning we cultivated wheat, rice, millets, pulses, and vegetables, some needing water and others not," said Bija. "But it took two years to get the soil fertile by using lots of cow dung and green manure."

Through her work as the seedkeeper, farmers who joined Navdanya were introduced to new kinds of seed. At the same time, the organization added to its collection from the discoveries of the farmers themselves. In addition to organizing the seedkeeping, Bija also chose what should be grown and where. She sowed, weeded, tended vegetables, screened special rice for the best seed, and gave food courses in the Dehradun area and in Delhi on Garhwali district food.

The produce on the farm, said Bija, keeps rising. In 1996, they got 250 kilograms per acre of wheat and rice and by 2004 they were getting 1,300 kilograms.

"From what we produce we feed 12 or 13 staff, plus people taking courses. And of course, we supply the seedbank," she pointed out. Surplus was sold at organic outlets in Dehradun and Delhi along with produce from Navdanya farmers from all over Uttaranchal and other states where Navdanya worked.

A typical day at the seedbank consisted of five people under her supervision making decisions about what to do on the land and with the harvest.

The first day I visited, two men were shaking the rice out of stalks that would serve as fodder for cows as well as compost. Bija was sitting on the ground, her legs crossed, separating the weed seeds from the chickpeas. My job for the morning was to shake out a bag of chickpeas and remove any that were small, withered, or cracked.

On the second day of my talks with Bija, three old friends — women that she knew when she was farming at her parents-in-law — joined her after lunch. All Navdanya members, the three were sisters-in-law married to three brothers. Each of them farmed an acre of land in a village four kilometres away.

Bija was giving them advice about the chickpeas she was sorting. These black ones mean that insects attacked the crop. "We need to use some neem," she said. Neem oil, secured from the pods of the ubiquitous neem tree, acted as an organic pest repellent.

But the women were most interested in information about new rice varieties for the cropping season starting in July. Indu Negi, a young woman in her 20s who served as a coordinator for the area, would set up a special meeting either in their village or at the Navdanya farm so that Bija could talk about the different varieties and what they could expect from them.

The women farmed alone without the help of their husbands who were working far away in hotels in other states of India. One had gone as far as Dubai.

"Our husbands make money for the extras," one of them explained. Extras included private education for their children. "The government schools aren't good enough," they said. All the women could read and write and wanted to make sure their children had the best education.

"Our children aren't interested in being farmers," they explained. "They don't like farming," said Bija.

Bija's daughter Rajni, a teacher, explained that because she was brought up in bustling Dehradun, the capital of Uttaranchal, she didn't have the training and experience of her mother to be a good farmer.

Later, while talking with her at her mother's home outside Dehradun where I was invited for supper and stayed the night, she expressed awe and respect for her mother's monumental knowledge and commitment to organic agriculture, including the electric energy she brought to it.

Now women like Bija were receiving international acclaim for the ecological way they managed their crops and land. More and more of the world was recognizing that organic produce was more healthful than the chemically laden food available in the big Western supermarkets. In addition, soil and water were being preserved for a sustainable agriculture that could not be maintained through soil-degrading chemicals that depleted water systems.

Bija's work in promoting organic farming in the state of Uttaranchal, which officially promoted organic farming, was feature news in agricultural and environmental circles.

In 2001 in Portugal, she won a Slow Food Award, given by the Slow Food Movement, an international organization that promotes biodiversity crops grown slowly and organically in contrast to the fast processed food that had come to characterize industrial countries.

A few miles from the Navdanya farm, on the wall of her small, lace-adorned, four-room house lined with blue striped curtains, sat the framed award given to celebrate Bija's seminal work with Navdanya, an organization that was reaching out to thousands of farmers all over India. She received her award to highlight the work of women whom Navdanya leader Vandana Shiva called "the primary food providers in the Third World. Contrary to the popular assumption," she wrote in an article in 2002 in the Slow Food magazine, "their biodiversity-based small farm systems are more productive than industrial single crop systems."

In Portugal, Bija was joined by other groups of women from Africa and Latin America who also won awards. One was a Moroccan cooperative that helped Berber women develop and promote argan tree oil with the aim of conserving forests and improving conditions for rural Moroccan women.

Dona Sebatiana Juarez Broca from Mexico rescued and disseminated knowledge about traditional processing methods for chocolate and helped install farmer cooperatives doing organic cultivation. And Adriana Valcarcel Manga, a chemistry graduate from Peru, ran a company that produced flour, herbal teas, baked pastries, and puffed cereals based on traditional Andean products.

But Bija, who was bold and decisive when it came to farming, was not used to the fame that had come with her receipt of the Slow Food Award. Like so many of the women farmers I had been meeting in India, joy for her came from working in the earth and making the land sing with tasty produce for the community.

The fact that she was becoming a household name among environmentalists and feminists around the world meant little. She was surprised and smiled only a little when I told her she was an international celebrity. "I found out about you first in Montreal by keying into the Internet. Suddenly," I told her, "there was your picture and a detailed story about your successes for everyone to read."

But the Internet was not where Bija tuned into the world. Rather, it was on the land tending ginger and millet and maize, with mist rising off the Himalayas in the distance.

She found the world of foreign countries strange although she was thrilled to see "all the different dresses and different kinds of faces" in Portugal and Italy at the two conferences she had attended. She was embarrassed that she didn't speak English and figured she would be quite left out when she went to Portugal in 2001 to receive the Slow Food prize, and then in 2004 as a participant from Navdanya to the Terre Madre organic conference in Turin, Italy.

"But I was astonished to find so many people who couldn't speak English!" she laughed as her daughter Rajni translated and Bija and I had a go at exchanging words in Hindi and English.

Then it became my turn to feel self-conscious. Here I was in India, a country of over a billion people (compared to my little country of only 32 million) to do research without a solid grounding in Hindi. My excuse was that most of the people I would talk to would speak only regional languages. This was the case in Andhra Pradesh where I met farmers in 2002, and would meet them again in 2005 and 2006, but it turned out not to be the case around Dehradun where most do speak Hindi.

Now it was breakfast time at Bija's house. In bare feet, she ran out to her miniature walled-in courtyard garden and picked some fresh herbs that she invited me to smell before throwing them into a delicious chapatti filled with potato. Every patch of earth in her yard was awash with green. "She sometimes gets up at 5:30 in the morning and works out there," said Rajni, who couldn't match her mother's energy.

"How long do you intend to keep up this pace?" I asked Bija as I thought of all the chores that I knew lay ahead of her at the farm. "As long as I am alive," she shrugged. "I don't want to be a burden to anyone. Besides, I love working on the land." And with that she cleared up the dishes and began a 15-minute walk to catch a rickety old public bus crammed with people that would drop her off at her 24-acre paradise.

Vandana Shiva, with her important national and international agenda, blew in and out of the centre although she did give some lectures to us at the end of the course, but we did not get to know her at all.

However, all of us who took the course on Gandhi, Cultures of Non-violence, and Globalization were inspired by meeting Satish Kumar, who gave most of the course. He was one of the most remarkable Indians I have ever met. His life had been an incredible adventure based upon Gandhian simplicity and non-violence. At nine years old he withdrew from the world and joined a wandering brotherhood of Jain monks, but left at 18 to campaign for land reform along with Gandhian activist Vinoba Bhave who became a mentor.

Most impressive was his decision in 1961 at the age of 26 to walk with friend E.P. Menon from Delhi to Moscow, Paris, London, and then from New York City to Washington in a protest against nuclear weapons; and without a cent in their pockets! He was inspired to do this by Bertrand Russell — who at the age of 90 had been put in prison because of his protest against nuclear weapons — and by Vinoba Bhave, a spiritual successor to Mahatma Ghandi who had walked throughout India collecting millions of acres from landlords that he distributed to the landless poor.

Vinoba told him that "walking is the simplest, the purest, and the most natural way to travel … it keeps you in touch with the earth, with people, and with the state of the world." He also advised him to do it without money, putting trust in people and the universe for well-being.

Satish Kumar faced hunger and heat as well as dust storms in Persia and snow in Russia, but he said he enjoyed generosity offered by people who took the pair in and listened to their message, even in Pakistan which was considered enemy territory. He said that perhaps the most difficult moment on this trip was when he reached the border between India and Pakistan.

"We were about to cross the frontier. One of my friends said: 'Are you out of your mind? Walking into enemy territory without an escort? You are reckless. We have had three wars with Pakistan in the last 20 years. They are Muslims, they will kill you.'" Then his friend gave him packets of food, which Satish refused, saying they were "packets of mistrust and fear." He said that he couldn't tell his Pakistani hosts that he did not trust them and so he had brought his own food with him.

He walked across the border without money or food, and the first person he met was a Pakistani man who asked if he was Satish walking for peace. Satish said yes, he was, but how did this individual know? The man said that a few days before he had heard this from a traveller who had met Satish and his friend in India. The Pakistani said he was also for peace and invited the pair to come for dinner and to stay at his home.

"At the border of India and Pakistan," Satish wrote in his book, *You Are Therefore I Am*, "I experienced a deep realization that the Earth is a Garden of Eden blessed by millions of diverse forms of life, religions, cultures, customs, costumes and colours. I wanted to celebrate the glorious diversity and embrace them all."

Inspired by the idea of peace, he went on to say in his book that "where there is peace, there is no fear of the Other — other peoples, other cultures, other countries, other religions. Because peace gives us a sense that there is no Other. What separates us from others is our labels, our conditioning, our identities."

The Gandhian feeling embodied in the outlook of Satish Kumar was reflected in other people that we met at Bija Vidyapeeth. One of them was the grandson of Mahatma Gandhi: Arun Gandhi, who lived in America, had started a Gandhi institute there, and ran a tour of India that went to places that reflected the Gandhi approach. Along with the 30 socially-conscious Americans he toured with, he dropped by to talk to us.

Unfortunately the divisive elements around caste and religion that Gandhi deplored were never totally absent and popped up even within an organization like Navdanya. One of the Navdanya community organizers was a young woman finishing university. She wanted to get married, and I pointed to two seemingly eligible unmarried male co-workers. Educated and attractive, the two men also possessed similar social values, and were fun to be with. But alas, one was Muslim and the other was Dalit, while she was a high-caste, Rajput Hindu. Her family, she said with resignation, would not agree.

All of us attending the course became so involved with the farm, with Bija, with Satish, and with one another that we forgot about the outside world. There was no regular phone or internet access at Bija Vidyapeeth, but eventually we heard about the devastation of the Tsunami where so many Indians had died or lost their livelihoods and communities.

After the course was over, I went off in a jeep to do research in the Tehri area of the Himalayas with a group of eight others from the course, including a young couple from Mexico and Spain shooting a film on the Ganges. We concentrated on talking to villagers who would be washed out when a big dam on the Bhagirathi river flowing into the Ganges was built. A highlight was meeting Sunderlal Bahuguna, an environmentalist who had fought the building of the dam and had lost.

It was a time of sleeping eight in a row on floors, and sometimes trekking at the end of the day through dark mountain goat paths to a remote village for the night. We ate chili-hot dhal from roadside stands, shared our caches of fruit and bottled water, and enjoyed warm welcomes wherever we went.

For Christmas, a group of us went to the holy city of Rishikesh on the Ganges and stayed in ashrams where monkeys wandered in and out of the rooms and sometimes grabbed fruit right out of our hands. They were cute, but scared me stiff because they could scratch and transmit rabies. We spent our days listening to lectures by swamis. Eventually we found a hotel where each of us prepared a dish for a vegetarian meal on Christmas Eve which we ate Indian-style on the floor of a terrace overlooking the Ganges.

That was my Christmas in 2004 and I will always remember it. We ended the night by going down to a remote spot on the Ganges where

Organic farmer Narvada, with a load of cow dung on her back, is ready to descend a steep path to her land in the Himalaya mountains.

we started a fire and told stories. I then went back to Dehradun to make arrangements to return to Andhra Pradesh.

My last experience in this hill kingdom on the edge of China and Nepal unfolded when I went to an enormous post office in Dehradun to send off a load of books and documents I had accumulated back home to Montreal. I was told at the hotel to visit a wrapping specialist with a cart crammed in with a lot of other mobile stands outside the post office.

The wrapping man took my books and packed them in newspaper. Then he drew out a beautiful beige piece of material, cut it to size, and like a couturier, stitched very carefully all around it. Next he took some hot red wax off a pan over a fire and sealed it in little circles all around the stitching as though it were a royal package.

In the middle of all this, surrounded by beggars and assorted hawkers, fruit sellers, women dragging kids, and the usual wild rickshaw traffic, another man appeared with a warm glass of Indian tea for which he wouldn't accept a single rupee. This was all part of the very genteel service not available back home even in the Westmount post office. I wondered if I was again being graced with the colonial lady treatment, but in gratitude I drank down the tea and was amazed when I was handed a second cup.

But the British legacy around bureaucracy which then followed inside the cavernous post office was surreal. To send this masterpiece of wrapping took an hour of laborious paperwork.

First I stood in line. Then a toque-headed clerk behind a big glass with a hole through it gave me a sheet of paper to fill out. Instructions were in Hindi along with incomprehensible English.

In India when these things happened, which was often, I would say in a loud voice to people in the line: "Anyone speak English?" And some accommodating person would always materialize to deal with the Hindi-speaking clerk and to help me fill out the form.

A nice man immediately stepped out of the line to help me. Once I'd filled out the form, the clerk seemed to want two photocopies of it. At least that is what I picked up.

"Well, actually," said the young university professor that was helping me, "the clerk ran out of forms, so he wanted you to make some photocopies for his next customers, but *before* you filled it out." But with his help I had already filled out the form. He had been smiling all the time we were doing it and now I knew why.

Next I had to paste this sheet of paper to the cloth package. And where was the paste? Oh, there was some on a desk if I waited in line while people with bigger elbows nudged in ahead of me. I felt I couldn't just say "Get to the back of the line," because then I might look like a colonial type. People were always so very nice to me, sometimes too nice, so I had better just go with the flow.

Vestiges of colonialism reminiscent of the British Raj were always around. I was reminded of it because Republic Day was coming up. But now it was the World Trade Organization Raj, and English-is-the-language-of-the-bloody-world Raj, even though I was in a country where there were over a billion people and only about a third spoke English. And why should they? I should speak Hindi.

These were my thoughts while I was standing in line waiting my turn at the paste. Never mind. It was better than going to a boring post office in Montreal where nothing at all happened. What made India fantastic were the constant dramas.

I stood in line, did my pasting, and returned to the line to pay. This came to quite a lot, 1,400 rupees. Divide by 32–35 rupees to the Canadian dollar.... Well, I didn't need the weight to carry around.

Unlike the Himalayan women I had met, who never had a day off from looking after land and cattle, I now had a chance for a small holiday in Dehradun. It was a relief to have my own bathroom in a heated hotel where I didn't have to go to bed with all my clothes on, including my Tibetan coat, the way I did in the mountains and at the Navdanya farm.

In this capital city with lots happening I enjoyed the streets filled with delicious food. I bought nectarous fresh juice (pineapple, pomegranate, papaya, and orange) from a little stand, and picked up delicious single sweets filled with nuts.

Every night I ate at my favourite Punjabi restaurant across from my hotel where they served great Tandoori chicken. The waiters always smiled when I came in. The best thing about it was that they used very little chili. Lots of Tibetans hung around and I had many conversations with them.

It was going to be very hot back in Andhra Pradesh, so I had to figure out where to dump my Himalayan wardrobe. This included a sweater, two toques (at night I put one on my head and one on my feet), plus my armless Tibet coat, which was great if you didn't have arms, but warm enough with a sweater. Around Dehradun, a city of about a million, there were women beggars with kids, so I gave my clothes to them.

I would have to start taking my malaria pills which I had stopped because mosquitoes did not thrive in the Himalayas or on the cold plains in winter. Two more days, and I would board one of those bumpy, windy busses at 5:30 a.m. for Delhi, then take a taxi to the airport where I would have to have my ticket "endorsed" at some place outside the terminal. Would I find the terminal? Maybe. Then it was off to Hyderabad where I would be greeted by Vithal's driver, a man I knew, as long, of course, as I recognized him.

11
"ROW, ROW, ROW YOUR BOAT"

Back in the state of Andhra Pradesh, January 2005 found me in the middle of dry scrubland a few hours from Hyderabad in Cherlapatelguda, a village of one-room huts with intermittent electricity. It was early evening and the village was swinging to the sounds and music of a wedding. On a specially-created stage, a beautiful bride in a red and gold sari adorned with jewels and flowers looked out with her new husband dressed in white and saffron over an expanse of about 1,000 guests. Around them on stage, men in clerical robes read from the Bible and proclaimed Pentecostal-style in between piped-in blocks of recorded Indian music that the guests swayed to in their chairs.

I was standing on the fringes of the scene next to Sugunamma, an accomplished Dalit woman leader I had just met. In this village and across the state she was helping to create a formidable cooperative federation run primarily by Dalit women. Along with her was Syamala, a community organizer and women's rights lawyer from the organization that had been assigned to me in Hyderabad to act as a translator and helpful friend.

During a lull in the proceedings, I saw one of the pastors on stage pick me out of the crowd as a western visitor and I knew I might have to rise to the occasion. He jumped down from the stage, waded through the guests, introduced himself to me as "the pastor," and, as though this were something I did every day, took my arm and escorted me to the stage to "bless the couple." I couldn't say I was not qualified to bless anybody. The village wanted to include me, to make me feel like an honoured guest; I had to be gracious and participate; so I went forward with the pastor and climbed on stage.

The newly married couple, like most people at the wedding, could not speak any English, but I stood in front of this very tired looking pair that had probably not slept for a few days, and wished them a happy life together. They smiled and I hoped that maybe they picked up the intention behind the words.

The pastor asked me to sit down next to them and announced that "Later on, we want you to sing a song, maybe a sacred song." A song, I said to myself? And a sacred one to boot?

In the wake of Christmas, all that came to mind was "Away in a Manger," definitely not appropriate, I thought, my mind drifting to the idea of an already pregnant bride. The evening wore on with Bible readings and exhortations, all in the Telugu language, when finally the pastor said: "We would now like you to sing a song."

I had been working on what I would do when this moment came. I couldn't say I didn't know a song. In India, everyone knew several songs. I had contemplated singing "Let Me Call You Sweetheart" which I had delivered to the village journalists on my first trip, but I couldn't remember all the words. My friend Salome from the Deccan Development Society had told me that when asked to sing, Canadians visiting India often sang "Row, Row, Row Your Boat."

Okay, I said to myself, and smiled at what my friends back home would think of my choice. I couldn't just launch straight into the song. Even to myself I had to justify it. I looked at the couple, and knowing that only the pastors and Syamala could understand, I said that my song was a lullaby for them.

"When all these celebrations are over, and you go home," I said to this pair who looked up at me with expectation, "this is a gentle song to lull you to sleep."

My heart went out to this girl who looked so young and vulnerable. If this were a traditional couple, the wife a scared virgin, maybe lullaby was the right metaphor for the bride's first night alone with her new husband. Who could tell? Knowing that at least I would not forget the words, I tore myself away from wedding night reflections, and launched into this children's song I had learned in kindergarten.

At the end of the event I started to take off toward "my sources" still at the edge of the crowd, when the pastor said that I must come to the sit-down feast in the adjoining tent. I was to be awarded the full experience. I said I was with my friends and couldn't leave them, so they invited them too. Along with the hundreds of guests sitting cross-legged on the ground, I enjoyed with my new friends a sumptuous dinner of curry dishes on large, flat, banana leaf plates.

After the evening was over we returned to the room I was to share with Syamala, which came with a wandering chicken that clicked in and out. I finally gave up trying to shoo her out when I discovered that an empty niche in a bookcase served as her nest to lay eggs. I would dutifully pick them up and give them to Sugunamma who was preparing meals for us.

Here and there, unaccountably, another woman from the village would come in and lie down for the night next to Syamala on a double bed. These women had their own huts to sleep in, but it was part of making me feel at home and not alone that extra women came in and out to spend the night.

This village had no toilets, so when necessary I marched with a flashlight to the fields, often accompanied by one of the ladies who made sure I knew where to go and came to no harm in the dark.

At a private home in the village there was an Indian toilet consisting of a hole in the ground next to a large bin of water. It was about a quarter of a kilometre away, and I was told I could use it any time, but all the houses looked the same, and I knew I would never find it in the middle of the night.

The crazy thing was that in the courtyard in front of the house where I stayed stood a tall concrete box for a toilet next to a shower area consisting of a drain and a pail of water. But the toilet stall was used for storage.

Syamala told me that the elders of the village found these concrete toilets provided by the government confining and smelly. But I discovered that the real reason for their unpopularity was because the fields served as the only place where women could get away alone together to talk without interruption from prying in-laws or anyone else.

For about a week I spent time with Sugunamma and other dynamic women leaders as well as the grassroots women in the community who were taking loans and starting businesses.

My idea was to focus upon a single village in this Dalit women's organization called Ankuram Sangamam Poram, or ASP, composed of 80,000 women who were saving money and taking loans in 1,500 Andhra Pradesh villages.

Ankuram in Telugu means sprout and stands for land development. *Sangamam* means rivers coming together and denotes community. *Poram* is the stool used by leather workers, who traditionally have been Dalits.

ASP was started in 2000 by J. Neelaiah and his wife Grace Nirmala, a Dalit couple that in 1994 installed themselves in a poverty-stricken village where they organized marginalized women into self-help groups and worked on the issue of temple prostitution. The organization grew from there with help from NGOs committed to working mostly with poor Dalits.

According to my friend Vithal Rajan, the *eminence grise* behind the organization and chairman of ASP's advisory committee, "The goal is to build an organization owned and managed by Dalit women so that they are not dependent upon either the government or men."

The next morning, a cool January day, I was sitting with 35-year-old village leader Sugunamma in her one-room house listening to how she had been a child labourer and married at seven. Her parents were poor Dalits that had leased land from upper castes. She grew up in a neighbouring village with four sisters and one brother who was the only one allowed to go to school.

At 10, when she arrived in Cherlapatelguda to live with her husband and his family, her job was to graze the family cattle and to labour as a coolie on a landlord's land, in addition to doubling as a servant for him.

In Cherlapatelguda village, leader Sugunamma of Ankuram Sangamam Poram encourages Dalit women to take loans for businesses and supervises a farm committee to promote better farming methods.

Her husband, who was then 15, had been a bonded labourer for five years, and like her he had never gone to school. He worked for 30 years as a virtual serf until he could finally pay off a debt to the landlord incurred years before by his family.

Suganamma's in-laws had one acre of land that she and her husband both currently worked on, but because the land was in the name of her husband's aunt, Sugunamma felt landless. She wanted to have the land transferred to her mother-in-law who lived with them, with the proviso that upon her death it would be transferred to her.

On the land, she and her husband grew *jowar*, an important cereal, tomatoes, and enough millet to make roti for a year, but they had to buy rice and vegetables, and therefore had to work for the major part of the year as coolies on landlords' land.

She was earning 30 rupees a day (less than $1 Canadian) compared to her husband who was paid between 50 and 70 rupees day.

Suganamma's goal was to be able to lease and then buy and develop more land and invest in a borewell for water. Through her self-help group she had started by taking loans for a small goat-rearing business that was bringing her extra money.

In her village, land was in the hands of 100 high-caste families and 400 "backward-caste families." The 250 Dalit families, at the foot of the caste scale, were mostly landless.

"Right now," she said, "during January and February there is not enough work for all the landless Dalits in the village." Over a period of a year, she said there was only six months total work available for agricultural labourers.

Through her hard work and vision, Sugunamma had made sure her daughter received a good education so she could become a qualified nurse. "I didn't want her to end up doing the same work I have had to do," she said.

Her daughter Mamatha had at first attended the primary school in the village, but Sugunamma said she wasn't working hard enough. Many families were yanking the girls from school and marrying them off early. So when Mamatha was 12 and in grade seven, Sugunamma packed her off to live in a special girl's residence (commonly referred to as a hostel) in Hyderabad where she stayed during high school, junior college, and her nursing program.

By October 2005, when I saw Sugunamma again, her daughter had a job in a private nursing home, making 2,500 a month with expenses for food and accommodation at 750 rupees a month. Her yearly salary was 30,000 rupees ($811 Canadian), which was considerably more than her parents could make as day labourers. Her ambition was to find a secure job under a government program.

Although she opposed child marriage, Sugunamma took a traditional view and favoured an arranged marriage for her daughter with a man who had a good job and came from an appropriate family. She worried, however, about the dowry she would have to produce, even though dowries were prohibited by law.

Sugunamma had taken good care of her daughter but she worked just as diligently for the well-being of her village. For four years she had been leader of her self-help group called Telangana.

In addition, across the village she had encouraged women from 200 poor Dalit families to become members in 14 self-help groups so they could start to rise above their status as landless coolies.

She said that for the previous year (2004) in the village of Cherlapatelguda, 85 members of the ASP self-help groups had taken loans amounting to 500,000 rupees (about $14,285 Canadian).

Because of her leadership qualities, she had served for three years as chair of the board of the ASP cooperative representing over 100 self-help groups in 15 villages in her region of Ibrahimpatnam. During the 2004 year, members had taken loans amounting to 2.5 million rupees, the equivalent of about $71,428 Canadian.

She was also an active participant on the state level ASP board that met in Hyderabad and represented women taking loans in about half the districts of Andhra Pradesh.

Partly through the encouragement of leaders like Sugunamma, the women in the ASP groups in Cherlapatelguda were expanding their economic horizons and looking for greater wealth-creating opportunities. Many were going beyond taking loans for the more traditional items associated with microcredit, such as tea stalls, mobile veggie stands, and acquiring small numbers of milk buffaloes and goats.

Under ASP's Ibrahimpatnam regional cooperative, women who had successfully paid off two loans taken as members of a village self-help group could join Ankuram groups, of which there were 10, allowing them to take bigger loans for larger projects.

For example, Syamalamma, a coolie with five children, had taken a loan of 10,000 rupees (about $275 Canadian) so that she and her husband could buy special wood-cutting machines for a furniture business and they were planning to take a 50,000 rupee loan in order to expand.

Anjamma, a 30-year-old woman with four children, was working with her husband toward creating a house building business with loans of 10,000 rupees. Both of them had also been day labourers.

Bugamma, 27-years-old with three children, and leader of one of the self-help groups, had taken a loan of about $550 Canadian for a second-hand rickshaw that her husband repaired. She invited me to take a picture of her inside it. He had been a coolie "bashing rocks," she said, "for 60 to 70 rupees a day. Now after expenses he makes 100 to 150 rupees a day with his rickshaw taxi." But she had her eye on something much grander. Her next loan, she said, would be for a seven-seater automobile taxi for her husband that she expected would bring in even more money.

But if businesses were growing in transportation and construction, the land, which many were depending upon for food security, did not seem to be producing very effectively. Many talked about lack of water, rocky land, and poor crops. This had been the lot of the Dalit women in the Medak district too, farming on similar dryland, but they had developed it and made it bloom.

I talked about this with Syamala, a community organizer with ASP in the West Godavari district. She was serving not only as a translator, but also my trusty guide in the village. I asked her if it would help if I contributed some seed money to cover initial expenses in order to create a village committee to tackle the issue of land development.

Sugunamma and the male staff person at the regional level of Ibrahimpatnam decided this was a good idea, but because I was contributing 500 rupees (a paltry $14 Canadian) they decided to include me in on an initial small meeting and encouraged me to contribute ideas.

I felt somewhat embarrassed by this. After all, what could I, a city lady from Montreal who knew nothing about growing produce on parched land in India, contribute? However, it was all part of the inclusive attitude so characteristic of Indian village women. It also turned out to be a lesson for me about the perilous problems of caste in a village.

In addition to the 14 ASP self-help groups with mostly Dalit members, there were another 16 self-help groups run under the government's

Department of Women and Children in Rural Areas (DWCRA) program in the village. I suggested to Sugunamma and other ASP women leaders that they invite the leaders of those other groups to join. Wouldn't it be a good idea, I said, to have all the leadership of women's groups in the village involved in improving the land?

They turned the idea over for a while, but I perceived considerable reluctance. Nevertheless because I had raised it, I could see they felt they had to consider it. Looking back, I think I was receiving special deference for being a member of the white-lady caste, as I sometimes saw myself, in this caste-riddled society that had had so many years under British rule. It was fine to include me, but if the white lady who didn't know very much came up with a rotten idea, it deserved to be summarily thrown out.

The source of concern was this: many of the leaders in the other groups were wives of landlords, and the ASP women, who were mostly Dalits, feared that before they knew it, the upper castes would control the group and turn it to their advantage. Over the years, on land questions the Dalits in the village had already been mercilessly cheated.

One of the SHG leaders said that 15 years before, another NGO working in the district tried to distribute 32 acres of land to Dalits under a government program that had placed ceilings on land holdings by individual landlords. However, the Reddy (a well-known high-caste name) landlords in Cherlapatelguda responsible for assigning the land kept control. She said that 20 acres of land that should belong to Dalit families were still under Reddy jurisdiction.

I was appalled at the thought of further exploitation. "Forget about including the other groups," I said. "Do what's best for you."

If they worked together, Sugunamma said, the farmers could get land development loans for borewells and irrigation and work together to fix up the land. Some were already saving seeds and could maybe start a vermiculture project using worms, dung, and green manure for fertilizer.

Subsequent to the meeting, a women's land group was formed and they worked together levelling stony land and creating water canals for crops. The government gave them wages to grow castor for oil, which does well on dryland, and Sugunamma said they were helping them form a bigger men and women's farmers club.

But if caste could create havoc in the village, so too could the older generation, namely the mothers-in-law in the extended families that most young brides were forced to join when they married.

In my peregrinations around the village talking to self-help group leaders, I met Lakshmamma, a woman who had started a mini phone business in a small kiosk that allowed her to run a paying service as a phone operator serving 10 residences.

Lakshmamma, 38-years-old and the mother of three boys and two girls, was the leader of a self-help group composed almost entirely of teen wives and mothers. The group had been meeting for two years and none of the girls had as yet asked for a loan. They just saved money, a requirement for every member.

Why? "Because they have no power over their lives," said Lakshmamma. Living in the heart of their husbands' extended families, they were under the thumbs of their mothers-in-law who would claim any loan money the girls brought in, she said, so they didn't dare apply.

The girls were all day labourers from Dalit or other backward castes, commonly called OBCs.

"Now they are working together to build up the confidence to hold their own," said Lakshmamma who was giving them all the support she could. "They have to consult their families, but four are preparing to request loans for buffaloes." Others were about to apply for a loan for a tent house for rental purposes, a rickshaw, and tools for carpentry. The girls, she added, had access to one to three acres of land and were also eager to take loans to develop the land.

But even older high-caste wives didn't always enjoy an easy ride. Domination by their husbands and other males in the extended family was often a problem.

At a spacious mansion with many rooms, I met the wife of a Reddy landlord, who was an OC, meaning other caste, or higher caste according to the Indian caste lexicon. She was a leader of an ASP self-help group composed of five landless women from backward castes, and seven other caste women with four or five acres. She was also on the village council.

Her husband with two brothers farmed 30 acres of land and they were, at the time, hiring up to 20 day labourers, and up to 60 at harvest time. One son was at university and the other was finishing grade 12.

She was not suffering economically, but with great bitterness, she told me: "I have less freedom than a Dalit landless woman, a coolie, working on my own land." She didn't elaborate, but I suspected she felt like a cog in the wheel ruled by her husband and her brothers-in-law. She showed none of the spirit of Sugunamma and so many other Dalit women I had met who overflowed with a mission to make a difference no matter what the obstacles.

In India, widows are another group of women that in the past have had a difficult time — as anyone who may have seen the film *Water*, by Indian-Canadian Deepa Mehta, could imagine.

One of the women that Sugunamma insisted I meet was Mangamma, a widow of 50 who had arrived in the village 20 years before at the age of 30, alone, after the death of her husband. She had five young children and her one connection in Cherlapatelguda was a sister.

Instead of becoming a shunned widow and victim, Mangamma carved out a position for herself as a promoter of good nutrition and reliable health care for families. She was also instrumental in starting government-sponsored women's self-help groups.

When she arrived in 1984, Mangamma learned about nutrition. With government funding and links to a health program and a nurse, she began to work with pregnant women and children under the age of five. She would weigh babies and children and graded them on their health from levels one to four, with one as normal and four as hopeless. Cleanliness was a problem, and people were afraid of using vaccines. She said there was no family planning.

By 2005 when I saw her, family planning included use of the loop and birth control pills, as well as tube tying and vasectomies. To respond to the growth of sexual activity among teens and the threat of HIV, she had initiated a sex education program for girls ages 11–18.

"She'd be great to have on our Ibrahimpatnam MAC board," said Sugunamma referring to the ASP regional cooperative covering 15 villages.

In talking to development experts in India, everyone kept telling me how important it was for women not only to gain more economic power, as the women in ASP were trying to do, but also to wield more formal political power.

"Only then," said Smarajit Ray, who had been instrumental in creating the Andhra Pradesh government's anti-poverty program for women's empowerment, "would there be major improvements in the fields of health and education."

The personal drive that marked the life of a woman like Mangamma needed legislative support so that it could flourish.

To advance female participation, the government had passed laws stipulating that one-third of village councils be composed of women. In addition, there were other affirmative action requirements to give Dalits and backward castes more government jobs.

To make sure I met the most important women in the village, Syamala and Sugunamma brought me to meet J. Lakshamamma, the female sarpanch, or village mayor. It was an impromptu visit, but Lakshamamma, who was outgoing and enthusiastic about her work, was happy to be interviewed.

The mother of four children, Lakshamamma and her husband owned one acre of land and leased five others. Lakshamamma, with a few years of elementary school education, could read and write. As head of an ASP self-help group where she had been active for several years, she had shown leadership in the village.

She was mayor partly because the post had been "reserved" for a backward-caste (BC) woman, so she had run and been elected, but she was also there because of the manoeuvrings of her husband. As soon as we arrived he suddenly appeared on their villa balcony along with a man who announced he was an important leader and head of a regional watershed committee struck under the government's District Rural Development Agency (DRDA).

I discovered that Lakshamamma's husband was a policeman with grade 12 who had resigned because he had wanted to get into politics. He was vice-president of the watershed committee and he had had his eye on becoming sarpanch himself, but since that position had been reserved for a BC woman, he had had to step aside.

I had heard that in situations such as this, very often the string-puller, whether husband or upper-caste conniver, sometimes "stood in" for the elected person on the council, thereby subverting the whole point of guaranteeing women's participation at the political level.

This, I discovered, was not the case with Lakshamamma and other women councillors in the village of Cherlapatelguda where a bevy of organized women's self-help groups in the village were quietly support-ing the basic rights of women.

But on their home turf, Lakshamamma's husband and this other man wanted the first and last word.

Whenever I asked Lakshamamma a question, through translator Syamala, one of the men would shout her down and answer for her. I tried to ignore them but I didn't want to shut them up the way I might have back home. Eventually Syamala, who was not easily intimidated, said: "We have come to interview the sarpanch and not you men."

The head of the watershed committee then announced that I should interview him, so to keep the peace I agreed to talk to him later. If the government water committee he was in charge of was effective, why was I hearing so many stories of parched land producing nothing and bore-wells only on landlords' property?

We got rid of the two men and settled into talking with Lakshamamma, who was into the third year of a five-year stint as sarpanch.

The majority of council members were women, she said, and they all came and represented themselves. Her biggest accomplishment was an agreement to set up a high school in the village. She was also working on the question of village drinking water that depended upon sources outside the village.

Along with Syamala, I then tramped out with the head of the watershed committee to a stretch of dried up land with nothing growing on it. He boasted that he had been elected by all the landowners in the area and said he commanded a yearly budget of 600,000 rupees, or $17,142 Canadian, a very hefty sum.

He claimed that 400 farmers had benefitted from more availability of water. However, there seemed to be no effort to coordinate issues of water, crops, seeds, fertilizer, organic methods, trees, and livestock.

He himself said that he had three acres of land, but because of no rain he wasn't using it, and when he did, he used hybrid seeds and chemicals. He had a borewell, but it had collapsed, he said. There were seedkeepers in the village keeping traditional seeds, but the government extension department and the companies were pushing hybrid seeds and chemicals.

As I saw it, here we were in a place where the farmers had to face the challenge of practicing dryland agriculture under the kind of conditions that favoured the use of organic methods. Yet the president of the watershed committee and his friend the vice-president were using hybrid seeds and chemicals, and large numbers of the farmers I had interviewed said their land was useless.

The combination of hybrid seeds necessitating chemical fertilizers and pesticides used up a lot of water, and in many places in India this was responsible for a disastrous drop in the water table.

The government watershed committee, it seemed, was not accomplishing much in this village. However, as I discovered when I returned to Andhra Pradesh several months later, the leaders of the ASP women's self-help groups, through their new land committee, ended up achieving what thousands of rupees and the males running things had not.

Across the ASP network in Andhra Pradesh, the women continued to improve their economic prospects. By 2007, members had taken $7.5 million Canadian in loans for enterprises and built up savings of $3 million.

"Through their businesses they have succeeded in doubling their incomes," said Vithal Rajan proudly.

But these figures illustrating the power of microcredit tell only part of the story. What I will remember most from my visit to the village was the driving determination of Sugunamma turning Dalits into leaders, mayor Lakshamamma leading the majority-women village council, Mangamma, the not-to-be-shunned widow, establishing better health for families, and finally, the teen mothers standing up to their mothers-in-law. These were the bright lights of the village that ever-so-quietly are dismantling the age-old social barriers keeping the massive potential of India's rural women in check.

12
TROLLING FOR YELLAMMA

The first Tuesday seven days after the full moon in February was an auspicious day for villagers in the Andhra Pradesh district of Mahabubnagar who were eager to seek favours from the goddess Yellamma at a temple devoted to her. Along with thousands of women and children in brightly coloured clothing crammed into bullock carts, tractors, and rickshaws, I was travelling comfortably in a car that slowly bumped along the road toward the village of Lingampalli for this *jatra*, or festival, in her honour. Trudging along beside us on foot, men in dhotis clutched sacrificial chickens, goats, and lambs. Next to them hundreds of swaying women balanced pots filled with flowers and herbs for the goddess.

This would be a 24-hour vigil.

Poor villagers were here to beseech Yellamma to heal their sick, bring rains, grow crops, produce baby boys, and avert natural disasters. After the sacrifices, the petitioners would cook and eat the animals and then settle down for a night under the stars.

According to legend, Yellamma was a young girl who one day, while collecting flowers in the forest, met a learned man that she married. Years later, down by a river to get water, she saw a king and queen bathing in the river, and thought, "Ah, if only I had married a rich man, then I would have a better life." Infused with these impure feelings she returned empty-handed to her husband who knew she had had these thoughts and beat her. But Lord Shiva, god of destruction and rebirth, rescued Yellamma. Her husband then ordered their son to kill her, which he attempted, but Lord Shiva again stepped in, made her immortal, and she became a goddess that people prayed to for protection from adversity.

For the poor in India, adversity was always on the horizon. If you were a fisherman in the south on the Indian Ocean a Tsunami could take your life and wash away your home. If you were a farmer in the Uttaranchal hill state your village and farm could be swept away by the Tehri dam. In Bihar your child could be kidnapped for ransom. And in Kashmir an avalanche caused by an earthquake could wipe out your family.

Lingampalli became the site for a Yellamma temple, so I was told, because of a thief who stole many things and put them in a box. He went to sleep in the forest, and when he woke up Yellamma came out of the box, so a temple to her was erected at that spot.

For the following four successive Tuesdays, people from different villages would come to Lingampalli to celebrate and sacrifice animals in a bid to gain favours from the goddess.

I was attending this festival to Yellamma for a special reason. Tied to Yellamma was an ancient, but now totally illegal, Hindu ritual built into India's caste and temple system whereby beautiful young Dalit girls were earmarked by high-caste men to become *joginis*, meaning servants of god. In special ceremonies, they were dedicated and "married" to Yellamma, and as Yellamma incarnations, it was believed that especially through sexual contact, they could deliver favours.

The ritual had a history. Dating back several centuries, female temple dancers called *Devadasis*, or servants of God, performed at weddings and festivals. They did not marry and instead served as the mistresses of the priests and high-caste elders associated with the temples. Some were poets and artists, but a few became highly educated and even acquired political power.

Later the landed gentry in the villages called for something similar, and so Dalit women were recruited to be dedicated to the goddess Yellamma. At first they were enlisted to clean the temples, but soon they were forced to consort with priests and become paramours of landlords. Eventually they were expected to associate with more than one man and became village prostitutes.

Former joginis and activists with the Andhra Pradesh Union for the Struggle Against the Jogini System wanted to make sure that no dedications to the goddess Yellamma took place at this jatra, and I was accompanying them.

The head of the group was Grace Nirmala, a Dalit herself, and former schoolteacher. With her husband J. Neelaiah, of Ankuram Sangamam Poram, they lived in Utkoor village in the heart of the poor Dalit community for four years in the early 1990s so that Grace could get to know jogini women. She supported joginis and their children by starting self-help groups and special schools and recruited former joginis to stop potential dedications. In her estimation there were 80,000 joginis in India, 21,000 in Andhra Pradesh, and 3,700 in the district of Mahabubnagar.

Though dedication of joginis was a criminal act in the state of Andhra Pradesh, enforcement was almost non-existent. Stopping the practice lay with courageous former joginis working to convince parents and elders in villages not to dedicate girls. These former joginis were also good at amassing evidence against delinquent priests engaging in the practice. As a result, several priests had served jail sentences and been permanently defrocked.

On the long trek to the temple in Lingampalli, we finally left our car a few kilometres away and walked until we came to a small walled-in outdoor temple surrounded by a courtyard filled with sad-looking, aging joginis plagued by villagers eager for a touch or a look. The scent of incense hung in the sultry air. Wandering bands playing drums snaked through a dense crowd.

Up some steps, looking down upon this melee, an imposing black statue of Yellamma draped in white, covered with garlands of flowers, her eyes wide and terrifying, sat on an altar chair.

A surreal atmosphere prevailed in the courtyard as women priests and joginis — to prove incarnation by the goddess — danced like whirling dervishes into a trance. Wedged into the throng, small children in bare feet desperately seeking lost parents tried to squeeze their way through adult legs. To create space, a police whistle occasionally rent the air, but no one moved. The women mesmerized everyone as they danced to the surge of the drums as though possessed.

Grace Nirmala and Hajamma, a former jogini, watched for the telltale signs of young girls spiraling into trances inside a parade of thousands of villagers circling the outdoor Yellamma temple. Once earmarked to be a jogini, often at a jatra to honour the goddess, a girl would be expected to play the part as a prelude to the "marriage."

Traditionally, young girls were also dedicated during these jatras, but because of the presence of Nirmala's organization, in several districts of Andhra Pradesh these took place strictly in secret.

Hajamma who ran the anti-jogini association in Mahabubnagar district noticed one girl going into a trance, and she was able to find out the name of her village. Grace talked to a young bangle seller peddling her wares on the fringes of the dancing. A revealing sign was that she didn't go to school. The child was with her father who hastened to pull her away the more Grace questioned her. But soon the families of both these girls would receive visits in their villages from Hajamma or Grace who would make sure that no dedication took place.

I was one of four Westerners, two female field workers, and a contingent of ex-joginis that accompanied Grace Nirmala to this jatra. As the hours slipped by and exhausted joginis ceased spinning, we repaired to the organization's tent to drink gallons of water and to talk to people who had lived the jogini life.

Hajamma, a woman of 33 who later married and had two children, had had the strength right from the beginning to refuse to cooperate with her family and the village elders. She attended school until grade seven, but at 11, upon her mother's insistence, was dedicated as a jogini in her village of Utkoor where more than 50 women had already been inducted as joginis.

In explaining why her mother chose her, she said: "My brother died at seven years old. I was born when my mother was 40. I had two older sisters, one of whom had polio. Since my mother had lost her son, she decided I should become a jogini and look after her in her old age." Her father, who had been a bonded labourer, had left and gone to Bombay before she was born, but returned to witness her dedication. One week later he died.

During Hajamma's dedication, a designated man tied a special ornament around her neck and claimed his right to be the "bridegroom" that would be the first to deflower the young girl. However, Hajamma's mother wanted to reserve her daughter only for those who would give her gold or money.

Hajamma refused to consort with any of them. She continued to go to school after becoming a jogini, "but because the other students teased me, I quit and found construction work in the village." But living as a jogini refusenik in the village created problems for her. She had a sister living in Bombay, and so at the age of 16 she fled there to find work. In Bombay she met Lakshmaiah, a man that she later married. At the beginning, she said, she lived with him without engaging in sex.

She came back to Utkoor when she heard that the government was providing housing for joginis. With the help of Grace Nirmala, who had already settled in Utkoor, Hajamma became president of a group of joginis seeking housing.

After that she began living openly in Utkoor with Lakshmaiah. In 1992 she had a son with him and in 1994, a daughter. The following year the pair married, even though her mother and the village elders insisted she was already "married" to Yellamma. She was, in fact, the first jogini in her district to defy the jogini system and marry a man.

For a long time, both she and her husband were forced to work as daily agricultural labourers on landlords' land. However, she had 10 acres of land that needed work before it could be cultivated. Through a village Farmer Friendly Committee, she was receiving government money to level the land and drill a borewell. When the land was ready, she would make it available for cultivation to relatives.

When I met her, Hajamma was a single mother. Her husband had died and she supported herself and her children with a full-time salary as a key organizer of joginis in her village and a supervisor of activities in the district.

Dalit self-help groups were now thriving because of Hajamma's leadership qualities and she continued to work tirelessly to save young girls in the district of Mahabubnagar from joining the jogini system.

Every week, with encouragement from people like Hajamma, joginis were learning how to turn their lives around.

A former jogini. Bugamma (with her son) is a member of the Andhra Pradesh Union for the Struggle Against the Jogini System which helped her to marry and start a new life.

Because of Hajamma, Bugamma, a 20-year-old jogini woman with a son, had had the courage to marry a man she had fallen in love with.

Kistamma, 55, was an example of a jogini from Utkoor village that at the age of 50 joined a self-help group, took a loan to develop her mother's land, and was able to increase profits from her crops. Her jogini mother, whose name was Yellamma, dedicated Kistamma at Lingampalli at the age of 13. "My mother thought it was a good idea because I suffered from epilepsy. No one will marry you," she told me. After the dedication the epilepsy disappeared.

Once she reached puberty, Dalit elders decided whom she should consort with. Her first lover was a backward-caste man who saw her for two years, but after she got pregnant at the age of 15, he left her with a child and no support.

"After that I had no sexual contacts," she said. "I stayed with my mother, did bidi work, and went to the fields as a coolie." Although she herself had never gone to school, she made sure her daughter received an education. Her daughter, however, was taunted at school for being the child of a jogini. "She suffered from a lot of discrimination."

Like so many Dalit women I met who joined women's groups, Kistamma never wavered in her support for her daughter who became a nurse. Happily married, she was living next door to Kistamma.

Women such as Hajamma and Kistamma are women of strength who were able to rise above the social and emotional assaults they endured as young women. But at the jatra in Lingampalli I encountered others too crushed to be able to break out of the bondage of the jogini system.

A 28-year-old woman said: "I met a man that wanted to marry me, but my family said that Yellamma would punish them if I left. I am afraid of what might happen to them."

An old jogini who looked as though she might die of exhaustion on the floor outside the steps to the temple was receiving a pittance for cleaning the temple and lived mostly on handouts. She lived in a shack not far from the temple and was now a beggar.

A 35-year-old jogini, whose mother of 62 was also a jogini, talked as though she had no choice except to continue living on the fringes of a Hyderabad Yellamma temple. Through a pimp she found clients among temple-goers who would meet her at night in a small room she and her mother shared near the temple.

"The priest lets us clean," she said, as though being allowed to clean the temple were an honour. "And sometimes the temple-goers will give us money." She had asked the temple committee to be on the payroll for the cleaning they did, but were told they had to work for free.

The woman said she made between 50 and 100 rupees from each client and saw an average of two or three a day. The pimp, paid by the client, received between 10 and 20 rupees.

"The men I see," she said, "are often drunk." But she felt her years as a sought-after prostitute were numbered, and she worried she might find herself joining the league of jogini beggars whose livelihoods have dried up.

The lives of these women, I thought, have something in common with young at-risk girls in Western metropolises that become enslaved by criminal gangs like the Hells Angels. I thought of some of the street kids in Montreal I have talked to, some of them teenage girls on the way to becoming prostitutes, drug runners, and gun carriers for criminal gangs.

Many came from families of poverty, neglect, and violence. Removed by social workers from their homes, they could spend many years being shuffled around from one foster home to the next, often ending up in detention centres after engaging in delinquent behaviour. Abuse within foster homes was not infrequent. Many became school dropouts simply because their lives were too chaotic to show up every day. Some didn't get enough to eat.

All of them longed for saviours and roots, and thought they had found one when a seductive older man befriended them and promised them affection and security. Once pulled into a gang that monitored their every move, these girls who often started off as strip girls then became prostitutes, as I discovered in research I did in the past as a reporter.

Indian women have told me they believe these Western girls have choices whereas the young Indians girls forced to become joginis do not. On the surface this may appear to be true. However, in contrast to life in a big western metropolis, where people can become very isolated, Indian villages exhibit a sense of community that can offer these women some support.

In the town of Utkoor, 56 former joginis found solidarity with one another and a supportive community that the Western girls associated with gangs in my country do not seem able to find.

I found another example of community spirit in the village of Chinajetram near Lingampalli.

After a heart-rending day encountering joginis at the jatra, we spent time with 29 child labourers, some of them children of joginis, who attended a night school in this village. Ten worked as bonded labourers and they all belonged to a children's club that Grace Nirmala's group organized.

Poverty plagued this village, but thanks to Ankuram Sangamam Poram, the Dalit federation of women's cooperatives, four women's self-help groups as well as a Dalit village committee and a Dalit education committee were working to create a better life for the Dalit inhabitants.

The kids had the strength and determination and group solidarity to tell us that they were fed up working in the cotton fields. Now they could read, they said, and they wanted to attend full-time regular schools. The education committee said they would work on it, and the community support that I have seen in India made me believe a solution would be found for these children.

The commitment shown by former joginis such as Hajamma and Kistamma, by field workers Subhashini and Suneetha that translated for me, and by leader Grace Nirmala, made the day I spent with them one I will never forget.

The mission of these individuals working so tirelessly for the empowerment of exploited Dalits contrasted with the glibness of two Western men who were part of our group at the jatra. Both were students at a university in Hyderabad and viewed the jatra as an exotic cultural event without trying to understand its history and its effects upon vulnerable women.

One student from New York City went so far as to doubt the survival the jogini system. "I talked to a Brahmin," said this supposed student of sociology, "and he contested its existence now. You can't just believe everything you hear here," he said, as though the heart-rending testimony of the women we spoke to were fabrications.

The other young man, a Danish student who claimed he was writing an article for a Dalit community in Denmark, wanted more proof of the jogini system than he could see at the jatra. Sitting in the tent on their haunches, neither made any effort to get to know the joginis, all with stories to tell.

Their callousness enraged me. I felt this was another example of men on the defensive about the behaviour of other men, wherever they were.

Luckily, an engaging and highly informed young woman doctoral student in anthropology from England was also present. She was quietly living in a village with a Dalit family and spoke Telugu, something that I had not mastered. She said very little, but she was in the centre of the crowd when the trances were taking place. Later I saw her talking quietly to people in their own language, watching, listening.

The personal dedication of Grace Nirmala and her husband Neelaiah to young Dalit women consigned to the pit of the Hindu hierarchy where Brahmins reign at the top and Dalits suffer at the bottom has never wavered. A few years later, in 2008, a young Dalit girl made pregnant as the result of a brutal rape died in child birth after delivering a beautiful baby boy. Grace and Neelaiah had already raised two children. Their son was studying medicine in China and their daughter was at an Indian university, but they decided to adopt and raise the orphaned child as their own. As a family, they decided that the baby boy would become an integral part of the family with the same rights around inheritance as their two grown-up children.

In a manifestation of their generosity of spirit, Grace and Neelaiah, who are both Dalits, asked their good friend Vithal Rajan, a Hindu Brahmin, to name the child at the baptismal service in their Christian church. In remembrance of how the Biblical David as a young man had been able to slay Goliath, Vithal chose the name David.

13
TSUNAMI HEROINES ON THE BAY OF BENGAL

In December, when I had been in the Himalayas, a Tsunami had wreaked havoc on the east coast of India, killing thousands and creating camps of refugees waiting for disaster relief. But people in coastal fishing villages that had survived were also in trouble. Huts had remained standing but fishing boats had been smashed or carried away, and the fishermen, who were married to the sea and a coastal way of life, were in despair about the future.

In the Guntur area of Andhra Pradesh on the Bay of Bengal, thousands of families faced the prospect of no income from the sea. Like our Newfoundland fishermen, the men feared they would never fish again. The image of city slums hovered like a cloud over the boatless shores. To rescue their husbands from gloom and destroyed livelihoods, Indian women in villages in the area were rallying with imaginative projects.

Nizampatnam, with 300 fishermen, was one of 22 villages in two Guntur districts where women in 350 self-help groups were responding to the crisis. The village was coming back to life because the women were taking charge. To save their husbands from paralysis and the community from starvation, Nagamani, a woman 25 years old, was calling for practical solutions. I decided to head off to meet her in her village on the shores of the Bay of Bengal.

Journeying from the city of Hyderabad to the town of Guntur, the starting point for my foray into coastal Andhra Pradesh, proved to be a freakish adventure.

I had enlisted the help of a government official with the state-wide anti-poverty program. Called Velugu in early 2005, it was coordinating women's self-help groups in affected villages.

I had asked for a booking in a separate air-conditioned compartment on the required overnight train from Hyderabad to Guntur. On other overnight train trips I had slept in a compartment with the usual four open berths, but I was always with people I knew. This time I thought a separate unit was necessary. Little did I know that in this country, where space was a luxury, separate compartments did not exist except perhaps for a latter day Maharani who might command an entire car. In India, you go with the maddening crowd or you don't go at all.

Catching trains in India requires a certain dexterity that white ladies without the local language do not have. Mercifully, four people from the ASP women's cooperative organization took me to the station in Hyderabad and found the unmarked platform where my train was due to come in an hour late, at 11 p.m.

A fast runner with an eye for finding the right notice on a hidden pillar found out the number of my car and the location of my berth. None of these things were marked on the ticket. You must "confirm" at the station, if you can follow the instructions from someone at the inquiry desk that might speak English and can also decipher a Canadian-English accent.

After my handlers left, I found a grungy but air-conditioned waiting room off the track sporting a Men Only sign but with a few women inside. To escape the sweltering April heat, I sat there until the train lumbered in, only to find out that though my compartment had AC, I had to share it with two men. One suddenly decided to leave, and I was left with a rotund middle-aged man who looked perfectly normal, or so I thought.

I settled in for the night on a bottom berth facing my compartment mate with only a two-foot space between us. He insisted on leaving on a small light on, which I don't normally like, but I agreed to it. I took off my glasses and stuck them in a small net inside, and fully clothed with my face to the wall, I pulled the supplied train blanket over me.

In the middle of the night I rolled over and opened my eyes to the sight of a naked man pumping away at what I will euphemistically call heavy going "flashing activities." I see poorly without my glasses, but the unfolding pornography was alarmingly clear, and without a doubt designed to interest the possibly loose white lady from the West in the opposite bunk.

Somewhat alarmed, I thought of lurching out of the cabin and calling wildly for the conductor, but I decided that a white lady on the rampage would only create a spectacle. The best thing to do was pretend I had seen nothing and turn over. When from time to time, in my sleep, I accidentally rolled back toward the aisle and opened my eyes, the parlour porno, like some grotesque Punch and Judy show, would quickly resume. Exhaustion and the knowledge that I would be delivered to my destination at 4:00 a.m. kept me stone-still.

It was with gratitude that at 3:30 a.m. I woke to the sound of the train conductor knocking loudly at the door to get me up. Through the myopic mist, I saw my naked compartment mate, with all the unruly folds of a British Colombia Doukhobor, leap up and unlock the door.

Good Grief!!! as the Peanuts comic strip character Charlie Brown would say. For five hours I had been locked up with this public masturbator! "Oh well," I said to myself as I removed my head from my computer, which had served as a pillow in the interests of not having it stolen, "Just another Indian adventure."

I was met at the station by a community organizer and taken to a Western-style hotel where I slept for a few hours, had some breakfast, and then travelled to Nizampatnam to meet women who were making a difference.

With simple thatched huts perched on rocky soil and only a few battered-looking boats resting at the shore, Nizampatnam was like a forlorn child looking out to the mighty Bay of Bengal. Because their huts were set back from the ocean, Nizampatnam families didn't lose their homes even though clothes and stored food were carried away when flood waters poured in.

To provide quick relief, non-government organizations had moved in. But incomes quickly came to a halt because many fishermen had lost their boats or found themselves with vessels that were too battered to brave the treacherous Bay of Bengal waters.

Most, however, didn't own boats of their own and instead depended upon larger mechanized boats owned by fish traders who were also the village landlords. But some of these boats were lost and several were too heavily damaged to go out to sea.

I spoke at length with 25-year-old Nagamani, a woman with two children who was head of the village organization that oversaw 28 village self-help groups. These met on a regular basis to take out loans to improve their livelihoods and to discuss the social and economic life of the community.

Nagamani's husband owned an inland water body and had taken leases on two others to grow and harvest shrimp. To invest in this project she had taken a loan, "but everything he set up was flooded out so now we are living on my tiny tailoring business," she said. "Since the Tsunami, my husband hasn't worked. During January and February most of the fishermen here were too scared to fish at all.

"After the Tsunami, people ran away from their houses, but eventually they came back. We women decided to get together and do something," she said. Along with a team from Velugu and the fisheries ministry, they mobilized to get subsidies and took out loans from their self-help groups to replace four lost boats and repair 13 that were damaged.

Then there was the problem of the complete destruction of four mechanized boats along with major damages to 11 others. The government wouldn't provide subsidies or loans for lost boats owned by the village elite, but knowing that their husbands needed the livelihoods provided by these boats, the wives of 250 Nizampatnam fishermen took loans of between 5,000 and 10,000 rupees ($139 to $278 Canadian) from their self-help groups to buy materials for the 11 damaged vessels belonging to what they referred to as "the rich guys."

Their husbands contributed five days of free labour to repair them and the owners provided five days of food while the fishermen worked. "Our husbands fought with the owners to get them to pay something, but they lost," said one of the women.

What a gift these women had given "the rich guys!" But the first priority of the women was work for their husbands and an income to feed their families. Some kind of justice might come later. The fishermen had to give the owners 25 percent of their catch. "Maybe they will be able to negotiate a better deal in June when the fishing season resumes again," one of the women said.

Women dry fish from their husbands' catch in the fishing village of Nizampatnam.

By mid January the boats had been ready to roll, but the fishermen were too scared to test the waters and it wasn't until March that the boats ventured out. There was a setback with a quake off Indonesia but no Tsunami resulted, even though villagers on the coast ran to the hills. The boats weren't catching a lot of fish but a number were out on the sea. Now it was breeding season with a prohibition against fishing from April 15 to May 31.

Close to the Nizampatnam harbour on a small island covered with about 60 one-room thatch huts, I watched about 20 women in the scorching heat drying fish on the sand.

I wanted to take pictures but the only way to get there was to wade through waist-high water. I gave my camera and my fanny pack to a Velugu worker, also wading across so she could translate for me, and I went for a swim. I had always wanted to say I had gone swimming in the Bay of Bengal. The water was deliciously warm and tropical. On the shore it was so hot that my trusty salwar kameez quickly dried.

The shrivelled-up fish that the women were carefully sorting came from the last big catch before the prohibition period began. The women would market the bigger dried fish in neighbouring villages and sell the rest to chicken farmers for poultry fodder.

Even at the best of times, fishing families in Nizampatnam weren't making much money. During the nine-month fishing season fishermen on the small boats could make between 50 and 100 rupees a day for an income of up to $779 Canadian a year, while in the bigger mechanized boats they could make double that. For another three months, all tried to fish on small inland lakes and streams which would yield about 20 rupees a day, about 75 cents Canadian.

Village leader Nagamani, who had a boy of five and a girl of seven, was suggesting to her colleagues in the self-help groups that they take loans for small manufacturing initiatives — making candles and incense, for example — to supplement fishing incomes. She said that money could also be made from making and packaging pickles and chili powder. The men, she said, could operate machines that would grind the chilies and carry the bags out for marketing.

"This way our village families could depend upon a variety of livelihood activities." There was room in the village, she added, for more tailors, especially those capable of embroidering saris.

"I think we could also consider buying and leasing land and forming farm collectives," she added. Most of the villagers are landless, "And I must say, also houseless. These thatch huts hardly count as a house."

For many of the men who were so demoralized they were taking to drink, the idea of leaving a life of fishing was unthinkable. They belonged to the Pallekaru fisherman caste, and none wanted to consider abandoning a way of life that had been in their families for generations.

"But a blend of things could be good," said Nagamma, a 40-year-old woman who worked at a local fish factory, but because there weren't sufficient fish coming in on the boats, she had been unemployed for two months. Her husband was a driver of a mechanized boat, but he refused to go out during January and February even though the boat he drove wasn't damaged. "Like so many others, he was just too scared," she said. In addition, the fishing net he used was torn beyond repair.

Nagamma took a loan to mend her husband's broken fishing nets after the tsunami took its toll in the village.

To feed her family she had taken a 2,000 rupee loan from a money-lender at 48 percent a year interest, and a self-help group loan of 10,000 at only 3 percent a year interest to buy a new fishing net for her husband.

Under Velugu, the Andhra Pradesh state anti-poverty microcredit program, starting in 2004, the government agreed to pay 75 percent of the usual interest banks would charge, but only to women who joined the Velugu self-help groups. When bank interest was 12 percent, the women taking loans through their Velugu self-help groups paid only 3 percent. "For the past six weeks," Nagamma said with a look of relief on her face, "my husband has been going out to sea."

But like Nagamani she felt that villagers would benefit from engaging in a mix of occupations. "I am happy to continue working at the fish factory, but I'd like to take out a loan for some buffaloes."

Nagamma had lived through several assaults on her Bay of Bengal village. When she was 10, a cyclone hit the village and fishermen were stealing from grocery stores in order to survive. "My family," she said, "lost everything."

Fifteen years before, when she was just 25 and pregnant, she lost her house when a cyclone hit and destroyed 80 percent of the thatch houses. "We had to go to special shelters," she said.

Despite the constant threats these women face, they still had time to be warm and hospitable. On the day I was there they were inaugurating the opening of new quarters for their village organization. It consisted of two rooms containing just a few chairs. As part of the celebration, I was asked to bang open some coconuts at the entrance and cut a ribbon. After failing to split the coconuts, and a lot of laughs, the village organization committee, headed by Nagamani who was wearing a stunning pale green sari, served a crowd of women a small snack. Later she presented a lunch of succulent fresh fish to her village board members along with me and the Velugu community organizers who were ushering me around.

Most of the women I met in Nizampatnam were illiterate but all their children were attending school: "Something that might open other livelihood doors," said Bharathi, a community coordinator and livelihoods specialist with the Velugu organization. An M.B.A. graduate now in her 20s, she had worked for the government's Velugu anti-poverty program for two years.

"The village organization here," she said, "took a pledge that all the children of the women in the self-help groups must go to school."

Andhra Pradesh had a bad record of child labour, but the women in the village self-help groups were part of the movement to stop that. Some of the children of the fishermen might go on to junior college and university. "Coming out of this village there may also be teachers and health workers," she added.

A few months later, recognizing that village high school graduates needed greater job opportunities, the rural development ministry launched the Employment Generation and Marketing Mission (EGMM). Linked to the state-sponsored savings and loans self-help group program, by the end of 2009, it had trained and placed in jobs, mostly in cities and towns, more than a quarter of a million young people under the age of 25, making at least triple what they could make in villages working on the land as day labourers.

"We realised that youth have different aspirations from their mothers," said Mission director Meera Shenoy, in an interview in December 2009. "The parents are mostly agricultural labourers, struggling with seasonal incomes and manual work. The sons and daughters want to lead a different kind of life and TV fuels their aspirations — they see the city youth of their age with a fancy motorbike and cell phone. This is the segment EGMM targets."

She pointed out that almost 50 percent of the trainees are girls and 37 percent are Dalits and Tribals. "The impact, especially on girls," she said, "is like magic."

The youth receive instruction given in part by companies in 450 centres across the state. On-the-job training is landing them work in telecom firms, department stores, pharmaceutical companies, security agencies, manufacturing, hotels, and restaurants. English instruction is included. To ease their way into cities, the self-help group federations buy the young people bus passes, set up safe accommodations, and also organize parental visits.

"When we began the program, girls would say they have to ask their mothers to take up a job. Today, go to any training class and girls boldly say: 'We will take up a job anywhere.' When the girls get a job, child marriage, which is common in villages, gets reduced. Their self-esteems and aspirations go up. Many of our alumni want a career path and have enrolled in Open University to get degrees. Today the EGMM girls are in sales, retail outlets, rural business processing offices, and banking. We have broken the myth that rural girls can only be nurses or teachers. When we invest in girls, we are investing in a new generation with better health and education," said Meera Shenoy.

I never told the Velugu people that took me around the village what had happened to me on the train, but maybe they guessed. After my very full day in Nizampatnam, they decided I should take a bus back to Hyderabad that night. They cashed in my train ticket and secured one for the bus.

Air-conditioned and too jam-packed with people for any unconventional activity, the bus took off at 11:00 p.m., and got in six hours later at 7:00 a.m. Courtesy of the bus driver, rock music kept everyone awake.

The hotel room I had reserved at the Minerva in Hyderabad wasn't ready when I tumbled in. For a few hours, enveloped in the rejuvenating spirit of Nagamani and Nagamma back on the shores of the Bay of Bengal, I dozed safely and peacefully in the lobby.

14
SARIS ON SCOOTERS

In my experience, I've found that social activists in India were always wary of Americans no matter who they were, but in this land of 600,000 villages, Indo-American Vikram Akula, who grew up in the United States and was trained there, has achieved enormous respect among community organizers.

Vikram started Swayam Krishi Sangham (SKS) Microfinance in 1998 in Andhra Pradesh. By the summer of 2006 he had lent out more than $50 million U.S. to about a quarter of a million women in five states of India, tripling the number from 2005 when I first started to visit borrowers in villages where SKS began.

In his mid-30s, Vikram, who was born in Hyderabad, comes on like an American factory owner on the go who won't rest until his widgets or lawnmowers are selling better than anyone else's. The difference is that the product he is hawking atop his Indian soapbox is bigger and better loans to more and more poor Indian women.

In recognition of his work, *Time Magazine* in 2006 named him one of the "People Who Shape Our World." His goal then was 1 million women borrowers by 2010.

Given the bullock-like slowness of India, and the derailment possibilities, Herculean effort is required to reach these numbers of women, but Vikram, with his Pied Piper charisma and his financial smarts, has what it takes.

I met him in 2006 at the Hyderabad Sheraton Kakatiya Hotel, a fancy place where I encountered cagey Americans preparing for U.S. President George Bush's visit which had already been marked by huge demonstrations against him in Delhi.

Vikram moved quickly in between wheeling and dealing for loans, introducing the latest technology, hiring village field staff and planning expansion. With no time to waste, he came with a special assistant, and answered questions at a rapid clip.

"You've heard of MacDonald's Hamburger University?" he began, "where they teach people to turn out as many hamburgers as possible? Well I'm going to do something like that," meaning use the factory model to place millions of rupees into the hands of thousands more poor Indian village women.

Two years later, by the middle of 2008, he had completely outdone himself. Nearly 3 million women in more than 36,000 villages in 16 states had taken a total of $838 million U.S. in loans, and a year after that the members had expanded to 4 million women.

But Vikram, who spends about a quarter of his time in the U.S. where his family lives, has an Indian heart that has not allowed SKS to turn into a factory.

He was inspired by the Grameen model created by Nobel peace prize winner Muhammad Yunus of Bangladesh where women in village microfinance circles composed of five members gather every week and require no collateral to take loans. Loan officers, meeting groups of 40 in centres, deliver doorstep services. Expansion of staff will mean more employment for village-based high-school graduates that will receive training in finance and technology.

SKS started as a non-profit organization and then became a Non-Banking Finance Corporation (NBFC). Access, says Vikram, to commercial and international capital markets will allow SKS to reach greater numbers of poor.

Women in Lingapur village meet to discuss taking and paying back loans to SKS for businesses.

Vikram's sympathy for the poor began as a child visiting India in the summers. He remembered meeting a street hawker in a torn sari with a young son in rags selling pots to his aunt who paid in the form of rice when he was just seven years old. The woman dropped a few grains of rice on the floor and knelt to pick up each one, making him realize that for her even one grain of rice made a difference.

He cut his teeth on development issues under the eye of Vithal Rajan when he worked in the Medak district of Andhra Pradesh for the Deccan Development Society helping poor Dalit women set up their own village system of grain distribution with a sliding scale of prices.

After a Ph.D. from the University of Chicago in development and microfinance, as well as experience in the American investment sector, he was ready to start his own organization.

SKS offers start-up money to the poor, but staff members don't tell them how to do business. Vikram says the poor know what to do, and if staff gave them advice and the business didn't work out, then the poor might not feel obliged to repay the loans. Typical loans go for tea stalls, mobile vegetable stands, milk buffaloes, goats, and chickens, as well as land improvement. Emergency loans are also available at no interest.

The interest charges for regular loans are 24 percent a year which is standard for NGOs and microfinance institutions (MFIs) that must pay staff and build an organization. Weekly payments are spread over 50 weeks. Loan sharks and banks, which sometimes demand bribes and are often far away, can bring the cost of loans much higher, Vikram said.

The minimum loan is 2,000 rupees ($50 Canadian), and the maximum for the first year is 10,000 ($250 Canadian), and then each year increments of 4,000 rupees are allowed, so in the second year the women could take a loan of 14,000 rupees ($350 Canadian).

Women with a good track record of paying back can take loans for bigger enterprises. In 2006, SKS started to give bigger loans requiring collateral to women and their husbands who wanted to undertake more ambitious businesses.

All this sounded encouraging, but as I saw when I talked in villages to very poor people too scared or discouraged to join a group and take loans, SKS wasn't reaching the poorest of the poor, estimated at about 20 million families across India.

"I have a plan to respond to the destitute," Vikram responded. A year later in March of 2007 he launched an Ultra Poor Program modelled after a program developed in 2002 by the Bangladesh microcredit organization BRAC.

One thousand very poor single women heads of families in 200 Andhra Pradesh villages in the drought-ridden Telangana area are participating in an 18-month program with an economic, social, and health component.

After initial enterprise development training, the women have each received a maximum "asset transfer," which they do not have to pay back, of up to $200 U.S. to start an enterprise of their choice. Most women have chosen to invest in livestock such as buffaloes, sheep, goats, and chickens, but some have opted to start small grocery stores and become fruit and vegetable sellers. For additional investment in their business, every month they can receive a monthly stipend of up to $50 U.S.

The women also save at least 5 rupees a week, earned from their SKS-supported enterprise, which can be withdrawn if needed. The women can also take a loan from group savings and repay without any interest.

The social component takes the form of meetings where the women learn about existing government and NGO programs, while the health part consists of monthly visits by a trained health professional.

Graduation, expected 18 months from the "asset transfer," takes place once the woman has shown she can sustain her business and has learned to diversify her sources of income. Children must be attending school and there must be sufficient food in storage for a month. If the women need further loans to expand their business, they would then be eligible to join existing SKS microcredit groups.

SKS depends upon working closely with women in villages, and Vikram owes his initial success to four strong-willed young women loan officers who broke all the rules about suitable women's conduct in order to pull poor women borrowers out of their huts.

In 1998, men in the villages were astonished when high-spirited women in saris and helmets rode into communities early in the morning and late at night on scooters carrying bags of money. Since village women borrowers were working all day in the fields, this was when the loan officers could conduct meetings to deliver loans and receive repayments.

In India, men from all castes felt that daughters, sisters, and wives should not be roaring around alone in the early hours of the morning or after dark. Even educated women were expected to stay under male protection in the shelter of the home attending to womanly chores.

As late as 2005 and 2006, these ideas still prevailed. To my surprise, male field staff dominated SKS branch offices in two different districts even though most of their clients were women. The reason?

"It's hard to find women for these jobs," said Sandhya Rani, one of the original women organizers. "The men in their lives won't allow it."

It was reminiscent of Canada in the 1950s when women were expected to go to university to find husbands, and then stay quietly at home to start families away from the turmoil of the labour market.

The first woman on a scooter with SKS was Rama Lakshmi who had been in the trenches as a development warrior since 1994 helping women make more money and carve out bigger spaces for themselves in their villages.

Lakshmi is the Hindu goddess of wealth. On behalf of poor Indian women, Rama and others like her have, it would seem, received the goddess's blessing. All of the original SKS women field workers eventually became top managers, directing SKS operations in the field.

Nevertheless, for Rama the road up the hierarchy was difficult. Though she came from the top Brahmin caste she still faced major obstacles.

Rama's grandfather had been a landlord with 100 acres, but by the time her father came along, the land had been divided up, and he became landless when he sold his share to buy medicines for his ailing father. At the age of eight, Rama was bundled up with her mother and four brothers and taken to Hyderabad where her father, who had a few years of education, found a clerical job.

In her teens, Rama's parents started worrying about finding her a distinguished Brahmin husband. Because the crème de la crème wanted university graduates for their sons, Rama was packed off to become a highly marriageable woman with a degree just like the Montreal girls who went to McGill University in the 1950s.

Her father expected her to marry and take her place in Hyderabad society after she finished university, but Rama had her own ideas. Her grandmother lived in a village, and by the time she graduated with a science degree, she knew she wanted to work in the countryside with rural people.

"I had seen people in my family with a lot of problems," said Rama, referring to her extended family. "I knew I needed independence." Her mother had never worked outside the home, but defying the rest of the family, she supported Rama.

In 1994, Rama found a position at a non-government organization called the Cooperative Development Foundation (CDF). In impoverished villages, Rama helped women who were making as little as 10 rupees a day (at the time less than 50 cents a day Canadian) as agricultural labourers form thrift and credit groups.

Rama was close to her parents, but from the beginning she had to hide what she was doing from them. In her first job, she was speeding from one village to the next on her own, in an area where she knew no one, sometimes at night, on foot or public transport. All of this was considered improper and risky.

When she started, 6,000 women were meeting in small microfinance groups. When she left two years later, 12,000 women were organized into cooperatives that Rama had helped create. In a second job, she did similar work for the government's Department of Women and Children in Rural Areas (DWCRA).

But Rama was always looking for challenges. One day in 1998, she saw an ad in the paper placed by Vikram Akula, then 27, who wanted to start a Grameen-style microcredit organization in the Medak district.

Rama, who was 25, decided to join him. "He really didn't know what he was doing," she said, expressing awe as she commented on her first experiences working with him.

Vikram had learned about poor people when he worked for the Deccan Development Society, but he knew nothing about how to set up an organization along Grameen lines.

"In the first village we went to, people thought he was an evangelical preacher and just walked away," she said. But the two of them marched boldly into other villages and learned on the job.

In Narayankhed, the impoverished area where they had chosen to work, they initially talked to reporters from local newspapers. Claiming it was too hazardous for women, the reporters discouraged them from working there.

Rama and Vikram didn't listen. In Narayankhed town the pair looked for three rooms — one for her, one for him, and an office — but no one would rent to them. What was this pair up to? And why wasn't the woman at home living quietly with a husband? Finally someone from a bank arranged the rental and they were in business.

The next thing Rama did was to hire three women with village backgrounds to work as loan officers and field workers.

Soon these women, including Rama, were zipping from one village to another on motor scooters, their long braids flying in the wind, scandalizing the men, but bringing hope and loans to women who began to establish successful small businesses in their communities.

Watching their wives being advised by these obviously adventurous women upset the men in the villages. Sandhya Rani, who had worked in villages as a teacher tutor in order to put herself through university, said that when she was first working as a loan officer she wondered whether SKS could survive.

"The men in the villages said: 'Why are you focusing on the women when men in the households make the decisions about money? You should lend to us.' The moneylenders and finance companies were also mad because we were charging a lot less interest than they were."

There was also mistrust, she said, because the SKS employees were women. The only man was Vikram. At night in the villages, she said, there were a lot of drunken men around. "I was a little nervous."

At one point, in order to put a damper on SKS, a man in a village called the SKS office and announced that a field worker had been molested. Nothing of the sort had actually happened. The village women in the microfinance groups were alarmed, but SKS women staff convinced everyone that no rape had taken place, and that they could take care of themselves.

The villages, however, *were* changing. The local women were gaining power and the men couldn't stop it.

"Social changes in the villages started right away," said SKS loan officer Nirmala who went from field worker, to cashier, to manager of four different branches, and finally to unit manager in charge of eight branches.

"Better wages was the first improvement," she said. "In the space of one year, the women went from earning 10 rupees a day as agricultural labourers to 15 rupees a day."

Loan shark activities dropped. "Now the women could go to their microfinance groups for loans." Although the major loans were for income-generating activities, emergency loans at no interest were also available.

She said that another big change was that the men began working. I saw this myself in interviews I did with women who had taken loans. Several had had husbands who had been wandering alcoholics, but in the wake of their wives taking loans, they started to earn money in order to make sure that there was enough money each week to repay the loan.

"The women made it possible for the family to have real assets: houses, land, animals," said Nirmala who pointed out that because of this, husbands and sons started to show much more respect for the women.

When Nirmala first began, most of the children of the women in the microcredit groups were child labourers. But soon they were sending them to school.

From three women's microfinance circles that she started in 1998, by 2005, Nirmala was in charge of a unit of eight branches with 7,000 groups and 35,000 poor women pulling themselves out of destitution.

Sandhya Rani also moved on to became a manager along with the fourth woman that formed the quartet of women that established SKS.

Rama herself continued to soar. She had no commerce degree or diploma in human resources, which we in the west would deem a requirement for the work she did. Nevertheless, she turned out to be a brilliant manager who also never lost sight of the needs of the grassroots women.

For SKS she started over 40 microfinance circles, trained 60 staff, created four branches, and became an operations manager in charge of SKS expansion, staff recruitment, and training. She also set up a head office for the organization in Hyderabad.

When I saw her in the spring of 2005, she had moved on to another challenge. She was working with an umbrella group called Andhra Pradesh Mahila Abhivruddhi Society (APMAS) that helped coordinate activities of NGOs and government programs devoted to empowering women.

Every month she was spending half her time in villages smoothing relations between organizations and providing services and community know-how to the groups working with women. I didn't quiz her on the marriage issue, but I knew that few men would accept her being away from home for half the month working on her own.

Her family always acted protective, as I discovered one night when I took her out for supper in Hyderabad at a Chinese restaurant near my hotel. Towards the end of our interview, her cell phone buzzed. It was her older brother waiting on his two-wheeler at my hotel to take her home. She lived about 10 minutes from my hotel but he didn't want her walking alone at night.

Her brother, waiting for over half an hour, represented to me one of the strengths of India. Whether in the village or the city, the joint or extended family took care of people and gave them identity. A sense of community in this country was still important, and Rama worked within it, whether in her work or in her private life, which in 2009 ended up including marriage as well as work at APMAS.

In addition to the field workers who first worked in the Narayankhed area where SKS began, I also met the grassroots village women whose lives changed because of microcredit. Here is one example.

Punnemma, 30-years-old, who went to grade four and could read a newspaper, operated a thriving mini animal farm that had quadrupled her income. She operated out of a small courtyard on some scrub land off the main road of Narayankhed town.

In 2001, when she joined a microfinance group at the age of 26, she was working as a coolie outside the town and living in a slum-like room. A SKS field worker told her about the program. At the time, her husband, with grade seven, was an alcoholic wandering the streets. He worked in the fields when he was sober, which wasn't often.

By 2005, Punnemma had a thriving mini dairy with eight buffalo along with four goats and 20 chickens. She had bought and sold buffaloes and calves and had her eye on a high-yielding milk buffalo that would require a loan of 20,000 rupees ($555 Canadian) that would give more than 10 litres a day.

By breeding and selling goats, she had made a profit of 15,000 rupees or $420 Canadian. Her 20 chickens were laying 15 eggs a day, bringing her 15 rupees from that alone.

As soon as she started to take loans, her husband gave up drinking. There were goats to be taken out and buffaloes to be milked. Fodder had to be bought and collected. Week by week, the loans had to be paid off.

In 2005 Punnemma's monthly income was 3,200 rupees ($90 Canadian) and that didn't count her sales of goats and buffaloes.

With microcredit loans from SKS, Punnemma graduated from day labourer in the fields to managing her own mini-farm. She also adopted a girl and sent her to school.

A careful manager, Punnemma made use of everything. Her buffaloes generated piles of dung that she sold at 10 rupees a basket. She also made cow cakes for fuel, selling them for 1 rupee each.

In 2004 she had been able to purchase 125 yards of land for 25,000 rupees. For less than 3,000 rupees, or $88 Canadian, she and her husband, with their own hands, built a house made out of green gram stems and cow dung. A tin roof protected it all from the rain and she was planning to rebuild later in brick.

But Punnemma was most proud of the fact that she had adopted two children, a boy of 11 in grade four, and a girl of six in grade one. She had no children of her own, and these were two of her sister's children. "They will never be child labourers. I want them to finish high school," she said.

"Back in 1999," said Sailu, the branch manager for Narayankhed area who also goes by a single name, "people had no confidence in SKS partly because it wasn't asking for any collateral. The moneylenders wanted gold, goats, and even children as bonded labour. The villagers didn't understand an organization that was asking for 5 rupees a week for group savings. They said, 'How can we trust them?'" But SKS gained the confidence of the women and by 2005, in the Narayanhkhed area, more than 5,000 women were members of over 1,000 groups in 68 villages.

For empowered women like those I met, educating school-age children became important. Young children weren't going to the fields, girls were marrying later than their mothers, childbearing was postponed, and the birthrate was expected to go down.

However, some women found it difficult to let go of the old traditions and were still pushing their daughters into child marriages despite the fact that for girls the legal age for marriage is 18.

One of them was Vaschalabai, a woman in her late 30s with six children. She was another microfinance success story. In the village of Thimmapur she had, with her husband, six acres of land that he farmed along with their oldest married son and their daughter-in-law.

For a long time, however, they were farming only two acres of the six because the rest was just scrub. Eager to make money from her land, she took a loan to develop the other four acres, sunk a well, bought two bullocks, and planted commercial crops.

Once her farm was thriving, she took a job as a cook in a preschool started by SKS and began attending a night-class for drop-outs and child labourers who wanted to get back into the school system. "I want to learn to read a newspaper," she told me.

Her two oldest daughters, ages 22 and 19, both married with children, never went to school. Her married son went to grade four and dropped out, but a boy of 10 was in grade five.

In addition she had Sojala, a 16-year-old daughter who had never gone to school and was working in fields as an agricultural labourer, and Gayabhai, a daughter of 13 who had dropped out in grade three in order to look after her older sister's children.

Both of these daughters were in the SKS night school along with their mother and they were determined to get an education.

The village of Thimmapur, which had been rife with child labourers, was no longer as traditional as it once was. In fact it buzzed with female

teachers promoting learning the three Rs as part of an aggressive education program run by SKS in 12 villages.

A night school for drop-outs and children who had never been to
school was bursting with girls who wanted to get into the educational
mainstream. Literacy in this village was only 35 percent, compared to 61
percent in Andhra Pradesh and 65 percent in the whole of India, but it
was on the way up.

The result was a growing crop of teen girls determined to escape the
drudgery of agricultural labour and child marriage and eager to enjoy
the benefits of schooling.

Vaschalabai's two daughters, Sojala and Gayabhai, had caught the
bug. However their mother was standing in the way. She wanted to
marry off her 16-year-old daughter as soon as possible. And I suspected
she was at the night school in order to keep her eye on her.

It was eight at night when I arrived at the simple stone and mud
walled schoolroom covered with white plaster. Seven girls who had just
completed an hour of study were sitting cross-legged on the floor with
small wooden desks. Their teacher, Sri Devi, was a role model for them
and the girls looked up to her. Married at 14, a mother at 15, and a widow
by 19, she was taking a junior college program by correspondence and
was determined to flourish as a teacher.

The school was also crammed with village on-lookers because they
had heard that a Western lady was coming to talk to the girls. Vaschalabai
was also present.

Gurumurthy, academic and administrative head of the SKS education program, and my translator for the evening, encouraged all the girls
to come forward and sit in a semi-circle near me. A man of 38 with children of his own, he encouraged these quietly determined girls, and created a spirit of solidarity and hope among them. But the girls seemed too
shy to say anything. Gurumurthy figured out the problem and sent the
prying rubberneckers away.

I decided to ask each girl about her circumstances and what she
eventually wanted to do. As I interviewed and he translated I picked up
the thread and told them I had been a teacher, and that education could
make a big difference. These girls were all looking for a future that didn't

include a teen marriage or working in the fields, but during the day all of them were at home looking after siblings, doing housework, or labouring on the land.

Ruta, 15, had gone to school until grade four. "My parents stopped me from going to school," she said, "so I could work as a coolie. Today I was in the fields preparing land for sowing. I also do housework, cook food, and clean the vegetables." She had a married older sister, two brothers in grades one and two, and a five-year-old sister.

Both her parents were agricultural labourers, and her mother was in a microfinance group. She decided on her own to go to night school. "I think they support what I am doing.

"I would like to keep studying until I am ready to take the grade seven exam. But," she said, with a catch in her voice, "that costs 500 rupees (about $15 Canadian). Will my parents be able to find the money to pay the fee?"

Kalavathi, 15, completed grade two and was forced by her parents to quit school to look after three buffaloes and five cows. "Today," she said, "I was in the fields harvesting Bengal gram." Avoiding the question of marriage, she said, "I want to complete grade 12."

When it was her turn, Sojala, Vachalabhai's 16 year-old daughter, stared down at the floor to avoid the gaze of her mother and said, "My mother wants me to get married." Sitting next to her were two other girls whose parents also wanted to marry them off. They wore blank expressions and refused to say anything when I tried to get them to talk.

In India people expect visitors to react and not sit there passively taking notes and staying on the sidelines. So I said what I thought. "You can always wait to get married," I said, "once you've finished your education."

Gayabhai, Vaschalabai's 13-year-old daughter, had been away looking after her older sister's children. To do this she had had to leave home. But now she was back, "because," she said, "the children are bigger."

She had her eye on a residential bridge school with a 10-month program run by SKS for girl child labourers. The last one to speak, she was resolute about her plans. "I want to get a good job," she said. "I will complete grade 12," she said firmly, "and become a teacher."

This allowed her older sister Sojala to speak up. She said, "I have decided I want to study so I can enter grade 10 and finish high school."

In 2006, when I revisited, Gayabhai had gone through the bridge school and was in grade five at a regular school. Sojala had avoided marriage but she was in Hyderabad looking after the children of relatives.

The future of children hinges very much on what parents like Vaschalabai decide. Among the group of night school students who completed the program in December of 2004, many had had to accompany their parents to other places in the state in order to find work.

"Migration is a problem," said Rajesh Kumar, who was coordinating SKS's preschools, elementary school tutoring programs, and night schools across 12 villages. He pointed out that during the winter months before the onset of the monsoons, there was not enough work for everyone.

But the microcredit groups were helping to change this. Loans taken by the women were creating businesses tied to the village and the surrounding area.

The key, from what I could see, was a new spirit of hope carried into the families by the women, but traditions die hard, and the girls were still struggling to make sure they weren't slated to remain the village's second-class citizens.

Boys were more encouraged to go to school, but they too could find themselves in situations of rank exploitation.

In a village in another district, I met a woman who had taken a loan for milk buffaloes and used her profits to buy her 14-year-old son out of bondage to a landlord. For five years he had received 8,000 rupees a year ($222 Canadian) for a 13-hour shift working every day of the year with only one meal a day.

In an attempt to give her youngest boy a future, she sent him to primary school but he dropped out because the kids at the school taunted him for being a Dalit. Unlike children from richer families, he went to school in bare feet and had no schoolbag.

He told me he had no friends at the school, though his teacher encouraged him and he had learned to read and write and do basic math. He had the same experience, he said, at a residential school run by the government. When I met him he was looking after buffaloes.

I was constantly running into little boys working as child labourers, bringing tea to offices, or working as waiters. They looked just as sad and lost as any of the girls I met in Hyderabad on the street begging.

Among the women involved in microcredit, for every Vaschalabai failing her daughters, there were many more Meerabais doing exactly the opposite.

Meerabai Rao, 28, was an example of a woman who was making sure her children received an education even though she herself never went to school. She was also an example of a woman who had, along with her husband, been able to parlay her loans into a bigger business linked to a thriving urban market.

SKS had, in 2006, added on a new bigger loan program for people who had done well with small loans, and Meerabai was taking advantage of that for a recycling business that was doing very well.

But Meerabai had had to break with her family in order to chart her own independent course. Meerabai was married at 15, had a child at 16 and two more by the age of 21. One of seven children, she was born into a rich family. Her father had 200 acres in the neighbouring state of Karnataka, about 60 kilometres away from the village of Sindol in Andhra Pradesh where she was living.

Meerabai hadn't been allowed to go to school because the class had boys in it, and she had been confined to the house because the daughter of a landlord and village mayor couldn't play with just anyone.

In faraway Sindol village, her father had found her a man to marry who was supposedly a government employee. However, once she settled in, Meerabai discovered she had married a man with grade 10 but no job, and virtually landless because the two acres his family owned weren't producing.

Sindol was a poor village with about 250 families, some of whom had a few acres of land, but most didn't have water and had to rely upon fickle monsoons. About 30 families had no land at all and worked as agricultural labourers.

Her dad said, "Come home, you've been hoodwinked, you're with a no-good. I'll give you 10 acres of land and find you another husband." Although she hardly knew the man she had married, she decided that she wouldn't go home and risk living in virtual purdah, stashed away in the drawing room of her father's house.

"It was a challenge," she told me, through an interpreter from her native Telugu, as she recounted her first year at the age of 15 in this village where she knew no one. "But I loved Yadav and I decided that we would make it."

The pair stayed with his parents for a year, and then moved out on their own. Meanwhile her landlord father had disowned her. "I have never taken a paisa from him," she said tossing her long black braid back with defiance. There was no dowry because her husband's family hadn't asked for one.

"To survive," she said, "we started a tea stall, even though I hardly knew how to make tea." She joined a microfinance group and borrowed $125 Canadian so they could expand it into a grocery.

Not content with that, a year later they decided to buy two acres of land and she borrowed another $625 over two years so they could have a borewell that would give them enough water to grow rice and as well as onions and chilies for commercial sales.

After a while her husband got the idea of starting a side business recycling paper, rubber, glass, plastic, and scrap metal. "We started it out of the grocery," she said. During 2003 and 2004, she borrowed a total of 40,000 rupees ($1,212 Canadian) to expand this business.

They created a mini warehouse on rented land eight kilometres away that cost them 1,000 rupees (about $30 Canadian) a month. To pay their growing number of collectors who scoured more than 10 villages in the area for material, they had to fork up around 100,000 rupees (about $3,000 Canadian) a week.

Six years after joining her microfinance group, they were making a profit of 10,000 rupees a month ($278) and after they'd paid for food, the kids' education, and their life insurance policies, they still had 6,200 rupees ($175) to invest in this ever-expanding business.

She recounted all this as we sat outside on the floor in a tastefully decorated, shaded living space with pale green walls painted with geometric patterns in turquoise, yellow, and pink. Meerabai herself was clad in a black and white stripped sari covered with bold fuchsia flowers, looking very much the business woman on-the-go, able to rattle off figures quicker than I could take them down.

Pointing to a man on a bike carrying a twisted piece of metal that would travel to their roadside warehouse, she described how they had recruited collectors from several villages that wheeled around on bicycles to pick up the materials. A permanent employee segregated the matter as it came in. Once a month, 10 hired labourers packed and loaded materials into a rented truck that travelled to Hyderabad where it was sold for recycling.

Meerabai and Yadav Rao needed bigger loans to pay advances to their collectors, so she had borrowed at 35 percent interest from a moneylender and had an outstanding loan of 100,000 rupees. In 2006 she was able to take a bigger loan from SKS through their new program.

With their profits, the pair bought a solid two-room house with colourful touches and original artwork created by her daughter. Made of stone and mud covered with cement, it had a terracotta-tiled roof and a red brick extension for the kitchen. The walls were covered with handmade clay pots and musical instruments, and a comfortable shaded area outside offered outdoor living.

Following Indian traditions, across the bottom of her door a yellow strip stained with turmeric promoted well-being, while mango leaves strung across the top were said to exude oxygen. Outside in her spacious courtyard surrounded by a stone wall, she had a Tulsi plant, a revered symbol of worship in the Hindu tradition and widely used for its Ayurvedic medicinal value.

Her children were all in school, and although her girls were seven and 12, she had enough confidence in them to let them take a public bus to school. In many villages as soon as a girl must take a public bus to go to school, she can find herself at home doing housework or looking after siblings or out in the fields slaving for 20 rupees a day. Or getting ready to be married off. Soon Meerabai would be sending her oldest daughter Preethi to a good boarding school.

Meerabai's family was thriving and now there was now enough money for holidays — something unheard of in Indian villages. Meerabai and Yadav took a week off to show their children the city of Tirupati and visit the world-famous Lord Venkateshwara Hindu temple. Several months later they all went to Maharashtra state to visit a second temple.

Though she still couldn't read, Meerabai knew exactly the financial state of the business, including expenses, profits, and what she had to pay every month on her loan.

Because of her flourishing business, they had been able to dismantle the tea stall and grocery kiosk. They leased out the land they bought, and as compensation get some of the crops.

"Now I can concentrate on bringing up my three children," she said.

15
LIFE AFTER CHILD LABOUR

Sakku, 11, Sabera, 14, and Santhosha, 13, were three girls among over 1 million child labourers in Andhra Pradesh who were not attending school. Instead they did housework and looked after younger children at home while others the same age or younger toiled in fields, factories, and restaurants.

These girls belonged to families so poor they couldn't imagine being able to save 5 rupees a week or take a loan as a member of a microcredit group. But when the parents of these girls were asked by teachers from the district to release their daughters from work so they could go to a special residential "bridge" school, they believed enough in their daughters to say yes.

I first met these girls in February 2005 at a school for 100 girl child labourers in the Narayankhed district of Andhra Pradesh. Started by the education wing of SKS, and funded in part by the government education system, the school was designed to teach the students enough in 10 intensive months so they could enter a class appropriate for their age in a regular school.

In the middle of fields, at this school outside the village of Anthwar, I stayed for several days in a Shangri-La atmosphere where the air was fresh and the food plentiful and nutritious.

I watched 100 grateful girls, colourfully dressed in their own individual outfits, sparkle with an inspiring liveliness as they worked on their lessons and joined together to play sports.

Classes took place in two bare one-room buildings that felt like gymnasiums. The walls were decked with educational materials, but there were no desks or chairs. Eight women teachers, ages 18 to 24, worked with small groups of girls seated on the floor with mini wooden frames they could write upon.

I arrived there with SKS education program coordinator Rajesh Kumar one night after the girls had gone to bed. I peeked into one of the gym-like spaces and saw them laid out on the floor, wall-to-wall on mats with their eight teachers. There was not an inch to spare between them. In the morning, each girl rolled up her mat along with her few belongings. Neatly tucked into the base of the four walls, these thin little bedrolls were a tribute to the non-consumer lifestyle of these girls aged nine to 14 who could look so lovely with so little.

I myself slept in a small office building with a flush toilet and a room with a regular bed for guests next to another small building with more rooms for overnight stays. The only two other structures in the complex were a hut for preparing meals and an outdoor row of toilets for the girls.

The next morning, the girls, who were keen to meet a Western visitor, gathered around outside before class to meet me. They could speak a little English, so I said, "Hello, my name is Sheila," which also happens to be an Indian name they can pronounce. Giggling, they gave me their names and, tumbling over one another, threw out their hands for a handshake.

Most of these girls were Dalits or Tribals at the bottom of the Indian pecking order. I sensed that they believed that they had been specially singled out, and in return they were heartbreakingly keen to learn and participate.

In a field on the property, using organic methods, they had sowed rice, rye, pulses, and jowar. Very proudly, they showed me how they were taking care of the new plants. SKS education administrator Gurumurthy,

At the "bridge" school for girl child labourers run by SKS, children plant organic plants and have a mathematics lesson.

who had worked at the Green School for DDS, taught them how to maintain records on sowing, germination, and harvesting, which also included practical lessons in mathematics.

Every day I did something with the girls outside on the grounds. Sometimes I played ring ball with them. Other times I would teach them a few words of English. One day I met them inside and taught everyone a song: it was "Row, Row, Row Your Boat," and more appropriate for these girls than those wedding guests I had entertained a few months back.

The second night I met some other little girls and one young boy that had not been as fortunate as these bridge school students. The occasion was a visit with Rajesh to a small hill village to observe five women meeting for the first time to learn about starting a microcredit circle. Their small children, some of them sleeping or nursing, were wedged between them.

But on the fringes beyond the circle, girls who looked no more than five or six years old were painstakingly making mats that they sold for 20 rupees, or about 75 cents Canadian. It took these small girls a day to create a mat made from leaves that their parents tore from spiky-looking trees that grew on scrub land.

A social work graduate, Rajesh was working in several villages where SKS had set up preschools, night schools, and tutoring for students who were falling behind in regular primary schools. The goal, said Rajesh, who also had degrees in management and law, was not to create a parallel system, but to push the regular government system to perform.

To make education accessible to everyone, Rajesh was ready to do almost anything. "Maybe these kids could attend our bridge school and teach the others how to make these mats," he said. "The money could go to the families of the mat-teaching children. We could run our school so that the kids could work during the sowing and harvesting season too," Rajesh added. "But then," he sighed, "lots of other NGOS would accuse us of supporting child labour."

After the meeting ended, Rajesh and I went to a restaurant in a nearby town for supper. We were served by a nimble and disarming child waiter of 12 that I met regularly because we went frequently to this restaurant. The boy had dropped out of school because his father had died, and he and his brother had to help his mother earn enough to eat.

I wanted to slip him 500 rupees (about $15), but Rajesh said it was a bad idea. First of all, the owner of the restaurant might take it, or the kid might use it to pay a prostitute. Rajesh had run a shelter for street kids in Hyderabad and the kids sometimes tried to bring girls there. He said it would be safer to give the boy clothes.

The next day I spent time talking with Sakku, Sabera, and Santhosha at the bridge school and then visited their families at their villages. All these girls were very eager to succeed and were working hard.

Sakku, a slight girl with earrings and bangles in bright yellow print pants and a green top, wore an especially eager, hopeful expression. One of six children, she had been pulled out of grade two to look after her older sister's child. When a teacher visited her house to see if she might be interested in going to the bridge school, she jumped at it.

Virtually illiterate when she arrived, she had learned the Telugu and English alphabet and could read and write small words. Her hope was to re-enter elementary school at the end of the 10-month program in December of 2005.

Sakku said, "My mother figures that at least one of us should get some education. Now I am meeting people from other villages. I like the food. It is better than what we had at home, and there is more of it too."

With Rajesh I met Sakku's family in Raparthy, a village of 500 families characterized by rough thatch dwellings or simple one-room houses made of stone and mud. Electricity was available only for those that could pay.

I talked to Sakku's father, Poul, 45, and her mother Ratnamma, 40, parents of six children, three of whom never went to school at all. This included an 18-year-old girl with one child, a 12-year-old looking after her sister's child, and a boy of 14 working as a bonded labourer. A boy, seven, and a girl, five, were in school, but who knew for how long.

In this village, 217 children were attending classes in an over-crowded four-room school. The headmaster of the school estimated that 22 others were child labourers, but Rajesh said the estimates were always low. "In many villages a quarter of the children are child labourers in addition to another 15 percent that are enrolled in school but never show up to class," he said.

I conversed with Sakku's parents through Rajesh in their courtyard, sitting cross-legged on the ground in front of their one-room stone and mud house with an outside thatch hut for cooking. In a corner outside a calf lounged on some hay. Crosses were etched on cement columns beside the door indicating they were Christian. A few years before, a priest had asked them for 10 percent of their earnings, and more recently wanted 500 rupees, I was shocked to hear, but they were too poor to pay.

We sat on a mat with relatives and neighbours listening in. Poul's sister, a leper that lived with them, was sitting there too, looking old and confused. A few times Poul avoided questions about treatment by land-lords, indicating he was afraid of repercussions.

He and his wife owned less than one acre of dryland and had let it go fallow because for the past two years there had not been enough rain. About 50 other farm households in the village were like them, he pointed out, with up to one acre. "We work as coolies for big landowners," he said, referring to 70 farmers in the area with four to five acres served by borewells that every year allowed them two seasons of harvests.

Poul and Ratnamma had owned two bullocks that their older boy took care of and rented out for ploughing, but three years before they had had to sell them.

In a good year they could work 150 days and make 18,000 rupees (about $500 Canadian), but in a bad year they might work only 100 days and together make only $375. It cost them $457 Canadian a year, they said, to feed and clothe seven people living in their house.

Because they were impoverished Dalits, the government had given them money to build a house, but unfortunately not enough to complete it. To make sure they had a roof over their heads, the year before they borrowed 4,000 rupees from a moneylender at 60 percent interest which brought the loan up to 6,400 rupees.

Because of poor monsoons, they hadn't been able to work enough days as agricultural labourers, so to make sure they would eat, they allowed their 14-year-old son to become a bonded labourer. This came with a 6,000-rupee advance. But their son had to work on a landlord's land every day for eight hours a day for a complete year, with no days off, for a daily wage that came to 16 rupees, or 50 cents Canadian.

What will happen when the year is up? I asked. "Maybe we'll see if we can get 8,000 rupees this time," Ratnamma said. The money, explained Rajesh, was guaranteed, which was what made it attractive.

While talking to Poul and Ratnamma at their home, I noticed Rajesh carefully surveying the on-lookers. Just before we left he grabbed a cousin of Sakku that he knew was in grade 10 and graduating from a government high school.

"I want you to mobilize those cousins of yours that I know have dropped out of school," he said. "We may have some openings at the bridge school for them."

In the same village we went on to visit the parents of Sabera, 14, who like Sakku, had been pulled out of grade one to look after the house and the children of her older sisters. Now that she was in the bridge school, her parents were keen for her to go beyond high school and finish grade 12.

Her mother Gousia, 45, who had married at 13, was illiterate, but her father, Babumiya, 55, had finished grade 10. They were poor Muslims living in a bleak single room with no electricity and no furniture. A thatch-covered area that looked suitable for animals was also used for sleeping and cooking.

One of seven children, Sabera had four siblings who never went to school. Of these, two sisters and a brother were married. When we were visiting, the youngest of these, then 19, uncovered two doll-like children lying on the floor inside the house. "Twins?" Rajesh asked. But they weren't twins, they were simply born very close together. "That's the nature of our family planning," was Rajesh's bitter comment.

Sabera also had an unmarried sister of 18 working as an agricultural labourer and another sister of 12 who went to grade two, dropped out to look after a sister's children, but was back in grade one. A sister, eight, was in grade two. And then there was Sabera at the bridge school.

Landless, Gousia and Babumiya worked as agricultural labourers, but depended upon moneylenders when there was not enough work.

"A few years ago we borrowed 10,000 rupees at 35 percent interest from a money lender. My husband took over a year to repay it. This year we borrowed another 7,000, but we hope to repay it next October at the end of the agricultural season." But if there were no rains they could find themselves even deeper in debt.

I asked them two questions. One was why she had seven children. "Traditions," she said, quite simply and without any explanation.

Later, over dinner, Rajesh blamed family planning strategies practiced by government health services. In the past he had worked on birth control projects in another district of Andhra Pradesh and he said he was appalled to see that the village women offering birth control advice "always had a baby in their arms and another baby already on the way."

He suggested that this was because those in the jobs were Dalits named through the policy of "reservations" or affirmative action. Many, he said, were Christian converts encouraged by their clergy not to practice birth control. But from what I could see in my journeys around villages where microcredit was flourishing, birth control was practiced mostly because of schooling and economic progress, regardless of religion.

My second question to Gousia was why she hadn't joined a microfinance group. "I'm too poor for that," she said. "Everyone has to pay 5 rupees a week into savings. Also, if I bought a buffalo, I would be afraid I wouldn't be able to pay back the loan." She was obviously a candidate for an asset transfer under the program for the ultra poor that SKS leader Vikram Akula was setting up.

We had a third family to visit in the village of Meerkhanpet, where farmers had a maximum of five acres, and 10 families had no land at all. There, I met the parents of Santhosha, 13, who had gone as far as grade two and then had been forced to stay home and do housework.

Her parents, both illiterate, had a half acre of land that they said "makes no profit" because of the lack of rain, so they made a living as agricultural labourers whenever they could find work.

During the off season in the winter they were often unemployed. Five years before, they borrowed a lot of rupees to pay for their daughter's marriage. "To pay it off, last year we had to go to Hyderabad for four months to work in construction," said Pochamma, who admitted they were forced to leave their two boys, then eight and 10, home alone cooking for themselves, but going every day to school. Neighbours made sure they were okay.

One of the villagers listening in piped up and said quite proudly, "We have our children in the government school. But there are two girls we know who aren't in school. They are working as coolies." Moving in close to Rajesh, she said, "Why don't you take them at the bridge school? But you'll have to pay the parents 20 rupees a day, because that's what they make in the fields. The families need that money."

Paying parents to send their children to school wasn't on the agenda, but Rajesh and Gurumurthy were willing to try almost anything in order to make sure the children of these villages had a chance.

Back at the bridge school, I spent time with the teachers, some of whom had had to fight hard themselves to get an education.

Manjula, only 18, lost her mother at four. Her father, who had remarried, was a drunk who lost the land he owned and a business he had started. He refused to pay for schooling past grade 10 and expected her to work as a day labourer.

She wanted to complete grades 11 and 12 for junior college, and received the support of her mother's sister who invited her to live at her home. But after a while, her uncle complained she wasn't pulling her weight and demanded money for rent. She insisted upon completing her grade 12, found a job teaching primary school, and was then in a position to pay the rent.

In India young women don't take rooms on their own if they are living in their home village, so she stayed on with her aunt and uncle even though she felt rejected. Everything changed when she got a job working and living at the bridge school in a supportive atmosphere with her fellow teachers.

Her goal, she said, was to complete university through the Open University program which had a flexible program that would allow her to continue teaching at the bridge school.

"I tell the children here that they have to learn to stand on their own two feet. And I tell them my story so they can see what they might have to do," she said.

Another exemplary story came from a teacher who described her experience at the age of 15 when she'd finished high school and married a man with a college degree. Living with him and his family on a farm, her in-laws forced her to work "as a coolie," she said. "But my husband, who was not working and not looking for a job either, was allowed to stay home and look out the window."

She worked in the fields for a while and then fled back to her village. "I had not finished high school to end up a coolie," she said. Even though an Indian woman usually stays married and does what her in-laws want, this young woman got divorced and decided to become a teacher.

The bridge school coordinator, Sangeetha, 23, was another example of a woman who had fought for her education. Her father died when she was four and her mother married her off at 15, but Sangeetha insisted on continuing to go to school after marriage.

She finished high school, became a preschool teacher, and then supervisor of 12 SKS preschools where some of the students learned to read so well that they were able to skip grade one in the regular primary school and move into grade two.

Mother of a girl, six, and a boy, four, Sangeetha not only ran the school for child labourers and acted as a counsellor to the girls, she also coordinated education committees in a number of villages, all designed to promote literacy and school attendance.

With her sari hiked up above her ankles, and her thick black braid of luxuriant hair blowing in the breeze, she rode around to the Narayankhed villages on a motor scooter.

When I met her she was wearing a beautiful orange sari, sparkling diamond-like drop earrings, and several multi-coloured bangles on her arms. The second day she was wearing a pale pink top and a contrasting pink and coral sari with it. Along with her students, who did not wear uniforms, she set the tone for a colourful campus of up-beat energetic young girls determined to read and write and re-enter the regular school system. A few years later, she moved on to work on SKS's new program for the ultra poor.

On my last day at the school, politicians and top representatives from the district's government school system were invited for a special inauguration ceremony to mark the start of this school.

Sangeetha decided I should attend and she wanted me to look elegant. Usually I wore a simple Indian salwar kameez tunic and pants that were looking a little faded. Sangeetha decided I should don a sari. The young teachers, aged 18 to 24, with characteristic enthusiasm, turned up a purple sari and a purple blouse with sparkles on it for me to wear.

The blouse was too small but Manjula got out her scissors and re-stitched it to fit. They wound the sari around my waist and pinned me in, stuck a bindi on my forehead, tied back my hair — since Indian women don't wear their hair "down" except in Bollywood films — and stuck in some fresh flowers.

One of the students noticed I had no jewellery, and ripped off her necklace. Another contributed bangles. They were very sorry my ears weren't pierced, otherwise they would have lent some earrings. The girls gathered round and were thrilled with the makeover. "Now you look like Sonya Gandhi," they said.

When the dignitaries arrived prior to the ceremony for a period of informal chit-chat, I scooted around like a journalist on a story for the next day's paper and asked them hard-hitting questions. I had gathered in advance all the figures on the gaping holes in the district's government school system. In some primary schools, for example, some teachers didn't bother to turn up. When students graduated from grade five there were not enough spots in grades six and seven to accommodate them. Schools with grades six and seven were sometimes so far away, attendance wasn't possible because there was no school bus system. The dignitaries assured me they were already working on all these problems.

For the ceremonies I was placed at the front near these guests, when suddenly, after everything had started, Rajesh, seated next to me, asked me if I would speak. I had about three minutes warning and scribbled some notes. My rule in India was to do what people asked. Rajesh had sacrificed many days for me. This was the least I could do.

I addressed my comments first to the high-caste politicos and school administrators. I commended them on paying the salaries of the teachers who were using SKS's innovative learning-to-read program that was enabling the girls to have a second chance. I added that it was great to hear they would address the rampant problems in the regular government system.

Then I spoke to the girls. I told them what a great job they were doing and how impressed I was with their perseverance. They were on the right track, I said, and they should stay there. In the cards, if they could stick it out, were better jobs for them in rural areas. Rajesh had confided to me that with the growth of microfinance circles, once the girls finished high school and took training, they could be eventually hired as loan officers.

Finally I spoke to the teachers, to Sangeetha, and to the academic administrators, Rajesh and Gurumurthy. "You are the ones carrying out the most important kind of Indian development. Once poor girls from rural areas become educated, India will really take off." Looking at the dignitaries, I added. "And I am hearing this from people like Amartya Sen, your Nobel Prize winner in economics."

The next day, on our way back to Hyderabad in a hired car, Rajesh and I dropped in for breakfast one more time to the restaurant where the very appealing 12-year-old child labourer waited on tables. I had not been able to buy him clothes and I was determined to make sure he got the tip he deserved for serving us so diligently on so many occasions. While I was paying the bill I gave him a smile and encouraged him to come over. Making sure that no one could see, I dropped my hand and quickly passed him 100 rupees, which was barely $2.5 Canadian. He gave me a quick smile and then, poker-faced, returned to carrying tea to his customers.

Andhra Pradesh had the second highest number of child labourers in India. Census figures reported 65 million child labourers across India but other sources estimated up to 100 million.

I stayed in touch with Rajesh after I returned to Canada. A good friend of mine, Pat Machin, a crackerjack high-school teacher of English from Montreal, wanted to support one child labourer going through the bridge school. She sent $325 to cover the cost of 10 months of education and room and board for one girl. Rajesh decided it would be for Sakku.

When I went back to visit the school in the spring of 2006, two of three girls that came from the poor families I had visited were doing well.

Sakku, 11, was in grade four and flourishing. Santhosha, 15, was still at the bridge school and preparing to take her grade 10 exams and finish high school. Her goal was to register in a nursing program offered at the junior college level.

Only Sabera, the daughter of the very poor Muslim family, had fallen back. She had gone into grade four, but as a tall 14-year-old, she felt too old for her class, so she had become discouraged and was working as a day labourer in the fields.

Out of all the of the girls I met at the bridge school, 69 percent were safely enrolled somewhere in school, and another 13 percent were taking tailoring courses back in their villages. However, 12 percent were working in the fields as child labourers, partly because, like Sabera, they were a little old for their grade level. Only 6 percent had gone to Hyderabad with families, and Rajesh assumed they were more likely to be working than at school.

However, everyone at the school had learned to read and write, a major accomplishment in a country where, according to the 2001 census, only 54 percent of the women were literate compared to 76 percent of men. In Andhra Pradesh, 51 percent of women could read compared to 71 percent of men, but the numbers were continuing to improve.

Rajesh was also continuing the fight to improve overall standards of education in the regular primary schools of Andhra Pradesh so that students in the schools actually learned to read. In a tutoring program he had installed in 12 village schools, a special program called Learning to Read guaranteed that students falling behind were able to catch up on their reading level. He said that studies showed that all over India, in grades two to five, 60 percent of students couldn't read, and that in two poverty-stricken districts where SKS worked, 70 percent couldn't read. He added that the drop-out rate between grade one and five was 40 percent in Andhra Pradesh and that parents with children in government schools felt the children weren't learning.

To help remedy this, during the 2005–06 school year SKS joined with the NGO Patham to teach 1,000 Andhra Pradesh primary school teachers in 300 schools how to use this highly successful Learning to Read program. He said that the Andhra Pradesh government subsequently introduced the program across the state, and that the NGO Patham went on to introduce the program across the country.

Meanwhile, the bridge school went on to educate 200 more girl child labourers so they could enter a regular grade in a government school in their villages. The success rate for settling permanently into regular schools went up to 81 percent for a group that finished in June 2006, and 98 percent for a third group that completed their work in June 2007. Another group was scheduled to start in November 2008 and move on to regular schools in June of 2009. "Our goal," said Rajesh, "is 100 percent."

By early 2009, Vikram had come up with another imaginative educational scheme to help the marginalized. Growing numbers of poor families wanted their children to receive a bilingual education so they could compete in the globalized world. In response, SKS began to set up a network of 1,000 affordable schools with strong English teaching as an alternative to the state schools.

"Wherever there is a SKS branch, we'll have a school," said Vikram. "Our goal is to eventually reach 1 million children." By January 2009, 20 had already been set up with special loans available so the parents could pay the required fee of $4 U.S. a month per child. Teachers for the schools were being drawn from local communities and were being trained by SKS.

16
ORGANIC COTTON'S SILENT POWERHOUSES

Late in 2005, as the international year of microcredit was drawing to a close, I was back again on a third trip to India where microcredit was booming. With World Bank support, the Andhra Pradesh government's own microcredit anti-poverty agency was reaching nearly 8 million rural women with loans for small businesses at 22 billion rupees, or about $550 million Canadian.

Renamed Indira Kranthi Patham (IKP), meaning Indira Revolutionary Path, the idea for it had originated with the late Smarajit Ray, a gentle but determined senior civil servant with a wealth of knowledge about villages and a belief in the capacity of women. In the 1980s he had seen the awakening of women in villages across the nation through non-government organizations that had fought for social justice. Under an Andhra Pradesh government agency he created called the Society for the Elimination of Rural Poverty, his dream was to use this NGO model to help women in rural areas to achieve greater economic and political power.

Unlike most government officials, Ray, who died in 2005, was a guru to Dalit women across the state and made a point of being accessible to them. Several village women in various organizations told me they turned to him for advice when bureaucrats slammed doors against them.

In an interview before he died, apparently because of inadequate hospital services, he told me that only when women in villages expanded their livelihood possibilities and became active in village politics would education and health services improve. "Women will exert the kind of pressure that the government will not be able to resist," he said.

Like Indian Nobel Prize-winning economist Amartya Sen, Ray believed that in rural India, where 750 million people dwell, good schools and solid medical care are crucial requirements for advancement of the Indian majority.

The trickle-down effects of city-based information technology companies and outsourcing for big U.S. corporations that Western journalists were writing about would not propel the poorest of rural India into economic development.

"Go out and find women who are moving into non-traditional fields and breaking into bigger markets," he told me after I had spent months talking to women that had subverted starvation by starting mini businesses. "They are the key to development," he said.

On the Bay of Bengal coast I had already seen how women under the anti-poverty agency he had started had rallied with the kind of leadership that was saving the day for fishermen after the Tsunami of December 2004 had ravished their villages and the fishing industry.

On my first trip to India, I had met first-rate village women journalists with only grade six who were turning out high quality social issue stories for a quarterly under the same organization. By 2008, some of these women were working for mainstream publications and breaking into the middle class.

Now, on the advice of senior officials with IKP, I was in the district of Adilabad where 92 mostly Tribal farmers in six villages were on the way to creating a farmer-run organic cotton growers producer company that promised to expand to include farmers from several districts in the state and beyond. By growing organic cotton on 455 acres and securing a fair trade price for it, they had in two years succeeded in doubling their incomes as well as improving their land and staving off ailments caused by excessive use of chemical pesticides.

The project had been initiated by the Indian Education Technology Centre (ETC) which trained farmers in organic agriculture and Solidaridad, a Dutch-based fair trade organization.

The two groups approached IKP in 2004 after hundreds of cotton farmers in Andhra Pradesh had ingested pesticides and committed suicide when their crops failed and debt overwhelmed them. The suicides had started six years before and continued in the wake of promises of high yields with a genetically modified cotton seed called BT cotton that worked well on irrigated land but less so in the dryland Deccan plateau.

But by 2004, the Andhra Pradesh Cotton Project (APCOT), another organization spearheaded by Vithal Rajan, was working with 650 farmers in an attempt to manage pests and grow cotton in the most sustainable way. A six-year project, it worked under the leadership of a group of NGOs, government agricultural agencies, and a forward-looking agri-business.

Creating an organic cotton growers producer company was another response, and it was presented to me by IKP as a flagship example of collective action by poor Tribal farmers slated to run an enterprise of their own that would connect to global markets.

At the instigation of Smarajit Ray, IKP had concentrated upon women, but the organic cotton growers' project was dominated by male farmers. Only seven out of 92 official members were women.

In my peregrinations around Indian villages I saw that for rural women the road to the establishment of upscale economic activity was strewn with barriers. Many in the development sector acknowledged that the key to food security and three meals a day along with greater social justice lay with women who worked first and foremost for their families and their communities. But I saw that officials shied away from paving the way for women to run enterprises that would connect them to urban and world markets and catapult them into the middle class.

I was sorry, but not surprised, to hear from one of the IKP organizers that ETC had favoured making the organic cotton growers company entirely male.

Despite this, the silent powerhouse behind the project was a Tribal non-literate woman of 48. Bhemmbai Sidam was president of a wide-ranging, woman-based cooperative society called Kerameri Mandala Samakhya that drew from over 100 villages.

It was clear that without the leadership of Bhemmbai Sidam and her messianic push to form a producer company and pull in hundreds more farmers, this organic cotton growers association in the Kerameri area of Adilabad district was going nowhere.

I also discovered that the backbone of the successful cotton seeding, weeding, and harvest lay with the brawn and brains of the savvy wives of the male farmers.

My first stop, accompanied by IKP community organizer Thirupathi Jetti, a sociologist with a long history of working with NGOS, was Peddasakeda village with its flimsy stick-and-tin huts inhabited by farmers of the marginalized Gond tribal group just two generations away from living in hill areas.

Crammed into the front verandah of a small school house, empty because of a holiday, the women sat on the floor on one side and the men on the other, with the male village leader between them. When I visited a village I often had to bow first before power brokers, in this case the village Gond leader who heard I was coming and insisted on being present. After a translation of my questions that went painstakingly from English to Telugu and then to the Gond language, he took it upon himself to answer mostly on behalf of everyone there, particularly the women.

After persistent prodding, and some help from Thirupathi, the women and men seated there did eventually reveal that in addition to cooking and overseeing their children, the wives of farmers in the organic cotton project worked many more hours a day on the land than their husbands: nine hours in comparison to their husbands' six.

The next day I dropped into Kothari village, a small hamlet where 16 farmers were members of the cotton project, three of them women. Ah good, I said to myself, I could talk to the women. But once again, the meeting was hijacked by the Gond village headman. Only by going off alone with two of the women members was I able to hear their stories.

Tanubai Marsukola, a non-literate woman of 27 with two boys aged six and two, had four acres originally in her husband's name but

Organic cotton farmer Sharja Bai in Peddasakeda village gets fair trade prices through her cotton collective started under the Andhra Pradesh government's Indira Kranthi Patham project.

transferred to her. "The Tribals," said Thirupathi, "are more equality-minded than the Hindus."

Before 2005, she and her husband were growing cotton with chemicals. "We made no profits," she said. "We had enough rain, but inputs were high and the prices low." For the 2005–06 crop, using organic methods and receiving more money under fair trade for their organic cotton, she was expecting to almost double her income per quintal (100 grams) of cotton.

A feisty woman with obvious leadership qualities, Tanubai was treasurer of her local self-help group and was taking loans for her cotton land under the Organic Cotton Growers Association.

Shakuntala Chahakati, 24 with grade nine and two boys aged six and three, leased 3.7 acres in 2005 so she could be part of the cotton project. Until then she had been working as a coolie at 30 to 40 rupees (about a dollar) a day.

My next stop was the village of Bheemanagondhi where I met Bhemmbai Sidam, the dynamic president of the Kerameri Mandala Samakhya (KMS) which oversaw seven organic cotton farmer associations covering 106 villages dominated by Tribal groups growing cotton.

A member of the very poor Kolam Tribe, Bhemmbai, one of the seven women in the organic cotton project, was born in a hill area village. Though she could not read or write she had proved herself a talented leader capable of promoting livelihoods.

Tall and slender, she looked elegant in a green sari and drop earrings, but her face wore an expression of grim determination. "Look," she said, as I accompanied her to her thatch stall where she proceeded to milk her milk buffalo, "I'm pushing 15 more families from this village to join, and by the end of 2007 I am looking for farmers from another 12 villages to get on board. Our farmers will form a producer company whether they get help from Indira Kranthi Patham or not."

She had two acres in the cotton project. A widow and the mother of three daughters and a son, she stood out as the only woman in her village who worked her land alone after her husband died of a heart attack 10 years before.

In addition to farming her land along with her 27-year-old son that she had sent to a residential school so he could attend high school, she played an important community role as head of the Samakhya, or women's cooperative. She helped over 100 families get loans to set up irrigation systems for the land. To avoid gouging middlemen, and secure the best price for local farmers, she had helped eight village organizations set up a marketing venture for the sale of local red gram, a staple legume of the pigeon pea family.

Although the cotton project was composed predominantly of farmers from Tribal groups there were also five Muslim farmers in the village of Surdapur.

In this village of 20 Muslim families I went to the fields and met Shaidabee Shek, 45, who boasted that she was the only woman in her village working in the fields.

"It's a lot better for us now that we're in the organic growers association," she said. "We were paying 50 percent a year in interest to moneylenders and we were stuck buying our chemicals from them. We are very happy with the Kerameri Mandala Samakhya."

Shaidabee had three married girls, 25, 20, and 18, with no formal education though she was proud that they could read Arabic. But a daughter of 11 was in grade six, and her three boys all had some education, though a nine-year-old son was helping her in the fields.

I cringed a little at the sight of this child labourer diligently weeding in among the plants. "He doesn't like school," she said, almost apologetically, "and now he's working with us because we are old and need help."

Most of the village women I met that were involved in community organizations and taking loans made sure their children were in school. This little boy was an exception.

The organic cotton growers project showed how NGOs and a government agency like IKP could work together to prepare marginalized rural people to start their own enterprise.

According to C.J. Robins of ETC, the goal was to gather organic cotton farmers working with NGOs in Andhra Pradesh and adjoining states into one farmer-run organization and eventually create an independent producer company.

A key player in the cotton project was the Integrated Tribal Development Agency, a state-wide outfit promoting the status of Tribal peoples. In an interview, District of Adilabad Project Director Saurabh Gaur said he was making sure farmer representatives were learning along every step of the way so they could eventually run an autonomous organization.

IKP also sent me off to an institution called Lace Park surrounded by beautiful gardens in West Godavari. In this district, an estimated 200,000 women were turning out handmade lace at slave wages for an estimated export market of 300 million rupees, or $7.5 million Canadian, and a domestic market of 100 million rupees, or $2.5 million Canadian.

In the late 1970s, German sociologist Maria Mies and Andhra Pradesh feminist K. Lalita produced an International Labour Organization study that documented the lace artisans' rank exploitation by exporters.

Later Lalita helped a lace worker called Hemalatha form a cooperative, but the women had to go on a hunger strike to get their cooperative registered by the government and were under constant threat from exporters. The group of 600 had survived and the women were selling their embroidery through fair trade organizations, but they represented only a fraction of the numbers of lace artisans in West Godavari.

Through IKP community workers, now 10,000 lace artisans had banded together into 51 cooperatives with the hope of getting a better deal for themselves.

The government had spent millions of rupees to set up a complex of buildings containing workrooms where the women learned new designs and a factory floor where they stitched together lace-and-fabric bedspreads, pillow cases, table cloths, and clothes. About 30 people, including some of the lace artisans, were receiving salaries.

A showroom available to individual buyers and exporters displayed their work. The promise was fairer daily wages for their beautiful handmade lace that their ancestors had learned from an Irish nun in the middle of the 19th century. But as I was to discover, it remained only a promise.

Initially under Lace Park the women advanced from 10 cents a day to nearly a dollar a day, but I arrived to find them making a paltry 50 cents a day under a contract to make cushion covers for the Swedish home furnishing chain IKEA.

The Indira Revolutionary Path seemed to consider this an advance because after all, IKEA was a big multinational and now the women were selling to a global market. Many of the women were high school graduates and from a middle-level caste, but they remained grindingly poor due to the continued control of greedy exporters.

When a senior rural development official at the district level told me the low wages of the lace artisans were justified because "they were just housewives," I was outraged.

These "housewife workers" who were being left in the lurch were no different from the piecework contract workers with no union to protect them currently working in their homes for slave wages in Montreal's low income neighbourhoods. They were part of the continuing international global sweatshop I had seen firsthand, when in the mid-1970s I worked undercover in a stocking factory in Montreal among immigrant women making far below the minimum wage.

At Lace Park, at first I thought there was hope for the West Godavari lace artisans because the project director of the district's influential District Rural Development Agency (DRDA) seemed committed to help them break into Western markets at wages that would pitch them out of poverty.

In Hyderabad I found Bina Rao, an experienced designer and market specialist with a proven record of tripling the incomes of equally-exploited Indian weavers. She was willing to open doors to lucrative markets in the West if she was approached and of course paid by this World Bank-funded government anti-poverty agency. But two years later, nothing had opened up, and the village lace artisans were still waiting. When I checked again in 2008, I found they had been virtually abandoned. Here is their story.

17
"BUT THEY'RE ONLY HOUSEWIVES"

At 9:30 p.m. at a broken down bus depot tucked into a grimy Hyderabad street that the autorickshaw driver had trouble finding, I met Srinivas Kondeti, a community organizer with IKP who promised to take me around by motorbike to the villages of the lace artisans. In store was a gruelling eight-hour bumpy bus ride to Lace Park near the village of Rustumbada in the district of West Godavari.

In India long bus trips take place at night so travellers can avoid losing a day's wages, still get a night's sleep, and allow the bus to avoid road hazards such as wandering cows and stray goats. But public transport, I found, was no more reliable than a bullock with a cart. The bus was supposed to leave at 10:00 p.m., but after several announcements of "only 15 more minutes" we lumbered off at midnight with every seat more than full.

Heavily fortified with many cups of tea, we settled into two seats and I took the opportunity to ask Srinivas, who was 29 years old, about himself. Armed with a bachelor of commerce and part of a law degree, Srinivas said he was engaged in development work because he cared about the poor. He wanted to see the women making lace start a company of their own that would propel them out of poverty and the clutches of exporters.

In 2004, as members of a conservative caste that favoured keeping them inside, the lace artisans had been working at home making 40 rupees for 10 days work, or 4 rupees a day (roughly 10 Canadian cents) for an array of handmade lace mats, curtains, and table cloths.

Now, by February 2006, they were making on average up to 35 rupees a day, the same as coolies in the fields. This gave them almost a dollar a day, but given their high-quality work, they still had a long way to go.

Srinivas had also started a small non-government organization of his own in the district and wanted to work for the poorest of the poor in his spare time — which I felt he didn't really have if he wanted to take on the forces that were holding back the lace artisans.

Married to a woman with meningitis, father to a new baby and with another on the way, Srinivas had been subjected to the kind of mishaps that befell people in this barely-pasted-together land. In the newspapers there were frequent stories about train derailments and Srinivas had been a victim of one of them.

"I was in this train accident," he told me, "and my foot was chopped off. I lay under the train for seven hours. When someone finally found me I told them to look for my foot," he said in a matter-of-fact way. "They found it and I was taken to the hospital where they sewed it on." He couldn't bend his foot at the ankle but he had learned to walk, and even run, so that it didn't show. For several days, with me pinned to his back, he would transport me on his motor scooter to remote villages.

Once the bus became quiet and children settled down, we drifted off to sleep. But thanks to the tea, after a few fitful hours I woke up with a desperate urge to use the facilities.

On an Indian bus, forget facilities. The drill was to waltz up the aisle to the bus driver and ask him to stop by the side of the road and hope you could find a bush. But as the only white lady on the bus, I recoiled at calling attention to myself by bringing the bus to a standstill on the barren land we were passing through.

Soon a couple of men were at the front asking the bus driver to stop. I quickly swung my leg over the sleeping Srinivas and planted my sandalled foot smack into the middle of soft Indian flesh! Terrified I'd just killed someone, I leapt like a rabbit into the lap of the mystified Srinivas. Mercifully I had hit a backside and not a stomach and the sleeper hardly moved.

I should have remembered that Indians who normally sleep on floors will lie down anywhere. On this narrow aisle, two or three quietly snoring men were stretched out asleep. I had to move fast or the pit stop would be quickly over. I picked my way down the dark aisle between the arms and legs, all the while searching my fanny pack for my tiny rolls of toilet paper.

Outside there wasn't a bush in sight and the lights of the oncoming traffic lit up the side of the road. Well, I didn't have a choice. I crouched close to the bus and was glad to be more or less concealed by my tunic-like kameez.

Once the bus was rolling again everyone was silent, including the aisle sleepers. A few hours of intermittent sleep later, punctuated by crying kids and smells of musky Indian food, we arrived at a small town where a taxi took us to beautiful Lace Park.

Walking under a glowing early-morning sky down a wide entry way of opulent gardens to the government-funded Lace Park buildings, I could have imagined myself in a corner of Versailles rather than a designer version of a virtual sweatshop.

Inside a small pastel-coloured building where women learned new designs and a showroom demonstrated their work, I was ushered past administrative offices to the one private guest room, tastefully-decorated in pink and pale green. On a double bed, a bright rose bedspread with embroidery and lace looked so lovely I didn't dare sit on it.

On the Lace Park computer in an office next door, I later discovered over the Internet that at a big store in Canada a comparable bedspread sold for $235 Canadian. A Montreal friend who used to work in the fashion industry in France, and now lived many months a year in Lisbon, later told me that one of their lace pillowcases would easily sell there for $135 Canadian.

But here at Lace Park the women were selling a double bedspread with lace for 1,100 rupees (about 27 dollars), a price so outrageously low that later during my stay I pumped them full of information that might spark them to raise their prices.

Lace makers working under the Andhra Pradesh government's Indira Kranthi Patham struggle to make fair wages.

Clearly they were still under the sway of middlemen who were controlling the show. Well, I thought to myself, even with a name like Revolutionary Path, could this government anti-poverty agency with World Bank money promote the kind of women's empowerment that would lead to a shake-up of the fortunes of the region's entrenched male lace exporters?

Later, on a walk down the road after a breakfast of an Indian porridge called *upma* and a tea, I was back to more Indian realities. Next door to Lace Park was a sign that read: SCHOOL FOR BACKWARD CLASSES GIRLS. Inside, the girls in their rainbow-coloured clothes reminded me of the enthusiastic students I had met at the bridge school for girl child labourers. Already meeting in classes under the trees, they ran to the fence to stare at me, the strange-looking, visible minority white lady that was just as captivated by them.

Later that morning on the back of Srinivas' motorbike, I took off with him down a dusty road next to a long canal lined with villages of thatch huts to the village of Darbharevu. At a "common production centre," 20 women in colourful saris sat closely together on a verandah doing lace crochet work.

These women said that in 2003, before Lace Park came into their lives, they were making 40 rupees a week working eight hours a day, six days a week. At 7 rupees a day, they had been making about 21 cents a day Canadian.

Now, in 2006, thanks to the efforts of the Lace Park organization, one third of the women were making 60 rupees for an eight-hour day (about $1.50 Canadian) but two-thirds were making only about 24 rupees a day, or 60 cents Canadian.

"We've improved," one of them said, "because we've learned new designs. We can work every day. If we worked as coolies we'd get 35 rupees a day but for only 200 days a year. So we're better off."

The women in this group had learned to read and sign their names but had had no formal education. Married to landless day labourers, they were still living in poverty and they said they weren't satisfied with the wages they were getting from Lace Park.

"Now private traders are willing to pay us more than Lace Park. We asked them why they didn't pay us more before. We're staying loyal to Lace Park, but some of us are now selling to both," they admitted.

But even for the women making more, life was difficult. Mani Madida, a woman of 30 who had had polio, said she was glad she was a lace maker because she was too disabled to work in the fields. Married at 15 and now with two girls aged 10 and 14, she and her family, including her landless husband who worked as a coolie, lived in a one-room thatch house.

Mani Madida's daughter, Laxmiteja Madida, was in grade 10, the last year of high school, and a good student, but Mani said: "She knows how to do lace, and that's what I want her to do. We need the money."

But Laxmiteja had other ideas. Tearfully, she told me she wanted to be a teacher. She wanted to do her "plus two," meaning grade 11 and 12 plus a three year B.Sc. university degree and a bachelor of education to become a teacher.

The fees, Srinivas told me later, for the whole process, would be 31,000 rupees, or about $775 Canadian.

At the meeting I also met master lace trainer Kanakdurga Penumatcha, a poised and confident woman of 38 with grade seven and the kind of energy that I felt could help propel the lace federation of cooperatives into the chips. Working six hour shifts for Lace Park 20 days a month at 500 rupees a month, and making lace herself for 200 rupees a month, she was making 700 rupees which was only $18 Canadian a month. Her husband, 45, with no education, was a landless coolie.

"Our federation," she said, "must become independent, and when it does I believe we can market our own handmade lace products for more money to the West and to upper class Indians and well-to-do Asians in other countries."

Married at 15, she had a son of 22 in a bachelor of commerce program specializing in computer studies. But the combined income of her lacework and her husband's daily labour was not enough to send her son to university.

Her son was benefitting from a higher education only because Kanakdurga never stopped working. Wherever she went, slung over her shoulder was a bunch of saris for sale that she peddled at every opportunity. This gave her an extra 900 rupees a month, and more than she was making from lace.

At her three-room house she served me tea and sweets in a living room that also served as a storage room crammed with bags of thread for Lace Park. She had a bedroom and a kitchen but cooked food outside with wood over a grill. The shower and toilet were outside. A plastic chair was produced for me to sit on but there was very little other furniture.

Back at Lace Park I kept hearing from the IKP bureaucrats about the famous IKEA contract that a middleman from Chennai had landed on behalf of the Swedish big box multinational home furnishings store.

Of the 10,000 lace artisans, 4,000 were in the process of turning out 120,000 lace and fabric cushion covers for 4,800,000 rupees ($120,000 Canadian).

I was told by Lace Park officials that a cushion cover cost 39 rupees to make and was sold to the middleman for 40 rupees ($1 Canadian). By this calculation the women were therefore making 1 rupee profit. In their discussions with me, the lace artisans who were always polite and inclined to be self-effacing, were nevertheless showing barely-concealed anger at what they were making from this contract.

Bina Rao, a graphic artist and designer in Hyderabad that was helping weavers market their products to the west, knew the quality of the women's lacework. A few weeks later she told me that the women should have sold the cushion cover to the Chennai middleman for 130 rupees, more than three times what was negotiated on their behalf.

Late one night at Lace Park, on a computer in an office next to my room, I discovered from the IKEA website in Montreal that the cushion cover was selling for 280 rupees, or 7 dollars — seven times the amount the lace workers procured from the middleman.

The head of Lace Park, a man that seemed discouraged about the plight of the women and felt helpless at the lack of resolve of the government to promote marginalized women, said he had no idea what the middleman sold the cushion for to IKEA.

A meeting of the presidents of the 51 cooperatives was being scheduled and the head of Lace Park begged me to talk to the women, hoping, I could tell, that I might spur them to fight for more. I had to find out from the women themselves what they were making a day to produce this cushion cover. Off I went the next day with Srinivas to the village of K.S. Palam where the roads were crammed with bullock carts carrying coconuts to markets.

Eventually we settled down in a two-room thatch hut to talk to Kanakalaxmi Inti, an executive with one of the 51 lace cooperatives. Called the Doddipatla Village Alankriti Lace Manufacturing Women's Mutually-Aided Cooperative Society, it represented five villages and 420 lace workers.

Like master trainer Kanakdurga, she had primary school education and her husband was a landless coolie with no education. By scrimping they had made sure two sons and a daughter completed high school from their combined income of $420 a year Canadian.

"In this village the women working on the cushions are making 80 rupees ($2 Canadian) for five days working six hours a day," she said, "16 rupees a day."

Translating this into a standard Western day (an eight hour day including an hour for lunch, and seven working hours), they were making 19 rupees a day. This was 49 cents a day Canadian and 41 cents a day U.S.

This was a dismal show for a World Bank-funded agency that claimed it was fighting poverty. IKEA, in its literature, prided itself on social responsibility and claimed it did not buy goods created by workers making exploitation wages. Well, they obviously hadn't taken the time to talk to any of the women in these villages.

"Instead of the daily rate of 16 rupees a day we are getting from Lace Park," Kanakalaxmi Inti said, "we could work for private traders who are willing to give us 30 rupees a day for lower-quality lace."

Working late that night on the internet, I looked at sale prices of comparable Third World cushion covers in fair trade stores. In the Ten Thousand Villages stores in Montreal, a cushion cover was going for $24 and $38, or 912 and 1,444 rupees, in comparison to IKEA's $7, or 280 rupees. Eventually the women's lace cooperative federation was supposed to take over Lace Park. They needed to learn how to make it work for them.

The next day at the meeting of the lace cooperative presidents, the room buzzed with anger and helplessness as the different presidents traded stories about the reaction of the women in the villages to the low wages Lace Park was giving them for this cushion cover.

Feeling like a union organizer, I showed them on a blackboard the difference in retail prices in my home city of Montreal for a cushion cover at a fair trade store and at IKEA. The issue, which they all knew anyway, was the amount gobbled up by the Chennai middleman.

With Srinivas by my side as translator, I told them that mostly male organic cotton workers under Indira Kranthi Patham were getting fair trade prices, so why not them? After all they were both operating under the same government anti-poverty agency.

Over the next few days I talked to some of the lace cooperative leaders. All literate, some had up to grade 12. With English and computer skills, administrative instruction and marketing knowledge, they could form their own producer company just like the organic cotton workers, and take off.

A woman with obvious potential was Managatayaru Polnati, an eager 22 year old with grade 12 who dreamed of going to Hyderabad and taking a design course at the National Institute of Fashion Technology. Hired by Lace Park as a quality control worker, she travelled to common production centres in 51 villages and had been making lace since the age of 13.

"But I can't afford to do it," she said. "My family is very poor and my salary helps support them." Her father was a landless labourer and her mother was making lace. On a visit to her thatch home of two dingy rooms with virtually no furniture I saw and felt the abject poverty of her family.

I spoke to Surya Kumari, the president of the federation of 51 cooperatives known officially as the West Godavari District Alankriti Lace Manufacturing Mahila (women's) Mutually Aided Cooperative Societies Federation.

"We know there is a problem with the middleman for IKEA," said this woman of 36 with grade 12. "We want to sell directly to IKEA ourselves. Indians," she went on, "want low prices. In this country, we're competing with lace makers making lower quality items. We have to go for the international market and the upscale Indian market."

She said that IKP was wasting money on a bureaucratic infrastructure that wasn't expanding the livelihoods of the women. "We need training," she said. "That's what we want. But they don't want to take the time to do anything special for us."

She said she had already approached the West Godavari District Rural Development Agency (DRDA), a key state player in the project, asking for courses in administration and marketing. "We got nothing," she said.

I wasn't surprised to hear it. Earlier I had spoken with a project director associate of the DRDA who had dismissed the women as "only housewives."

"But now," said Surya, perking up considerably, "there is a new project director that looks good. We hope he will help us."

Srinivas immediately put me onto Sreedhar Cherukuri, the new DRDA project director. I showed up twice for appointments at his office in Eluru, the main city in the West Godavari district, but both times more desperate matters pulled him away. The first time, a bedraggled throng of worried villagers showed up to see him on a pressing question. The next day he was hauled off to deal with a mafia that had taken over government land, instituted commercial prawn fishing, and polluted the waters.

Finally I was able to arrange a meeting with him at Lace Park. By now I was almost an ex officio member of Lace Park and I knew my lovely guest room was there for me.

Waiting for him to show up I decided to have another look in the Lace Park show room at items the lace artisans were producing. I fell in love with a blue double bedspread trimmed with exquisite handmade lace and decided that even though I would have to buy an extra suitcase to take it back to Montreal, I would buy it.

The women wanted to charge me 1,100 rupees (about $27) for this exquisite item that would cost me $235 at a big Montreal store. Time for a lesson, I said to myself.

"Look," I told them. "I'm not your middleman. I'm your Western buyer. Think of this as your retail store. You have to sell at Western prices to Western people. This bedspread would sell for 9,400 rupees in my country. Maybe more." Very reluctantly they agreed to take double their asking price, 2,200 rupees, which meant I paid $56 Canadian for it. It was not enough and I felt embarrassed at how little I had given them.

But this was India where even the poorest people put hospitality and friendship before filling their own stomachs. I had become their friend but now I felt I was also an exploiter! They took the bedspread away in order to iron it and then gave it to me in a bag I didn't look at until I got back to Hyderabad. What did I find? As an extra, they had added two beautiful lace pillow cases, which my Montreal friend later said would each fetch $135 in Lisbon.

With this largess coming from the lace workers, I began to think of Laxmiteja, the girl whose lace-making mom couldn't afford to let her go to university to become a teacher. One night over dinner with Srinivas in Narsapur, I proposed that I help her with fees for higher education. I gave him 10,000 rupees (about $250 Canadian) to cover the first two years of her post-high school education and he gave me a receipt from his NGO. I would add the rest as time went on.

"I will make sure that she really wants to do this, and monitor it along the way," he told me. But a year later, he informed me it hadn't worked out and he had given the money to another deserving student. I never found out what had gone wrong, but a lesson I was starting to pick up was that community solutions work better than one-to-one charity.

When Sreedhar Cherukuri showed up, his opening words were, "We're going to take your advice because you're from the West and you know a lot more than we do." Here I was back to being pegged as part of the white-lady caste that knew more.

"Look," I said as I settled down in an office alone with him. "I don't know anything. I know nothing about business or fashion or marketing. What I *do* know is that you have a core group here of capable women who are educated and dying to get out there if you'd help them. Without your support they won't advance."

The artisans, I felt, were like 1950s Canadian women with education that were being held back by social attitudes about the role of women. They weren't like the fearless Dalits I'd met. I paused for a moment and thought of Anusuyamma who had forced mean-spirited government bureaucrats to come across with a promised loan for land purchases by staging a rowdy sit-in. Then there were the fearless village journalists who didn't care who they offended when they published an investigative journalism piece documenting government corruption.

Emboldened with these examples, I said: "With training in English, computers, administration, and marketing, the lace makers will be willing and capable of taking over. They are *not* housewives hiding away making lace," I added, thinking of the nasty remark from the DRDA project director associate I had interviewed. "Give them a hand and they'll take off."

"Okay," he said. When I dragged in Managatayaru, and told him her story, he promised to pay her fees for the designer course she wanted.

"We'll set up core committees in marketing, design, and administration," he said. "I would be ready to set up exposure visits for the women in India and the West. I'll make sure they can speak English and use computers." Wow. This was 49 cents a day be damned! It almost sounded too good to be true.

Sreedhar Cherukui, at 35 with a degree in veterinary science, experience as a university professor, and eight years in rural development, was new to his job at the District Rural Development Agency. I sensed he wanted to make a difference.

"My job," he told me, "is to figure out how to eradicate poverty through the organization of poor in groups." He talked about milk collection cooperatives that had been set up and a supermarket in Eluru I had already visited that was run by women.

"I know that what we've done at Lace Park is just 10 percent of what can be done. However, we've organized the women into cooperatives and improved incomes." On the issue of middlemen, he said: "We've replaced the village middleman and the local exporter. Now the women want to replace the port exporter." He sounded on track.

The next day, feeling hopeful, I made arrangements to return to Hyderabad. I had decided against the tiring overnight bus and opted to spend the equivalent of a bus ticket to Toronto on a hired car. While waiting, I was approached by a lovely 24-year-old woman working in the accounts office at Lace Park. This woman had a B.A. degree and was waiting to enter an M.B.A. program.

On a bench outside the Lace Park buildings, she sat down beside me, and in a hushed voice, as though admitting to a sin, she confided, "I don't want to marry." Clinging to my arm, she poured out her thoughts. "I have no one to talk to," she began. "I want to help poor people. I am a convert to Christianity. I want to be a nun." She looked up at me imploringly.

The response to this would normally take a while, but I jumped in, and breaking the advice Vithal had given me, I told her that I had been married, but I no longer was, and that I had a fine life as a single person. "I have family and friends. I can travel and do what I want."

"Oh," she breathed, and looked up at me as though I had escaped to some wonderful place. "You're not married?"

"No, I'm not, and I'm perfectly okay. Having a wonderful time, in fact. If I were married, I probably wouldn't be here meeting all you people."

Thinking again of forestry manager Anusuyamma from the Deccan Development Society, who had remained single, I said: "And I see more and more Indian women, even in villages, opting not to marry."

I told her she could work for a Christian organization if she liked and certainly some kind of NGO without becoming a nun which would tie her down and restrict her options. "At 35," I said, "you might change your mind and want to marry."

I was taking on the whole Indian social system, I knew, by telling her all this. Most women in India, particularly those in villages, felt they needed the protection of the extended family. But because they were being forced to live with their husbands' families under the heavy hand of mothers-in-law, some were in frantic search of alternatives.

Some of the unmarried women in their 30s that I had already met in India lived under the umbrella of an NGO. A nunnery, I realized, was another option. In the past, French-Canadian women chose careers as teachers, nurses, and administrators under the protection of a convent, rather than take on the weight of being mothers with 12 children.

"Look," I finally said. "There is a lot you could do here at Lace Park." She spoke English, was educated, and very attractive. Maybe she could have a wonderful career as a lace executive negotiating better terms for the artisans. I hauled in Srinivas, and, hoping he was broad-minded on the marriage issue, asked him to support her in the choices she wanted to make.

As I eased my way into the car, and waved to her, I was sorry I didn't ask her for an email address. I have often thought about her.

Back in Hyderabad I felt obliged to try to push the dossier of these downtrodden lace workers. I was staying at an NGO called Vista that helped non-literate villagers use visually explicit maps to pick up relevant agricultural and social facts about their surroundings.

Anne Chappuis, a French woman who had started her own NGO and had had years of experience in Andhra Pradesh, put me on to Bina Rao, an Indian woman that she and many others believed could help the lace workers find markets at fairer prices.

I spent four hours with Bina Rao who ran a design studio in Hyderabad called the Creative Bee that had succeeded in connecting weavers to lucrative western markets after she had helped them develop designs suitable for foreign tastes.

A woman with impressive credentials, including a degree in textile design from a National Institute of Design in Gujarat, she also advised government-level organizations promoting handicrafts and textiles.

"Lace," she told me, "is an in-thing in Europe now. There's growth in handmade products and it's an up-market thing. High prices and limited production is the way to go. If the women from the lace artisans' federation come to see me, I'm quite willing to help them."

I then fired off a letter to Sreedhar Cherukuri, Surya Kumari, president of the lace federation, Rama Rao, then manager of Lace Park, and Srinivas Kondeti, IKP's "livelihood associate" and community organizer. I told them about Bina Rao and suggested they form a team to consult with her. I also sent a copy of this letter to Vijay Kumar, head of Indira Kranthi Patham.

The letter mentioned the fact that the lace workers were making less than 50 cents a day under the IKEA contract.

During an interview later at his office Mr. Kumar could not understand why I was so riled up about the situation of these 10,000 lace workers. Given the fact that IKP was helping nearly 8 million women take loans across the state, he saw the plight of the lace artisans in the overall scheme of things as "trivial." In addition he didn't believe that these workers on the IKEA contract were making less than 50 cents a day and called Sreedhar Cherukuri to check it out.

"Look," I told him when he made the call. "I've talked to the artisans in the villages, I've interviewed the cooperative presidents. It's true."

Before I left he agreed that if a team from the lace federation lined up Bina Rao to help them he would make sure she was paid. On the advice of my friend Salome Yesudas, who knew the District Collector of West

Godavari — the top dog in the area — I fired off a letter to him asking him to intervene.

I had done what I could, but a year later, in May of 2007, Vithal Rajan contacted Bina Rao to see if anyone had talked to her. Nothing had happened. Srinivas, who could have organized it all, was no longer working with the lace workers.

"Well," said Vithal, "in India, you can lead a horse to water. But in this country, you also have to open up the horse's mouth and throw the water down."

Vithal also talked to Vijay Kumar who repeated that if a team from Lace Park recruited Bina Rao, he would pay. I emailed Sreedhar and Meera Shenoy, the head of employment generation and marketing for rural development in the Andhra Pradesh government, and heard nothing.

A few months later I approached APMAS, a state-level organization designed to help SHGs and SHG federations like those formed by the lace workers. N.V. Srinivasa Rao, manager of their livelihoods division, wrote me and said, "Since it is an institutional model involving 10,000 women under 51 Cooperatives, we shall certainly look into it and hope to do something positive." But he said it would take time, and I heard nothing more.

In August 2008 I found out that the lace artisans had become the victims of bureaucratic bungling. Sreedhar had been transferred out of DRDA to Hyderabad and subsequent DRDA project directors had done nothing. The head of Lace Park had changed and the new one had not been helpful. The Self Employed Women's Association, whose embroiderers had crashed into global markets, had offered to help, but the Lace Park administration had stood in the way of that too. Once again, it looked as though the powerful exporters were winning.

I thought of the four dynamic lace artisans I had interviewed — Surya, the lace federation president, Kanakdurga, the master lace trainer, Managatayaru, the quality control expert, and Kanakalaxmi, the lace executive. Why couldn't they forget the male bureaucrats, take a bus to Hyderabad, and get hold of Bina Rao? That, I felt, is what some of the feisty Dalits I had met might have done. However, quite probably the email I had sent to Surya via the Lace Park organization telling her about

Bina Rao's offer hadn't even reached her. And who knew what dangers the women might face if they did in fact strike out on their own.

I was gunning for a successful ending to this story about the lace artisans, but as of August 2008, 10,000 lace artisans tied to the Lace Park enterprise seemed to be on the shelf, their hopes on hold. Maybe by some miracle someone hell-bent for a breakthrough would finally rally to the cause. Back in Montreal, I waited for news.

Finally in December 2009, through an insider friend, I received a copy of a government of India report that laid out a business plan whereby lace artisans, exporters, and government bureaucrats responsible for development would work together in a cluster to expand the lace industry and break into new markets.

The 51 lace cooperatives, which have grown since I was there to 25,000 artisans, would work along with 75,000 other lace makers organized into a producer company. According to the plan produced by the ministry of textiles' development commission for handicrafts, the lace workers would by 2012 be earning 10 times more and turning out four times what they do now.

However, the report estimated the average current income for lace artisans at 500 rupees a month, working four or five hours a day, six days a week. At the current conversion of 44 rupees to the dollar, that would be $11 Canadian a month, or 11 cents an hour, calculating four hours a day for a total of 104 hours a month.

Under the new scheme, four years from now, these lace makers would be expected to make $1.10 an hour and $114 a month for a four-hour day and $200 a month for a seven-hour day, which even with inflation might mean a substantial increase in earning power.

However, extensive power would remain in the hands of the exporters who have traditionally kept the artisans subservient. To wrench fair compensation from a combination of the exporters and the development bureaucrats, I figure the 100,000 lace artisans might eventually have to do something drastic, like threaten to strike.

To find out whether the proposed scheme, estimated to cost over $20 million, was moving ahead, I wrote to the chief bureaucrat in West Godavari, Jaya Lakshmi, responsible for chairing a lace cluster coordinating committee, and to the project director of the District Rural Development Agency in charge of Lace Park. No response.

I also wrote to the head of Indira Kranthi Patham, expected to play a key role. Silence. Finally I faxed the executive at National Resource Center for Cluster Development under the federal ministry of small scale industry, which has been given the mission to "develop this cluster and help the women artisans." Nothing from there either.

18
WE WANT TO BUY A BUS

It was among the exploited Dalits who have always had to fight for every-thing that I found women making the most headway in breaking into non-traditional businesses with links to bigger markets. Three hours away from Hyderabad, 33,000 mostly Dalit and Tribal women in 400 vil-lages in the district of Nizamabad were taking astonishing leaps through a federation of 15 women's cooperatives supported by an NGO called Gram Abhyudaya Mandali.

Though mostly illiterate, the women had had the smarts to win a contract to run a sand quarry and were starting their own producer com-pany dairy. They had been building roads and had successfully negoti-ated with a big company to buy a bus in order to take a leasing contract with an Andhra Pradesh transport agency.

Always practical, the women hired accountants to do their books, and when the system routinely stabbed them in the back, they turned to Samson Nakkala, their Dalit leader/coordinator who helped them look for alternatives.

Untouchables were expected to "know their place" and not move into domains commanded by upper-caste, educated men. But sustained by group solidarity and a belief they had nothing to lose, these women never gave up.

In the face of astounding odds, they mobilized with grace and courage, sometimes against the advice of the more conservative staff they hired. When bribes were required, for example, they formed a bribe committee. When they needed to muster hundreds of women for a demonstration in order to get the attention of a state cabinet minister, they knew how to do it. They could have taught the equally poor but higher caste and more educated lace makers how to burst through barriers and win.

During my encounters with the Gram women, I met an Indian professor of business administration who taught in Delhi. He was not surprised to hear how well these unschooled women were doing. "What's an M.B.A.?" he scoffed. "Simply common sense institutionalized." Along with a passion to win, and a sharp knowledge of human nature, common sense always kept these resolute women on track.

Observing the women at Gram was a roller coaster ride into the inner workings of an unsung brand of Third World women's liberation. But in Hyderabad I had my own little obstacles to cross before I could even get to Nizamabad. Securing a map of the district was my first chore.

From my trusty Minerva hotel I marched along a road crammed with cars, scooters, and autorickshaws sweeping like giant insects in all directions. In my salwar kameez, I wove around rickety veggie carts and beggars along with barefoot swamis in dhotis, beautiful women in colourful saris, and the occasional full-length burqa.

Up some stairs and past a guard that kept out the unwashed, I was inside Bookpoint bookstore where the owner, who remembered me from an earlier visit, treated me to a Deccan Chronicle so I could learn about a festival celebrating the many-armed goddess Durga, the embodiment of feminine creative energy who rides a tiger and defeats demons.

But he did not have a map of Nizamabad District. He wrote down an address for me, walked outside, hailed an autorickshaw, and gave the kid-driver precise — well, Indian-style precise — directions in Telugu.

We were off to a place called Tarnaka in this sprawling city looking for Survey of India, Map Sales Department, which was supposed to be beside the Aradhara Theatre in the twin city of Secunderabad.

After a rocky ride around bullocks carrying straw, honking trucks, and street venders sitting cross-legged selling flowers, bananas, and clay pots, we pulled into a theatre courtyard. I waited for a business person that spoke English to show up, and he told me to go around the back. On foot, past tea stalls, broken down clinics, and a second-hand bookshop, another English-speaker told me Survey of India was several kilometers down the tangled road we had been on.

Back on the thoroughfare, the rickshaw did a U-turn designed to turn us into fodder for a funeral pyre in Varanasi and soon we were in a new alleyway. I corralled another man who said, "Oh, the Survey of India moved." The poor rickshaw driver who looked about 12 years old listened carefully to the new instructions from this very agreeable man who was willing to help out. Indians were always willing to help out.

Once again we were wheeling down a jam-packed main drag, when lo and behold, opposite Little Flowers College, was a sign marked Survey of India with guards outside towering gates reminiscent of a Canadian maximum security prison.

The rickshaw was ordered to remain outside, and I was ceremoniously directed to a small concrete security building. The way the security man behind a desk was looking at my fanny pack and me, I was feeling like a Saudi with a mysterious backpack en route to London.

"Passport please?" said this large man in uniform. Luckily I had not left it in the hotel room. "What do you want here?" he asked.

"I need this map of Nizamabad," I said.

"Why?" he wanted to know.

Vithal had told me that I was always a tourist, and I had suddenly made the mistake of telling him I had an appointment to visit an NGO. Oh dear. In Bangladesh anyone wanting to visit an NGO was seen as a troublemaker and denied entry. Oh well, I seemed to be "passing." He filled out a paper, gave it to me, and returned my passport. Outside, a guard looked at my "entry pass," and I was allowed to walk down a road to a place marked Map Sales Department, a musty place with a long counter where a young man disappeared and actually found my now-to-be-treasured Nizamabad map. It was 25 rupees. Victory! I ran back like a child with a prize, handed in my entry pass to another guard so I could exit, and I was back in my rickshaw holding up my precious map.

The rickshaw kid who had wasted another 20 minutes wasn't impressed. Now it was back to Hotel Minerva where I went to bed and then ordered in. But elsewhere in the subcontinent, another disaster endemic to this part of the world was unfolding. In Pakistan-occupied Kashmir and parts of Indian Kashmir, 40,000 people had just lost their lives in a huge earthquake and thousands more were homeless. The eventual death count would be 75,000, with 3 million homeless. I had to be grateful for my map, my air-conditioned room, and my Tandoori chicken meal.

A few days later I was in the village of Suddapalli near the town of Nizamabad in a very poor part of Andhra Pradesh getting to know Samson Nakkala who had provided a car to get me there. I was scooting around villages listening to the tales of the Gram women and watching them take the first steps in the development of their very own producer-company dairy.

The women in Gram were feisty freewheelers willing to try anything, but the green light to break out of their caste straitjackets came from Samson Nakkala, whose mission was to propel Dalit and Tribal women into the economic and social mainstream.

Samson's grandfather had been a Dalit day labourer in agriculture that had converted to Christianity, but Samson still identified as a Dalit and always felt up against the upper-caste establishment. In India, once a Dalit, it would seem, always a Dalit.

Samson came from Guntur on the Bay of Bengal in the region I had visited after the Tsunami. Like the women in Gram, Samson knew what it was like to be a child labourer, even though he and his siblings went to school. He was 12 when his father died, leaving a family of seven children.

Samson's mother, who had grade three and could read, made a living growing rice on a few acres of land and stitching clothes. She owned a four-room house that included a kitchen, but she rented out two rooms and the family of eight lived in one room. To put enough food on the table, all the children did odd jobs before or after school. Samson milked the family cows and made cow dung cakes for fuel while his brothers and sisters made match sticks or helped stitch and then deliver their mother's handmade clothes.

Like the Gram women, his mother was tough and willing to fight. Samson remembered an incident when a man charged his mother three *paisas* (cents) for a soda when the regular price was only two. "When my mother realized she'd been cheated, she stopped the fellow even though he was accompanied by a group of rowdy men. She said, 'If you think you can do that, I'll beat all of you up.' And they gave her back the extra paisa."

While studying for a bachelor of commerce, Samson ran into government corruption when he bottled ink for fountain pens and sold it to government departments. Officials demanded a kickback as a condition for taking his ink bottles, and Samson said he would have to deliver an inferior product so that he himself could make a profit. The response of the officials was: "Sell it to us cheap, we'll take our kickback, and then we'll just throw them away."

He enrolled in law school upon graduating with his commerce degree, but dropped out to do volunteer work after a 1977 cyclone in Andhra Pradesh killed 10,000 people. Promoting development among the poor, whatever their caste, became his goal.

After a workshop course at a social institute in Bangalore run by Jesuits, he was hired as a sociologist in the Nizamabad area with a community health project working with lepers. During the day he went out with health workers to village meetings, but in the evening he would return alone to talk to marginalized groups.

In one village he helped form a union of poor coolies that went on strike and won higher pay rates from landlords. In another he encouraged Dalits to go to court against caste leaders for discriminating against them in teashops.

In Dharmaram village where he eventually settled with his wife and two children, he started a cycle rickshaw cooperative for 29 poor rickshaw pullers who were renting vehicles. So they could buy their own rickshaws, he helped them get a loan from the government.

It cost 6 rupees for a train ride to Hyderabad where the rickshaws were sold, but the rickshaw pullers resolved to ride the train free. Only Samson bought a ticket. In Hyderabad, they all slept on the ground in front of the rickshaw store. After buying their rickshaws they proudly returned in a fleet, travelling 150 kilometres over 18 hours, sleeping by the side of the road.

In the middle of working with the rickshaw pullers, Samson quit the health project that had hired him because the health workers were uncomfortable with his hard-hitting activist work. The rickshaw pullers suggested he become a rickshaw puller himself. Instead, he took a cheap room in Dharmaram and borrowed from friends while he continued his work as an organizer.

Six months later, in 1980, an Oxfam funder who had supported the health project convinced him to start his own non-government organization and said Oxfam would fund it.

With Ellaiah, a man who had been a bonded labourer but became a rickshaw repairman and secretary of the rickshaw cooperative, Samson started Gram Abhyudaya Mandali, which means village development council.

Samson at first worked to make health services and education accessible to women and children in the villages of Nizamabad district where village sanghams were started. Rights were a priority. Men's groups that focused upon agriculture were also developed along with women's groups that saved money for emergency loans.

By the mid-1990s thousands of women were meeting in self-help groups and taking loans from banks for small income-generating businesses. In 2001 Gram won an award given by the National Bank of Agriculture and Rural Development for best performance for facilitating links between self-help groups and banks.

In 1995, the government passed a law allowing for the formation of cooperatives with an independent legal status. In India they are known as MACS, or Mutually-Aided Cooperative Societies. Using that law, Gram helped the village self-help groups band into 15 cooperatives in the Nizamabad district and four cooperatives in neighbouring Adilabad district.

By the end of 2005, Gram staff that had swelled to around 60 people had organized 40,000 mostly Dalit and tribal women across 506 villages into two federations for a total of 19 cooperatives. In 2004–05, borrowings by the women were almost 1.5 million Canadian dollars.

Each cooperative hired five or six staff, paid for in part by themselves and in part by Gram under an Oxfam Netherlands budget in 2005–06 of 8,000,000 rupees or about $210,526 Canadian.

But the Gram women went way beyond simply promoting their own financial interests. Across the villages they had become activists practising thatch hut justice. In addition to marriage counselling, they helped widows remarry and divorced women retrieve their dowries. One group went after a low-caste girl who had run away with a high-caste boy, brought them back to the village, purchased everything needed for a wedding, and married them off. A woman who had lost her husband to AIDS and was being shunned by everyone in the village was invited to join one of the self-help groups. In a village where police were torturing an untouchable man at night, the women hired a farm tractor, packed it with people, and showed up at the police station to demand that the injustice be stopped.

While all this was going on, the women kept building up their small businesses. But after they organized into cooperatives, Samson felt the time was ripe for them to expand their horizons. The tea stalls, grocery kiosks, mobile fruit and vegetable stands, chicken shops, and mini milk selling businesses they had started improved their incomes. But once they had done that, they could only imagine expanding into areas already dominated by other poor people, and they were reluctant to do that.

This was when Samson gave them a lecture about the possibilities of leaping out of their box at the bottom rung of the social and economic ladder and reaping the benefits of working at a higher level.

"It is critical to the process of redistribution that the poor enter market-driven businesses," he told me, and he believed that to facilitate this, NGOs such as his Gram Abhyudaya Mandali had to be able to accompany the women.

In advising the women, he pointed out that people already in other boxes were not going to quietly accept the entry of newcomers.

"But you have a right to be there," he insisted, and he added that they would have to learn how to make alliances with the players in the higher boxes.

The push by Gram women into competitive business took a dramatic turn in 2001 when four Dalit women boarded a train in the town of Nizamabad en route to Hyderabad and the Ashok Leyland bus company.

"They were off to buy a bus," said Samson.

"A bus?" I wasn't sure I had heard right.

"Yes, a bus," he said, smiling.

A few years before these women had been working as day labourers in the fields for less than a dollar a day and their subsequent loans had been for modest village businesses. How were they going to buy a bus? I thought, but I kept my white lady biases to myself and listened.

The four women taking the train were members of the Nandipet Mutually-Aided Cooperative Society, or MAC, composed of about 3,400 women in over 200 self-help groups. Their cooperative was among the first to consider such an ambitious endeavour.

The Andhra Pradesh State Road Transport Corporation that hired busses from private parties looked like a good place to start. When the women heard about a newspaper advertisement for a tender to operate under the corporation they decided to make a bid.

But first they had to own at least one bus to lease out. A bus would cost 1 million rupees, about $33,000 Canadian at the time, and they decided they should buy two of them. Their dream was to have a bus going to the temple city of Tirupati with a big sign saying NANDIPET MAC.

The women who boarded this train to Hyderabad were not wearing slick gray business suits or carrying polished leather briefcases. They were simply in their very best saris, looking as beautiful as Indian women can look. Only one of the four was literate.

But thanks to their parsimony, good business sense, and unwavering saving strategies, the cooperative they were part of was holding over 9 million rupees of savings, reserve funds, and share capital. This rather

Satyagangu (holding train entry bar) and her team take a train to Hyderabad to buy a bus.
Photo courtesy Kongara Srinivas.

impressive amount of around $300,000 Canadian gave them the confidence they needed.

When they arrived at the gate of the Ashok Leyland bus company a guard identified them as low-caste women with no business credentials and refused at first to admit them. "Why are you here?" he asked.

With a confident toss of their plush black braids, they proudly announced, "We're here to buy a bus," and he let them in.

Once inside, they negotiated a deal with a company manager that included a loan for the financing as long as they did in fact win the contract to lease a bus.

With this offer from Ashok Leyland, the women sent a letter to the chairman of the AP State Road Transport Corporation asking for a preferential allotment, meaning a contract without a tender. Dalits could sometimes benefit from a "reservation" or affirmative action, but the transport corporation said they had to go the normal route.

They submitted their tender before the deadline with the required deposit to go with it. However, the government bureaucrats told them that they had drawn the money from the wrong bank. When they returned with the deposit from the designated bank, they were 10 minutes late and their tender was refused.

Samson Nakkala was outraged on behalf of the women. "Where was the commitment to the Beijing Declaration?" he asked, referring to the Indian government's supposed support for marginalized women made in 1995 during the International Women's Conference in China.

Walls, I saw, went up like lightning whenever grassroots women threatened to move into corridors of expanded economic and political power. But as I would discover, the Dalit and Tribal women of Nizamabad's Indur Intideepam (meaning light of the home) Mutually-Aided Cooperative Society Federation (IIMF), composed of their 15 lively cooperatives, were a powerhouse that would not be stopped.

The Andhra Pradesh State Road Transportation Corporation ran leases on a five-year basis and the women decided that they might try again five years later unless they became busy with something else. Buoyed up by their support from the Ashok Leyland bus company, they weren't inclined to throw in the towel.

19
CHILI IN THE EYES

While the women from the Nandipet cooperative were negotiating to buy their bus, women from four other cooperatives in the Nizamabad district were mobilizing to win a licence to run a sand quarry. If they won, they would take loans from banks, hire and pay hundreds of workers to dig sand, pull in construction company trucks from several states to buy the sand, and bargain with municipal officials over daily technicalities like waybills.

This sounded wildly ambitious but apparently not for the venturesome Gram women who were fired up to crash into new economic boxes.

To hear how they had fared, I went to the village near the sand quarry to meet 10 women who had been involved in the sand contract enterprise. After several years, the women did in fact eventually make a huge profit, but the process as they described it felt like a cliff-hanging climb up the Himalayas with the gods arrayed against them. Eventually, they succeeded because they made a strategic alliance with players already in the sand quarry box, so to speak.

Here is how it went.

In January 2001, a staff person with one of the cooperatives saw a tender notification in a Nizamabad paper to run a sand quarry in a village in an area where Gram members lived.

In the past, about 500 coop members had worked as labourers making 60 rupees a day in the quarry and they knew what was involved. The executives of four cooperatives, representing 8,000 members from 650 self-help groups in 125 villages, decided to go for it.

The women put in the highest bid at 600,000 rupees, but the top government official in the district said that at this figure the government would lose money. There were two quarries in the same village, and the bid for the other quarry had gone for 1.4 million rupees, so the official told the women they'd have to pay an extra 300,000.

Strike one against the Dalit women. One of the Gram staff noted that the authorities didn't appreciate Dalit women moving into the male-run sand quarry business, so they upped the price. The officials, she said, were also worried that the women might not come through with enough bribes in the proper places.

Instead of outrage, the attitude of the Gram women was to jump right in and turf up the required cash. The women hired a bookkeeper and a chartered accountant to manage the cash flow but they decided to make all the key business decisions themselves.

The women paid for the bid in 40 days by taking 280,000 rupees from the four cooperatives, and had enough credibility to swing a 750,000-rupee loan, the equivalent at the time of $25,000 Canadian, from a government rural development bank.

On March 1, 2001, the contract started.

Their next task was to find 300,000 rupees to make the area accessible to trucks, including ramps. With no operational money, they hired 30 workers from the quarry village on credit, paying each one, for a start, 333 rupees for a month's work.

By May five trucks were buying the sand, but that wasn't enough for them to make a profit and they were competing with contractors at two other nearby quarries. To pay their workers, they took a loan from Gram for 230,000 rupees.

To drum up business, the women sent around pamphlets reading "Sand for Sale." By June there were 30 trucks per day and they were making 4,500 rupees a day, but all that went to pay their workers and their bank loan. No profits yet.

In July and August, heavy rains and flooding prevented any work being done at all, but they were still in the game. Strike Two.

In September work resumed, with 25 trucks per day and more trucks lined up to roll in. Things were looking up with profits on the horizon. Suddenly goons hired by a rival sand contractor began to beat up the male sand labourers working for the women.

Under Gram Abhyudaya Mandali, grassroots leaders Saraswati (right) and Lakshmi (middle) worked with hired manager Alivelu (left) to run a sand contract.

The Gram women went to the police who said, "Protect yourselves. You're on your own." The police, said Samson Nakkala, who monitored the project, lined up with the vested interests in the municipality where there were family connections and baksheesh flowing between the contractors and government officials.

The women told the workers: "We can't protect you, go home, we'll do the work ourselves," so 150 women from the Gram cooperatives went out to dig sand and throw pails of it into trucks. Always brilliantly creative, the women came up with a novel tactic to shield themselves from the lurking goons.

"A few of us carried red-hot chili powder and we announced that if anyone tried to stop us, we'd throw chili powder in their eyes," said Saraswati Wagmari, the 26-year-old president of one of the cooperatives involved in the contract. When the men who had been working there saw this, they joined the women and went back to work.

The next thing the rival contractor did was to grab half the women's quarry by throwing up stakes around it.

When the women complained to a top government official, he responded with brutal verbal abuse. Not willing to tolerate this, the women took him to court. This resulted in the women losing the support of the entire municipal power structure, including elected representatives.

The women sent a letter to the chief minister of Andhra Pradesh detailing how they had been abused, and this resulted in an apology, but they were still stuck with half their territory lopped off, in addition to continual raids of incoming trucks by two rival contractors. Strike Three, and it looked like they were out.

During the first year of their contract, the women had lost 1.5 million rupees and still owed money to the bank and to Gram, but they dismantled the illegal stakes that the rival contractor had put up around a hunk of their quarry and vowed to continue.

When another 900,000-rupee fee to operate came due, they fought to have it waived. The women argued with the transport minister that they'd had to deal with excessive flooding and less available sand than the rival contractors, in addition to work stoppages because of constant intimidations.

They took their case to state assembly members as well as elected representatives at the federal level, but in 2002, they were given no contract to quarry sand.

In June 2003, however, the Gram women were suddenly graced with a 165-day contract, thanks to their continued pressure on the administration. The reaction of their enemies was to burn their offices to the ground, but now everyone rallied to their side. This included the municipal authorities, the state anti-poverty program, and all the NGOs in the region. On a wing and a prayer, and with an office provided by the municipality, the women hunkered down to continue the battle.

It was time for a home run. For 40 days, the women soared. Every day there were 400 trucks and 3,000 labourers. From the four cooperatives, 44 women made all the management decisions and they hired 10 extra technical employees to help them.

Not willing to deal with the usual snags, they formed a bribe committee in order to grease the palms of officials who demanded bribes in order to issue the necessary waybills for the trucks. Every night two different women went out to take care of that.

At one point, one of the staff they'd hired objected to a decision they'd made. The women said, "Look, we hired you. Do your job. We're making the management decisions, and we'll take the consequences."

When the staff person complained to Samson, he said: "The goal of all this was empowerment of women. Now that they're becoming empowered, we must not stop them."

Baiawwa, a woman on the sand project management team, made this comment: "Gram organized us into cooperatives. They also showed us the path to business, however, in business their advice didn't always work. We have to do business with our own ideas. Sometimes we have to find our own way and maybe take a crooked path," she said, referring to the bribes they had to pay.

In reflecting on this, Samson said, "I was not going to recommend bribes, but the women had to get out there and learn how business was done. So no judgements passed."

The women also faced stiff reaction from the local men in their villages.

First of all, the labourers doing the work weren't accustomed to working for women. One worker put it this way: "We men would prefer to have a man boss," but he admitted that the women had brought them good jobs and good pay, which was, in fact, five times a day more than they would have earned a day as labourers in the fields. "In the end we were very happy," he said.

Secondly, the husbands of the Gram women weren't used to being married to adventurous business managers who weren't always available to do the housework and make the meals. Eventually, they also adjusted.

Sitting on the ground with his wife Chandrawwa who worked day and night for several weeks, Sailu admitted that he now helped with the household chores. With wavering pride he added: "When people ask where my wife is, I tell them she has gone to work."

This was the first time village women had been out after dark directing labourers in sandpits and instructing truckers on the roads. After sunset, women were supposed to be inside their houses. As a result, some village men spread rumours that the Gram women were engaging in "immoral" activities.

After 40 days the women faced another setback. The rival contractors took the women to court saying their activities were depleting the groundwater. The women replied in a counter case that all the quarries were under the same river. As a result, the municipality decided that quarrying in the region would be closed for an indefinite period and the women had to pack up.

Despite all the reversals, the women made profits. After recovering their 1.5 million-rupee loss, they made a profit of 900,000 rupees or about $27,273 Canadian, over this 40-day period. The four executives representing the four cooperatives were each paid 3,000 rupees. Up to then they'd received no pay at all.

But the most significant benefit to the women came from the thrill of hearing people addressing them with respect as Madame, and referring to Madame's Quarry. In their villages these Dalit women now enjoyed a whole new level of esteem.

Because of the water table issue, from January 2004 a ban was placed on all sand contracts in the area, but the women got a court order saying they could resume for another 125 days when it was lifted. Because of their phenomenal success, various politicians were lining up to seek a partnership with them so that they, too, could cash in on the rising expertise of these new entrepreneurs.

After spending a day with the women in the area where the quarry was located, I saw that 26-year-old Saraswati, one of the movers and shakers in the sand contract project, was shaping up to be one of the leaders of Gram.

Back in the town of Nizamabad, where I returned to a hotel to type up my notes, I asked Samson whether it would be possible to arrange another meeting with her. Samson decided she should come to nearby Suddapalli where Gram had a training centre and someone available to translate from Telugu to English.

Working as a tailor, Saraswati had orders to fill for blouses and wall-to-wall work at home with her four children. She would have to travel 180 kilometers on a sweltering bus just for me to interview her. This would put her back 300 rupees in lost wages and travel expenses, representing about eight days of work for an ordinary day labourer.

On my account, about 10 Gram women who had worked on the sand contract had already given up a day of their precious time. Any more time, I decided, would amount to white lady exploitation of the colonial variety. So I made a deal with Samson that a condition of the interview was that I paid for Saraswati's lost wages and travel expenses.

I had become a friend, and Saraswati didn't want to take a single rupee of reimbursement from me. Only by twisting her arm did I manage to get her to accept my paltry $8 Canadian.

It was always an empowering experience for me to meet the likes of Saraswati, who reverberated with such hope and tenacity to succeed no matter what. I had started my adventure in India four years before when I met the Saraswati that had cleared the bootlegger out of her village and for a while turned the men in the village against her. Now here was this Saraswati, who had gone from Dalit child bride married just out of elementary school, to fireball CEO turning villages upside down in the Indian countryside.

A woman of sparkling energy and quiet beauty, Saraswati, who came from the village of Eklara with a population of 2,000, was small and lean but carried herself with the grace of a ballerina. When I interviewed her she was wearing a saffron-coloured sari with a coral and green rainbow curling through it. Her thick black hair was pulled back to feature beautifully decorated gold earrings and smooth, flawless skin.

Her serene appearance, however, hid an entrepreneurial dynamo and social justice advocate that had been everything from goat herder, municipal sand contract manager, and self-appointed ombudsman of her community.

She even managed to mastermind a demonstration of 500 women who stopped the car of a state cabinet minister in order to make him aware of unjust treatment of their cooperatives running the sand contract at the hands of bureaucrats. And she did this while toting around a three-month old baby that was constantly in her arms.

A Dalit, she was married at 11 just after she had finished grade seven, and had had a child by the time she was 14. At 15 she joined a Gram self-help group in her village and took a loan for a goat, and then another loan, until she had a herd of 30 goats that she sold to buy and lease land.

Thanks to that first loan for a goat, a thriving cotton crop was growing on the land to support an extended family of 11, including her four children who were enrolled in good private schools. The profits from the goats also allowed her to buy chickens that multiplied to over 30.

Her parents never went to school and neither did her older sisters, who were child labourers, but her father learned to read and write on his own, and he made sure his last three daughters received basic education.

Saraswati, named after the Hindu patron of the arts and goddess of learning, was able to jump from grade seven to first-year university by enrolling in an Open University program that admitted mature students capable of doing the work. She did this all while having children, running a rickshaw leasing business of her own, sewing clothes, and serving as president of her women's cooperative.

For five years, starting when she was 21, she organized women into self-help groups in five areas in the Nizamabad district and also worked on social issues.

"Samson always told us that women must develop socially, politically, and financially, and that we must focus on everything from proper health to economic activity," she said.

Through her work on the sand contract, she learned about government programs and the problems people had in accessing them. By observing the conduct of elected officials and bureaucrats, she saw how a parallel system of bribes and influence could prevent ordinary villagers from receiving what they were entitled to.

Over the years she fought for poor people with rice ration cards that were getting short-changed by government shops, she mobilized to help older people get their proper pensions, and she helped pregnant women take advantage of a program allowing them to have their babies safely in a hospital. As a member of the board of an Andhra Pradesh federation of women's NGOs, she also worked to solve common problems across the state.

"Because of caste discrimination against Dalits, most of the men in municipal services or even in my village would ask: 'How come Saraswati isn't staying at home? What's she doing running around like this?' I've always tried to stay in the good books of people," she explained, "but I also want justice to be done."

In the 2004 state elections, she decided to try to become a candidate for the party in power at the state level. "I wanted to run because I saw from my experience with the sand contract that the elected people were not helpful." She gave speeches during the elections and people were interested, but in the end she wasn't chosen to run.

But Saraswati was a born leader and I knew I would be meeting her again soon. Three weeks later she was standing before 3,000 grassroots women and a full array of politicians from the area. As a Gram leader, she was inaugurating the beginning of an innovative producer-company dairy enterprise started by Gram women who owned milk buffaloes. I was lucky to be there on the first day that the milk started to roll in from the villages. It would be another roller coaster ride.

There was a proud addendum to the sand contract saga. Three years later in January 2007, the women were back in the sand business, this time for three months in a partnership deal with a group of big contractors. The "sand moguls," as Samson called them, agreed to handle technicalities with bureaucrats and politicians while the women managed the basic work. The Gram women made a profit of 3 million rupees, or about $79,000 Canadian.

"The lesson to the women taking the sand contracts was this," said Samson. "First you prove what you are capable of doing and then people in the new boxes will accept you for an alliance."

For the women in Gram who were banding together with the dream of starting their own independent Dalit-run dairy that started with milk collection in the villages and would end with a plant that shipped processed and packaged milk with their own trademark to supermarkets, it was a lesson they, too, would have to learn.

20
POSANI STARTS A DAIRY

In the village of Suddapalli, Posani Mekala stood in front of the building where her shiny bulk cooler was waiting to be filled with milk. Rickshaws were pulling up with 40-litre pails of milk from 1,000 women across 33 villages with another 1,000 women signed up to join. She could hardly believe it was really happening. She hoped the *palamitras* (friends of milk) in the village collection centres had been able to properly measure the fat and quantity on those new electronic milk-testing machines. The power failure that morning had created a problem. Tonight she would send the technicians out to troubleshoot.

Later, after the evening milk deliveries, and once they had 2,000 litres, a truck would take the milk to the Mulkanoor women's dairy, but that was just for now. Eventually they would have all the modern machinery to process and package milk right here in her village of Suddapalli. The Intideepam Mahila (light of the home) Dairy Producer Company would be India's first women's Dalit-run dairy selling milk with its own label in supermarkets.

She took a deep breath and thought of her years working in the fields as a coolie for 30 rupees a day. But then Gram came along and that had led to self-help groups and loans, and then her leadership of the Dichpalli cooperative that was overseeing the producer company. Now she was head of the Indur federation of cooperatives which had advanced the money for the bulk cooler from the women's savings.

The National Dairy Development Board had promised a big loan so they could take off. But would they really come through? She wasn't sure. If not, they would have to look somewhere else. Samson would help. She felt confident. Samson had showed them they could be more than coolies in the fields, more than small people taking small loans for small things. They could trust him because he was a Dalit like them.

The survey they had commissioned showed there were thousands of women in Nizamabad District with milk buffaloes. Under their producer company there would be no middlemen and the women would get all the profits.

Already they were shaking up the villages. Greedy middlemen in some villages were threatening to punish the women by withholding money they still owed. In one village the women had agreed to keep giving middlemen some milk, at least for a while, even though that meant less milk for their producer company. In another village a high-caste landlord demanded 40 litres of milk right away, but the women told him that now he would have to let them know in advance and he'd have to pay the market price. No special deals, they said.

The National Dairy Development Board had given advice and was still onside but they themselves had hired a manager. Posani smiled to herself. Dalit women that everyone wanted to kick around would show the world that they could do it. Poor women of higher castes were in this with them; Muslim women too. They would all work together.

She looked off in the distance and thought of how her village of Suddapalli would change. There would eventually be lines and lines of trucks hauling in milk and leaving with boxes and boxes of milk packets of all sizes to sell as far away as Hyderabad. They would need a big restaurant and maybe a hostel where people could stay.

At the Kapila Hotel in Nizamabad I had woken up at 5:30 that morning in time to climb into a Gram car that picked me up and brought me to Suddapalli village. Standing at the door of the building containing the bulk cooler, Posani, looking every inch the CEO in an elegant brown and gold sari, was welcoming everyone that had come to witness the event.

This included high-caste men from India's National Dairy Development Board, the District Rural Development Agency (DRDA), and from Indira Kranthi Patham, the state anti-poverty outfit that was supposed to be helping the lace artisans earn fair wages in global markets. Some of these guys, I could tell, weren't entirely comfortable with the prospect of these untouchable-caste women crashing into a new box. Getting them out of abject poverty was one thing, but encouraging them to run a big competitive business was another.

The men watched as the proud owners of this incipient dairy scrambled off rickshaws that had carried them in from the surrounding villages. The women had milked their animals very early in the morning and taken the milk to the village collection centres. Now in their multicoloured saris, looking like jewels, they were here to celebrate.

I milled around and watched.

On-the-job experience had turned Posani and her Dalit colleagues into smart entrepreneurs that could not be suppressed. The men were outclassed and I think they knew it. They were there because the event could not be ignored, but they were also curious as to how this humble Posani Mekala, who lived in a two-room hut in the Dalit corner of the village, could march like this onto centre stage.

I walked away from the bustle of the chilling centre into the courtyard in front. Across the road, on a barren tract of land, a wiry middle-aged woman in a lime green sari was perched on a hill of drying buffalo dung patties surrounded by about 100 buffaloes. I wondered who this woman was. I bounded over and through a translator met Shusheela, a woman of 45 with four boys and three girls. Of these, three were in school, and a son, 23, was a bonded labourer making $270 Canadian annually, slaving every day of the year for a local landowner.

Helping her and her husband mind and graze these buffaloes were two sons and a daughter of 20. Some of the animals, I later discovered, had been milked early that morning by members of the producer company. Most villages hired buffalo grazers at varying rates per buffalo.

Shusheela and her family received, she said, 5 rupees a month per buffalo for a total of 6,000 rupees, or $166 Canadian a year. She made a lot more from gathering and selling the cow dung for fuel or manure, which got her 20,000 rupees a year, or $555 Canadian. The total income for this came to about $722 Canadian annually, or 71 rupees a day, which was barely enough to feed her household of nine.

According to an NGO fieldworker, for the daily required rice, dhal, tomatoes, chili, oil, milk, tea, and firewood, without counting sugar, other vegetables, or fruit, it would cost 39 rupees a day to feed a household of five (63 rupees for nine) in the villages in late 2005. Oranges for five, I discovered, cost 30 rupees. Clothes and transport, not to mention books, would all be extra.

A lonely figure, a look of worry etched into her face, Shusheela seemed resigned to her fate as an impoverished buffalo herder and stood in sharp contrast to the Gram women of her village participating in the producer company. She had only a vague idea of what was going on across the road and was not a member of a self-help group. Was she too poor and tired to think she could buy a buffalo and pay back the loan? One of the poorest of the poor that microcredit was not reaching?

I wandered back to the chilling centre where women were celebrating. Later that evening a truck from the Mulkanoor women's dairy about three hours away would drive up and take the first load out.

But the day's work wasn't over. That evening technicians were scheduled to visit the milk collection centres in villages where there had been problems with the state-of-the-art electronic milk testing machines. I decided to go with them.

The sun had set and I was in a car with two technicians en route to village collection centres experimenting with the milk testing equipment. The animals had been milked before sunrise and now they were being milked again.

We entered the first village through a hard mud road that during the day was crowded with bullocks pulling carts and milk buffaloes going out to graze along with herds of goats.

At the collection centre I was spirited away by a young villager who took me into a spacious-feeling house where 10 people were sitting on the floor, some of them women holding babies. I was in the abode of a joint family composed of four brothers, each of whom had a few rooms attached to a large communal family room with no furniture in it. Three brothers worked on 10 acres of land with their wives. A fourth brother was a librarian working on a B.A. "Thirteen people live here," said a boy of 12 attending an English school and eager to practice his English.

I accompanied Devakarn Nalavalla, the mother of the sons, to a thatched area and watched her milk her two buffaloes. She said she was 45 but her weary, lined face looked at least 65.

She was earning 500 rupees (or $14 Canadian) a month from selling milk to a middleman, she said, and hoped to make 1,000 rupees with the producer company. In addition to her milking chores, she looked after six grandchildren while her sons and daughters-in-law worked in the fields.

After the milking, I walked with Devakarn to the small milk collection centre with her pail full. The tester was on a table, and on the wall a panel indicated the number of the milk producer, the quantity, fat content, and the amount that she would eventually be paid in rupees. About eight other women who had already brought in their milk gathered around.

Devakarn presented her pail of milk to the paid *palamitra*, a local village girl with high school education. She took out a small bottle, poured some milk in it, and tested it for fat. Devakarn's milk was then poured into a 40-litre container that measured the quantity. All of it was computerized and registered on Devakarn's smart card that she carried with her. Everything, according to the technician, was now working well.

We had two more villages to visit. Supper tonight would have to be the salty biscuits we had picked up from an outdoor kiosk and cups of hot milk.

As we rolled into Yanampalli, the last village on our circuit that night, the air smelled of hay and flowers and crickets were singing. Village buildings were compact concrete boxes in pastel colours along with thatch-roofed huts with buffaloes lolling outside or cached away under thatch.

At the collection centre 118 producers had already brought in 80 litres that night. Inside, about 10 women were arguing. A local woman who did not own milk buffaloes was saying: "But we want some of your milk. You can't sell it exclusively through the producer company."

At a quickie meeting, the women from the producer company decided that the neighbours had the right to milk, but they would have to pay the market price, which was 15 rupees a litre. One woman countered that she would give very poor neighbours a better price.

This new company was a chance for some women to move into a better income category, but against all this was the prevalence in many of these villages of landlessness and coolie work at 30 to 50 rupees a day, as well as the likes of Shusheela minding those buffaloes back in Suddapalli for a pittance.

However, a hopeful spirit was in the air. The educated daughters of the women in the producer company were now being hired to do a survey about the possibilities around starting goat and turkey producer companies that could draw in more poor people.

Inside the collection centre the palamitra was continuing to ask questions about the testing machine and I knew we would be there for a while. Off in front of the village square, I spied a STD/ISD kiosk. This meant Subscriber Trunk Dialing and International Subscriber Dialing — in other words, a handy and cheap public phone. I decided this was a good time for me to make a phone call to Canada.

It was now 10:30 p.m. The village was silent and everyone had settled in for the night. The kiosk was a three-minute walk away and I had started to take off for it when one of the technicians said: "You'll need a chaperone." I was suddenly accompanied by one man along with another 10 who had been watching from their huts. The kiosk was in an open area with a table and phone in the shadow of a statue of Mahatma Gandhi in a dhoti looking out into a square dominated by the village water pump.

While I made my call, I felt the eyes of the Mahatma along with 10 men that stared with fascination as I called a friend and related my most recent experiences. From time to time I connected with friends back home for only a few dollars from one of these ISDs.

Explaining the behaviour of the village men, Samson later said: "All their women were inside. Women don't go out at night. And when they do go to meetings the men aren't that comfortable. Also you're a free woman, on your own," he said. "And that makes you a curiosity."

The next day, in this country of continuing colourful drama, rickshaws, bicycles, bullock carts, and busses crammed with women converged upon the little village of Suddapalli. The sisterhood from the surrounding area was moving in for the inaugural ceremony of the Intideepam Mahila Dairy Producer Company. Representing over 400 villages in Nizamabad district, they drew from the 15 Gram Abhyudaya Mandali cooperatives with its membership of 33,000.

I arrived in Suddapalli to a giant patchwork tent of many colours. Inside, 3,000 women in saris and salwar kameez along with Muslim women in scarves were sitting on the ground with their legs tucked beneath them. A stage had been set up in front and while the women waited for the dignitaries to arrive small groups from the different coops sang songs. High-flying Saraswati of the sand contract saga was in charge.

Eventually a full complement of village, municipal, state, and federal politicians showed up. In addition, Vijaya, the president of the Mulkanoor Women's Cooperative Dairy that was taking milk from the Dalit producer company, arrived with members of her executive. In a great show of support, Vijaya, whose dairy drew from high-caste women, had cancelled an important board meeting so they could attend the inauguration. The size of the crowd astounded the politicians who always had trouble attracting even a small crowd to political meetings. The sheer numbers of these women who were taking a day off from work were a testament to the women's growing economic and political power.

From the speeches, translated by Samson's wife Mary who sat next me, it was clear that the women were succeeding where the establishment had failed. The Suddapalli sarpanch talked about how the Andhra Pradesh government had tried to start a milk collection business and dairy in the district and failed. Unreliable men that transported and sold the milk apparently watered it down and cheated the women buffalo milk producers. But the Dalit-run organization had representatives in every village that monitored the activities of eight hired supervisors and other employees through a vigilant board.

M.R. Arulraja, a seasoned community animator that Samson had hired to help the women envision creative solutions, stood up and told the women to stand firm no matter how they were treated. He talked about how the Small Industries Development Bank of India (SIDBI) wouldn't give the producer company a loan because the cooperatives weren't operating according to the same rules as a standard microfinance institution or bank. The self-help groups in the cooperatives made allowances for late payments of loans in situations of emergencies, for example.

"But you started your organization despite them," he said. "Now you are owners of this company and not coolies. You must earn lots of money. And keep in mind, you are asking only for loans and are not begging." Speaking into the crowd of women, he said: "Don't expect anything from others. Stand on your own two feet. If you can't buy buffaloes, get something smaller, two hens. Start small."

The MP representing the federal government for Nizamabad got to his feet and commended the women for envisioning a dairy in the poor Telangana area covering several districts that would eventually bring in 250,000 women. Afterwards, in a reporters' scrum that I attended, he confirmed that the women could depend upon funds from the federal government and from his own special fund. He said he would also support women starting other kinds of producer companies. "It's not sufficient," he said, "for the women to be just coolies and bidi workers."

As I lumbered back in a jeep to my hotel in Nizamabad later that evening I reflected upon the success of the past couple of days that I had been privileged to witness. I was the outsider, the white lady from Canada in unruly mouse-brown hair wearing the scuffed salwar kameez with the worn fanny pack around my waist. But in their contrasting lush black braids, the Dalit women in their saris and jewels made me feel like a member of the team. It had been an empowering time for me, too. People from my tribe, after all, were kicking out from under the male boots of caste and class. The new feminists who belonged to India's 600,000 villages, and were part of the forgotten 750 million rural people of this country, were on a roll, and I hoped that the likes of Shusheela would eventually be included.

I arrived back to the hotel starved and tired and went straight to bed, but in the morning when I came down for breakfast all the staff quickly surrounded me. I had been a hotel guest off and on for several days and everyone knew me. One of them brandished a copy of a local newspaper. To my astonishment there was a colour picture of me talking to the federal MP.

I had done nothing of note. I would have been glad to be interviewed about the accomplishments of these Dalit women, but no, just the fact that I was talking to an MP was news. I was back to being a vestige of the British Raj. The message behind the picture seemed to be: WESTERN LADY MEETS FEDERAL BIGWIG AT WOMEN'S DAIRY INAUGURATION.

Back in Suddapalli the next day, village representatives were sitting in a circle on the floor at the Gram training centre sharing tales about how they were rallying women to participate in their burgeoning milk producer company. Encouraged by animator Arulraja, the women were not only imagining more earnings, but also better clinics, schools, and higher education for their children. Among the women in Gram, social improvements were just as important as expanded livelihoods. They never ceased to be activists and promoters of social justice.

Sitting on the floor myself, I listened as Poorovva, a beautiful Lambada Tribal woman in her early 40s, wearing a green and gold sari with a rose in her hair, talked about how nervous five of the Tribal women in her village of Argul had been about visiting the Mulkanoor women's dairy.

The Tribal women were even lower on the economic and social totem pole than Dalits and were not used to venturing out to meet people like the high-caste, fearless Reddy women who flashed with confidence and ran the Mulkanoor dairy.

Prior to the opening of their new producer company, a group of 30 women who owned milk buffaloes had bundled off in jeeps to witness the workings of the dairy where they would send their milk until their own dairy was up and running. I had gone too.

"I encouraged them to come, and they loved it," said Poorovva, a day labourer who had spent her childhood looking after the family buffaloes. Married at 16 and with three children, she looked like the fiery Mexican artist Frida Kahlo. "They could see all the possibilities. And right away they started talking about buying more buffaloes."

In Argul, her village of 700 families, 200 milk buffalo producers of mixed castes had signed up to give milk to the producer company. Of the Tribal women, 10 out of 15 had signed up for the producer company and Poorovva was eager to pull in the others.

Poorovva stood out for her spunk and infectious determination and I wanted to hear more from this dynamic village leader. A few days later, with Samson's lively college student daughter Sumitra at my side as translator, we headed off to the village of Argul with its 23 Gram self-help groups.

Inside this village of mud and brick houses, we pulled up to Poorovva's simple three-room abode that looked into a bald courtyard with a clothesline where a single shirt waved in the breeze. Leaning against the door in a tattered dhoti stood her husband, an ailing man that had not worked for 10 years. Inside, curled up in a corner, Poorovva's frail mother-in-law cried when she told me how her husband had left her just before this depressed-looking son of hers was born. All her life she had worked as a landless day labourer.

In the course of hearing about Poorovva's life I discovered that her oldest son, 21, was in Dubai. He had left her with a debt of 100,000 rupees, or about $2,777 Canadian; an enormous sum of money that she hoped to pay off over five years, but creditors were already threatening to take away her house.

It was close to Christmas when I heard this story. My heart chilled as I suddenly imagined Poorovva and her family of seven sleeping with the two buffaloes she owned in her bald courtyard. In my mind she had become part of the New Testament's "no room in the inn."

Unlike others that had gone to the Gulf states, this son of hers was sending home no money at all. His one remittance had been a television set that sat on the floor in a bare house with intermittent electricity and only a few sticks of furniture.

Left behind for Poorovva to take care of were his two small children and his young wife, working as a bidi worker making cheap cigarettes out of tobacco fragments and bidi leaves for less than a dollar a day.

In addition, she had a son of 17 doing first class work in junior college, and hoping to attend university and become a teacher. More than half his 5,000-rupee fee ($136 Canadian) was paid by the government since she belonged to a Tribal group, but she had to pay the remaining 2,000 rupees and buy his bus pass.

Poorovva earned 2,283 rupees, or $63 Canadian, a month by working 15 days a month for less than a dollar a day as a coolie as well as growing corn on her half-acre plot of land. By joining the producer company and avoiding middlemen, she was making 50 percent more on the milk from her two milk buffaloes. Her daughter-in-law's monthly 400 rupees additional income brought the family total to $74 Canadian a month.

But on a regular basis Poorovva ran out of money for food for her seven-member household. When that happened she took emergency loans through her self-help group or from moneylenders in the village.

Despite this incredible load, Poorovva had enrolled her granddaughter in a private kindergarten and her grandson in a government nursery so they would get a head start in education. She admitted that she would have liked her son of 17 to go to work in order to pay off the debt that threatened to engulf the family, but she wanted him to realize his dream of becoming a teacher.

In what little time she had at the end of her working day she was village leader for the producer company encouraging other tribal women to buy buffaloes and join in order to improve their earning capacity.

As Sumitra and I rumbled out of the village in a Gram car I felt overwhelmed by Poorovva's story. If anyone deserved help it was this woman who did not present herself as a victim and was turning herself inside out in order to give the younger generation of her family a solid future. In

Poorovva is a village leader for the Intideepam Mahila Dairy Producer Company started by Gram Abhyudaya Mandali and composed of almost 12,000 mostly Dalit and Tribal women cow owners.

addition she was struggling to improve her own earnings and dreamed of expanding later into turkeys.

I knew that without difficulty I could raise from my own savings and those of my friends the $2,777 debt she was saddled with that might bury her and her family. I mentioned it to Sumitra and later to Samson and to Arulraja.

"There are other people in the village facing just as big difficulties as Poorovva," said Sumitra. "People will ask why she deserves to be rescued."

According to Samson, the community has to solve these problems. "When the creditors really threaten to take Poorovva's house, her self-help group and her cooperative will help her to find a solution."

My encounter with Poorovva, whose remarkable enthusiasm masked a life of heartrending hardships, became perhaps my most important lesson in India around the issue of empowerment of women and community development. The point was: community development of the sustainable kind is not promoted by charity. It is advanced by the village self-help groups with the wider area cooperative working alongside the individual woman to come up with solutions.

William Easterly, who worked as an economist for many years at the World Bank, corroborated this general principle in his book called *The White Man's Burden* where he argues that only local initiatives accountable to users promote development.

I forced myself to forget about Poorovva, but a few days later, by chance, I was back in Argul village, this time with Samson. In Argul only 33 out of the 200 women that had signed up for the producer company were delivering milk and he wanted Poorovva to find a way to persuade the others to contribute.

We arrived at Poorovva's house to find two 10-year-old friends of her son horsing around in the front room where she kept corn. She insisted we settle on some flimsy chairs while she sat on the floor.

In explaining the low participation rate, Poorovva said, "During the first days of the milk collection, the women didn't trust the milk testing machines. They felt they were getting low fat readings and therefore a low rate of rupees per litre. That's why some of them have gone back to middlemen who are ready to pay 8 rupees per litre no matter what the fat content."

"Look," said Samson. "The machines are now accurate. The women will discover they have good fat content and the producer company will pay them a much higher rate than the middlemen. We have to find a way to convince them to come back." Women were receiving an average of 12 rupees per litre and those with as high as 10 percent fat content were earning 17 rupees a litre.

How would Poorovva find the time, I thought, to talk to 167 women buffalo owners in between her work as a coolie, labouring on her own half acre, milking her two buffaloes, and cooking for her family of seven? She slumped a little and sighed.

"How are you doing?" Samson asked.

Poorovva paused. "You know, I'd really like to buy a third buffalo but I can't afford the 24 percent interest rate," she said. This was a standard rate among cooperatives so they could hire necessary professionals and allocate a percentage to be set aside for savings for the women. "But I could do it on 18 percent," she said.

She stood up to prepare some tea for us and while she was away I told Samson I felt badly that I couldn't do something for Poorovva. It was just a few days before Christmas, and so Samson, the Dalit Christian that he was, came up with an idea to give Poorovva what she needed, assuage my Western soul, and still promote community development.

The deal was this. I would give 10,000 rupees (about $278 Canadian) to Poorovva's cooperative. It would lend Poorovva the required money at 12 percent (half the going rate) so she could invest in a third buffalo, and this would become an experiment for the cooperative in lending at lower rates. Samson said that this 12 percent interest rate would start a policy discussion among the cooperatives. The producer company needed women to buy more buffaloes in order to increase the litres so the new venture could make a profit, but the women didn't want to pay the 24 percent interest.

If the cooperatives could reduce interest rates, Samson said he could approach banks for a lower interest rate for low-income women. At an 8 percent loan from the bank, for example, the cooperatives could charge 15 percent, or even less. We would have to go to another village to get the okay for this from the manager of Poorovva's cooperative.

But Poorovva wasn't about to receive this lowered interest rate for nothing. This was to be no gift. She would have to take on extra community responsibilities in order to earn it.

She came in with the tea and while we were sipping it, Samson looked at the two young boys that were sitting with us. One boy was the son of a Muslim and the other the son of a "backward-caste" shepherd whose aunt was in the producer company. "I have something to propose to you boys," he said. "Would you be prepared to go around the village and get samples of milk from women with milk buffaloes and then take the milk to be tested for fat levels at the collection centre?" The boys quickly said yes.

"This way," he told Poorovva, "the women will find out they're better off with the producer company."

"In the next few days I'll visit the school and I'll talk to the teachers about getting boys across all castes to help the producer company," he told me. "Poorovva can teach the boys and work with the man from the company that provides the testing machines."

Samson's idea was to get all the castes to work together across the village so that caste would become less of an issue. In Argul half the women contributing milk to the producer company came from high castes but they were working under Tribal Poorovva as village president and Dalit Posani, the producer company coordinator.

The next task was to test out the idea of the low-interest loan with Suhasini, the general manager the women had hired at the Jackranpalli cooperative representing 16 villages and more than 2,500 women in 193 self-help groups. At the coop offices in another village, she said okay and I hightailed it off to Nizamabad in a jeep with Samson to get the money from the ATM, or what Indians called the Any Time Money machine.

In Nizamabad town at my trusty ATM I pulled out the necessary 10,000 rupees from my savings account back in Montreal so that Poorovva could take a loan for a third milk buffalo and a chance for higher earnings and then I went back with Samson to the Jackranpalli cooperative. Suhasini received the money and I took my receipt. I had taken care of Christmas. Now I would board a bus for Hyderabad and then for Zaheerabad to spend Christmas with my friend Salome Yesudas.

A month later, in early 2006, the trials of the Dalit women who needed dairy, marketing, and loan support from the Indian business and public community were coming to a head. The Intideepam Mahila Dairy Producer Company needed a solid loan to take care of the loan it had taken from their Indur cooperative federation for the bulk cooler in Suddapalli.

The National Dairy Development Board (NDDB) had promised a low interest loan for a few bulk coolers so that thousands more milk buffalo producers in the Nizamabad district could join the company. The organization had given the women invaluable technical help in the beginning, but their promise of a loan fell through. Unfortunately, Posani's fears about the NDDB were right.

The advisor from the dairy board that was closest to the producer company was in full support of the women and dreamed of helping them expand into a huge enterprise in the impoverished Telangana region of Andhra Pradesh, but in the end the board's top management decided that unless the board had virtual control of the company they would not lend. They were not going to nurture this freewheeling producer-company child of the untouchables.

The message seemed to be either they didn't trust the women or they didn't trust the Dalit leadership. However, women buffalo milk producers from all castes were voting shareholders of the producer company. Though born of Dalit cooperatives, this was an all-caste enterprise.

Posani turned to the indefatigable Samson Nakkala, who in the spring of 2006 sprung for loans from Indian financial institutions and the international community. Based on the strong track record of business activities started under Gram cooperatives, a whole range of institutions responded.

The Friends of Women's World Banking, which gives money to NGOS working with women, came through with a loan of 5 million rupees, or about $125,000 Canadian at the 2006 exchange rate of 40 rupees to the Canadian dollar. India's Housing Development Financial Corporation Bank lent over 12 million rupees or about $300,000 Canadian. ICICI bank offered loans to the Indur cooperative federation so that the women could take loans to buy more milk buffaloes.

"In order to get out of poverty, each woman in the producer company needs to own four buffaloes," said Samson, who wanted to see each woman earning 3,000 rupees a month from her animals. "Now they average only one buffalo." As a result of ICICI's loan, between April 2006 and March 2007, women were able to purchase 1,000 new milk buffaloes.

The producer company then became a member of the Andhra Pradesh Matha Dairy Federation which provided a loan of 1 million rupees, or about $25,000 Canadian, to equip more villages with testing machines.

At the international level, the American Ford Foundation gave $200,000 U.S., or about 8.4 million rupees, for education and training so that up to 50,000 women could eventually participate in the enterprise. Finally a trio of Dutch aid and financial institutions said they would give grants and loans to the Indur federation that would in turn provide loans to the producer company for 20 bulk milk coolers.

The delivery arrangement with the Mulkanoor dairy had ended. As of August 2007, 2,500 milk producers were delivering 3,700 litres a day of milk to milk cooperatives under the Matha Dairy Federation until the Dalit-run producer company found the money to build its own dairy that would process, package, and sell the milk to retail outlets.

The individual women continued to improve their earnings. Under middlemen the women had been making an average of 6 to 8 rupees per litre. When they launched their producer company in 2005, this went up to 13 rupees per litre. By June 2007, they were making an average of 17 rupees per litre because the average fat content per litre stood at 7.5 percent, due in part to better feed strategies adopted by the women.

Posani's dream of a Suddapalli village bursting with new life was starting to come true, but not because the plant for the dairy was under construction.

By the end of 2006, a livelihoods resource centre sponsored by Gram was operating in the village with training programs to help women improve their productivity so that they would be ready to start producer groups around turkeys, goats, and sheep as well as crops such as oil seeds.

But when it came to the dairy project, Posani continued to face constant challenges. The Andhra Pradesh government suddenly banned Mutually-Aided Cooperative Societies (MACS) such as the one run by Posani from entering the dairy business, but the milk collection enterprises functioning under the MACS Act challenged this in a high court, which in April 2007 set aside the ban.

Through all this, Posani Mekala, Madame Promoter and CEO of the Intideepam Mahila Dairy Producer Company, remained determined and hopeful. Her goal now was 40,000 milk producer members delivering 100,000 litres of milk a day out of 500 villages by 2010. Once all that was in place she felt confident that money would come through for a modern dairy facility.

I kept in regular touch with Samson about new developments. By December 2008, the producer company was operating with five bulk coolers in five villages and had expanded to a whopping 11,589 women milk producers across 175 villages.

During the flush season of October to March the women were contributing up to 15,000 litres a day, and during the leaner season between April and September, as low as 5,000 litres a day. The women were making an average of 18.4 rupees a litre, almost triple what they earned before they started their producer company.

Two international NGOs, Agriterra and Rabobank Foundation Netherlands, donated 85,000 Euros (about $138,550 Canadian) for staff support and capacity training for the producer company which will be completely independent of Gram by 2011. Thanks to a grant of over 9 million rupees (about $225,000 Canadian) from Tata, the multinational Indian conglomerate, Gram set up a three-year training program to increase dairy productivity for women across 450 villages in 2009.

In the spring of that year, Samson registered a private limited company called Deccanstar Rumenavian with the majority of shares owned by the women producers. *Deccan* stands for the Deccan plateau in Andhra Pradesh, *Rumen* stands for ruminants (cows, goats, and sheep), and *Avian* stands for birds such as poultry and turkeys, which the company will eventually market.

According to Samson, early in 2010, with a commercial loan of 50 million rupees, ($1.25 million Canadian) Deccanstar will set up a small dairy plant that will market milk out of Suddapalli — with the brand name Intideepam — producing packaged milk for the Andhra Pradesh market.

"Our women have travelled a long way from a simple, village-level social group to self-help group, cooperative, and producer company, to private limited company and in [the] future they will also join public limited companies," Samson told me.

Central to the process is the Indur Intideepam Mutually-Aided Cooperative Society Federation (IIMF) of 20 cooperatives representing 47,000 women in the Nizamabad district in 2009. Since April 2006, the federation has been operating independently from the Gram NGO. Their focus, says Samson, is on finance and nurturing new businesses.

Samson points out that to advance on the scale of development, the self-help groups that joined together in the past to create the cooperatives have had to reorganize completely into producer self-help groups. "Availability of credit and access to it," says Samson, "will not alone drive development."

Thanks to Samson's push to find the grants to train the women, and because of the determination of the women to work together so that they can enter competitive markets, Posani's dream of a Dalit-run women's diary will be a reality in 2010.

The Gram women plan to launch other businesses. In the spring of 2009 the 20 women's cooperatives began to consider creating a carbon reduction enterprise that would sell thousands of fuel-efficient biomass cook stoves with the goal of seeking carbon emission reduction certificates through the UN convention on climate change and the follow-up to the Kyoto Protocol.

"After rolling out biomass wood stoves," says Samson, who has been helping the women, "we plan to take up biogas plants, wormi compost, and other natural resource management under Clean Development Mechanisms that will sequester carbon and the world will pay our women for making it more livable."

21
VILLAGE EMBROIDERY GOES GLOBAL

In the middle of January 2008 I was back in India for a return visit to the state of Gujarat to hear how 3,500 embroiderers that had been starving in village deserts because of droughts, cyclones, and earthquakes had formed their own company. Where in the past the women had sold to gouging traders when they were desperate, now they were supporting their families by selling colourfully embroidered, contemporary Indian clothes and home accessories to India's rising urban middle class as well as to outlets in the West.

Here was another inspiring example of how marginalized women were banding together to create a competitive business that rose beyond the horizons of microcredit. The women were all members of the Self Employed Women's Association (SEWA) which had grown to about half a million members in Gujarat and another half million in eight other states.

My starting point was Ahmedabad with its rich heritage in textiles and weaving going back to the 17th century. Known for historic mosques and temples, the city also attracted visitors to the famous Mahatma Gandhi ashram on the banks of the Sabarmati River.

On my first visit to the city in 2002, communal violence had stopped me from meaningful encounters with members of SEWA, but the situation was more stable and I was eager to meet not only embroiderers in villages but also street vendors and construction workers in the city that were finding innovative ways to benefit from the expanding Indian economy.

I was spending every day at an embroidery production centre lodged in a refurbished textile factory on the old side of the city. Called the SEWA Trade Facilitation Centre, the shop floor featured a team of sewers on machines using hand-loomed cloth to stitch up tunics, salwar kameez, jackets, skirts, handbags, wall hangings, bed sets, and cushion covers, among other items, in preparation for embroiderers in villages.

Indian designers with fashion technology expertise, who worked from traditional embroidery motifs passed down through the ages to the village women, created product lines for an upscale Indian and Western market. When the final product returned from villages, it passed through quality control, was washed and steam-pressed, and then shipped out to SEWA's high-end handicraft shops in Ahmedabad and Delhi, to big Indian retail stores, and to growing numbers of Western boutiques and department store outlets.

Getting to the place, in a neighbourhood called Saraspur where the textile mills used to flourish, usually meant that before the day even started I was exhausted and covered with a thin film of dirt. I was thirsty all the time, mostly, I think, from breathing in dust from the air. My mode of transport was the usual autorickshaw motorized taxi. On my first day I noticed several women in burqas on the backs of motor scooters with a protective mesh across their eyes and thought of how clean they'd be, unlike me, when they reached their destinations.

I hung on to a bar as the rickshaw joggled around busses, other rickshaws, motorcycles, cars, clumps of cows, the odd racing camel, a slow bullock hauling bags of stones, and Ahmedabadis of all backgrounds and religions in saris, salwar kameez, dhotis, and hijabs, along with smiling barefoot children who were trying to cross the road without getting killed. It was all part of my reawakening to the India I would live in for the next three months.

The ride to the SEWA Trade Facilitation Centre pulled me back into the chaos of an Indian city that felt like a village writ large, Ahmedabad being a growing metropolis of 6 million people, but with the sights and smells of a village at every turn.

On one side of the Sabarmati River running through the city was the new city, with its flourishing middle class, its banks and better hotels and restaurants, its call centres, universities and colleges, and its CG Road reminiscent of Madison Avenue in New York City. On the other side was the poorer, but historic, old city with its Hindu, Muslim, and Jain traditions where I would later meet street vendors looking forward to selling organic produce from SEWA farmers to the Indian upper-middle class in their own self-styled bazaar or mall. I would also spend time by the river with construction workers that had created their own company and were learning new skills that were winning them lucrative contracts on a big river construction project.

In thriving Ahmedabad, embroiderers with the Self Employed Women's Association sell their work at their own boutique in an upscale area.

I was staying on the new side in a modest but modern hotel close to the Ellis Bridge to the old city, where now, in my lurching autorickshaw, dust was flying into my face as we ploughed past rickety shops and one-room huts with rag roofs held down with rocks in traffic bursting with rickshaws, bikes, busses, and cars, all blowing horns.

On the old side of the city sculpted entryways dating back to the 18th century led to heritage buildings inside *pols*, or neighbourhoods, with families linked by caste, profession, or religion. Narrow roads were alive with street vendors and shops selling everything from vegetables to drums in between Hindu temples in bright colours and mosques with minarets.

But now, along sidewalks flanking the din and chaos of the wider thoroughfare we were on, thin aging men in rags lay asleep on the pavement while others were sitting up cross-legged and bleary-eyed. Concrete buildings were streaked with black fungus created by monsoon humidity.

The smaller connecting roads we took were packed with cupboard-sized stores wedged up together, everything awry and bursting out or hanging off. But then, to remind me that I really was in a city, off in the distance I saw an arrow for the Hong Kong and Shanghai Bank of China (HSBC), my favourite bank, since I knew I could withdraw rupees from it with my Canadian bank card.

Animals were everywhere and a regular feature of the traffic. More than one camel roared past my humble rickshaw, one carrying steel rods, and another a pile of rocks. Camels, I had been told when I was last in Ahmedabad, were very cost-efficient since they don't eat much and run fast. In the past, on streets with magnificent villas, I had seen temple elephants wandering about begging for rupees for food. Then there were the cows, sometimes eight or nine huddled in some naked space between shops. Each cow, I had heard, belonged to someone that milked it morning and night, but during the day, the animal roamed the streets dropping cow pats and looking for handouts from friendly Ahmedabadis.

We passed a market where women in colourful saris or salwar kameez were curled up with baskets on the pavement selling fruits and vegetables. There were more than 150 street markets of varying sizes in Ahmedabad and this was one of them. Smiling kids spied my Western face, and when the rickshaw slowed down they scampered up close and wanted to know "my good name," meaning my first name. I could never ride or walk around incognito. Already I felt quickened by the pulse that makes India a place where anything can happen.

I arrived at the production centre after the poor rickshaw driver had asked several people for directions in between cranking up his ailing rickshaw motor when it periodically conked out. The half hour ride had cost me just 40 rupees, about $1 Canadian, and the daily wage of millions of poor Indians.

I was now in front of a handsome red brick building with a modern business inside where college and tech-educated staff were linking up in villages to traditional embroiderers that had become top-flight barefoot managers, even though most of them couldn't read and had never seen the inside of a schoolroom.

The goal of this SEWA Trade Facilitation Centre was to eventually give as much high-level lucrative work as possible to 15,000 women embroiderers in desert Gujarat and a few hundred cloth stitchers inside the city that had been victims of those anti-Muslim riots I had covered in 2002. For now the business was operating with 3,500 shareholding grassroots women artisans set up in response to ecological and social distress, with a capital D. The goal of it all was development, and I was at the beginning of three of the most exciting months of encounters with grassroots women in India.

At the production centre I spent time first with Villoo Mirza, a designer who had run a prestigious Indian fashion technology institute and who had played an important role in training the women at the centre and setting up the supply chain that started in Ahmedabad, jumped off to 45 villages in the desert districts of Patan and Kutch, and came back again. Villoo showed me around the various departments, among them the sample department, where designs came to life, and the kits department, where packages containing garments along with a stencilled embroidery design and thread were assembled for the village women embroiderers to work on.

Several days later I sat down with CEO Mona Dave, a 38-year-old business graduate who got her feet wet with SEWA in desert areas setting up daycare centres for salt workers. A single woman living in an extended family that included a widowed mother, she seemed to devote her every working hour to making the embroidery company sing. When I was there, this included flying off to Spain to meet buyers at a big retail store interested in SEWA products in between talking to "spearhead" leaders from the villages about a new line of high-end clothes that the embroiderers would be making for their boutique in Delhi.

The embroiderer company's three-year strategy included creating 100 one-of-a-kind items with gems that would cost anywhere from 15,000 to 100,000 rupees ($375 to $2,500 Canadian) for a high-end niche market. Wall hangings inspired by mythology for corporate lobbies and possibly the mansions of India's new billionaires were also on the agenda.

From 2003, when the embroiderers became part of a non-profit company, to 2008, yearly sales had doubled with total sales for the five-year period reaching over 70 million rupees, or about $1.75 million Canadian.

Most important, the embroiderers, who worked on a rotating basis, had an income of 1,500 rupees a month they could count on for up to eight months a year, working about five hours a day, five days a week. Calculated on the basis of a 10-hour shift, they were making the equivalent of 150 rupees a day, almost four times what they could command as day labourers. "The goal," Villoo told me, "is for them to make 2,000 rupees a month for the whole year."

Through special training, many of the grassroots women had acquired the management skills to handle village accounts and guarantee quality production at the village level, which was the key link in this unique supply chain. In addition, all the embroiderers were shareholders with a say on the future of their company. Share capital invested in the company by the embroiderers totalled about 14 million rupees, or $350,000 Canadian. Each had shares of 4,000 rupees, or $100 Canadian.

Mona wanted to protect the heritage of the artisans, but she often pressed the village production supervisors, called spearhead leaders, to make the grassroots embroiderers work faster, and she always had a beady eye out for the slightest flaw in a garment. In the middle of one of our interviews, she suddenly hauled out a camera and took a picture of me in my embroidered kurta with mirror work in blue, orange, and pink. In preparation for visiting Vauva village where the enterprise first took off, I had bought the outfit at Banascraft, SEWA's embroidery shop on fashionable CG road.

"Look," she said, showing me the picture she had taken. "The mirror work should be on both sides of the opening down the front and not just on one side." I thought it looked fine as it was, and the next day Villoo had to convince her that this was a deliberate part of the design.

I got a taste one day of the passion of SEWA grassroots women from the villages as well as from the city of Ahmedabad when I sat in on a meeting of 35 SEWA women, some of them barefoot, who gathered at the Trade Facilitation Centre to meet Isabel Guerrero from the World Bank in India. SEWA's membership is one-third Dalit, one-third Muslim, and one-third low-caste women, and all these voices were represented.

One of the most articulate was Puriben, a wiry woman in her 40s and a leader of the embroiderers from the remote village of Vauva in Patan district. I had already read about this single-minded lady on the internet. She said that because village women were making money from embroidery, now families weren't migrating away for several months a year to find work.

"Now we can afford to send our children to school, and this," she said in a ringing, high-pitched voice, "includes the girls." Mme Guerrero asked another embroiderer leader what her husband did. "He works in the fields and helps me," she said proudly. "He takes care of the children and does household work. Husbands do that more and more."

The tone of the women who spoke in Gujarati (with translation to English) was wonderfully militant in describing their accomplishments. They recounted how in the past their husbands and communities had not allowed them to venture out beyond their homes and communities, but now, by banding together under SEWA, they were on the march creating farmer produce groups and businesses that were getting rid of middlemen. They were confronting bureaucrats that were standing in their way. Some were travelling across India and even going to abroad.

A construction worker told of how they had challenged the Gujarat labour department around enforcement of labour legislation and now

Master embroiderer Puriben is a barefoot manager for the embroidery company with a head office in Ahmedabad.

under her construction collective she was making more than three times what she had in the past.

A street vendor, who was a member of a SEWA union of 57,000 street vendors, spoke about how they were bringing abusive police to heel through the courts.

A farmer reported how SEWA women had started village committees to monitor school attendance and the work of primary health care clinics. "Sometimes the clinics will advertise immunization programs and then there is no doctor or nurse there to do the work," she said.

Several women also talked about how the bank they had started back in 1974 had helped them escape debt and moneylenders through microloans and was giving them an opportunity to protect themselves through a health, life, and disaster insurance policy as well as pensions.

Three Muslim women in colourful hijabs stood up and described how SEWA had helped them during the riots of 2002 when they became widows. One of these women said that until she joined SEWA she had rarely come out of the house. "SEWA helped me set up a home sewing business. I have seven children to feed and my goal is to make sure all of them, including the girls, finish school." A Hindu woman talked about how during the riots her rickshaw driver husband had been helping two Muslim ladies return to their huts when he was gunned down and killed. "I heard about SEWA and they helped me set up a business too."

On this sensitive communal issue, another woman reported that Hindu and Muslim women in SEWA had started a peace initiative in several Ahmedabad neighbourhoods in order to effect healing in the wake of the trauma of the riots. "We focus upon Hindu, Muslim, and Christian folk stories showing how much they all have in common," she said.

At the end of the meeting pictures were taken, and then all the women held hands, and as I would see them do time and again at other meetings, they sang "We Shall Overcome" in Gujarati. As their voices washed over me I was moved to recognize that these women *were* overcoming: the hymn was not simply a faint hope for the future.

These, I felt, were the voices of a grassroots women's movement seeking to make progress through practical action, thanks to the hard-nosed guidance of their leader, Ela Bhatt, a woman of 76 who sometimes came to meetings, and whose spirit was always present. Later, also inspired by what she had witnessed, the World Bank woman wondered aloud why she was working at the World Bank and not at SEWA.

That afternoon, back in Mona's office, and still in the wake of the women singing, I couldn't help being struck by how much her office was a testament to the fusion of the traditional village with modern fast-track India. An imposing portrait of Mahatma Gandhi looked down over her at her desk and computer where she faced an embroidered flower wall hanging made by village women. In contrast, financial sections of newspapers, including the *Economic Times* of India, were strewn across her desk next to a bookcase crammed with fat volumes on the Indian income tax and companies acts.

SEWA does not stand for remaining hostage to the past, but it does believe in justice for the village and city poor. Gandhi's penetrating gaze in my direction was also a reminder about why, for the second time, I was in Gujarat. I had enjoyed many days in the city at the Trade Facilitation Centre, but now it was time to get to know the feisty and famous village leader Puriben, and her aunt Bhachiben, in the remote village of Vauva where it had all started 20 years before.

22
THE BAREFOOT MANAGERS OF VAUVA VILLAGE

It took five hours from Ahmedabad in a SEWA jeep to get to Vauva village to meet Bhachiben and Puriben, the two earliest members of the SEWA embroidery collective. The dried up Banas River was the gateway to the desert-like district of Patan where they, and about 1,500 other SEWA embroiderers, were making a living in more than 20 villages that had suffered drought, cyclones, and a major earthquake. Travelling with me was translator Heena Patel, whose usual job was to provide various kinds of training to SEWA members through the SEWA Management School.

Seventy kilometers from the main town of Radhanpur and Handicraft Park, where SEWA had set up a regional production unit for the embroiderers, we turned into a bumpy road that until three years before had been no more than an eight kilometre cow path into the little village of Vauva. Whether under monsoon rains or blistering sun, embroiderers for years had had to tramp by foot down this path carrying embroidery materials in and finished materials out. Anyone with a medical emergency faced the same exhausting trek to the main road where they would stand by the side of the road hoping for a bus, tractor, bullock cart, or maybe a camel to pass by and take them to the nearest health clinic.

A couple of brightly painted autorickshaw taxis, signalling better times and more reliable transport, decorated the entrance to this village famous for its embroidery. On our way in, looking beyond the surrounding sandy scrub land, we glimpsed patches of green — the result of good rains over the past year and plentiful harvests of cumin, fennel, chick peas, and castor for oil. Set back from the road stood an elementary school, middle school, and high school where many girls now attended.

The SEWA embroidery company started in Vauva village. Where farmers used to have to migrate to get work because of drought, they can now rely on income from embroidery.

Inside the village, one-room tile-roofed huts made of rocks and brick held together with mud prevailed along with houses of concrete built after the 2001 earthquake when three-quarters of the dwellings had collapsed. Roofs of thatch sheltered cows, goats, and chickens.

We pulled to the side to allow a camel hauling a cart of vegetables to pass, its proud head towering above the simple huts. High in the sky in a field beyond stood a steel contraption for cell phone reception.

Along the narrow dusty roads stood vegetable stalls, a flour mill for grinding millet, a goldsmith, a carpenter making beautifully carved high-standing wood cupboards, and convenience stands selling sugar, small-quantity grocery items, and cosmetics. Every woman on the road was busy carrying something on her head, holding a child, or eagerly conversing with someone. Looking idle, several older men were hanging around the village square where I noticed an STD/ISD. Behind the village square rose the saffron dome of a temple and deeper into the village a mosque.

We got out of the jeep in order to walk deeper into the village where Bhachiben, the veteran embroiderer, lived. I was wearing an embroidered salwar kameez made by Ahir embroiderers from this village that I had bought at Banascraft, the SEWA embroidery boutique in Ahmedabad. Despite my Indian clothes, I looked unmistakably Western and children gathered around to stare. Wending our way by foot through narrow dusty paths between huts we came to a little courtyard and a one-room hut open on one side to the elements and the other huts. Bhachiben Bhurabhai Ahir, wearing an embroidered dress, was sitting on a rope mattress bed in front of her hut busily embroidering a piece of cloth.

A woman of 55, Bhachiben was so lined and weathered from the sun and back-breaking work that she looked 20 years older. She saw my look of surprise when she later told me her age. Stating it matter-of-factly, but without complaint, she said: "It's because I've had a hard life." Bhachi was her first name but everyone at SEWA had a *ben*, meaning sister, attached to her name, and so I became Sheilaben.

Bhachiben's husband had died three years before and her mother-in-law two years before that, so she lived alone. Her two sons had died at three and four years old when they became ill with a disease. Each of her boys had died in her arms while she was tramping on the old cow path to the main road in search of a lift to a hospital. Though she lived by herself, Bhachiben never felt alone because she had become the beloved neighbourhood grandmother for the children of families living around the courtyard. A little boy of five clung to her when I visited, and didn't let go until it was clear I would not spirit her away.

Her hut had no furniture except for a belt bed cot with a "spring" made of woven pieces of cloth sitting on four short wooden legs that she took down from a hook on the wall to sleep on at night. But an exquisite embroidery panel hung across the entrance to a kitchen corner festooned with several copper pots that years ago she had exchanged for treasured embroidery. She had no electricity and cooked over a grill with wood. At night she lit up her room with a kerosene lamp suspended from a hook on the wall.

She treated us to delicious Indian tea with lots of milk that she prepared for me and Heena along with some neighbours that had crowded in. There were not enough cups so some of the tea was served in saucers, a godsend for me because it allowed the scalding tea to cool a little quicker.

Here is her story, recounted as we sat cross-legged on the floor together, along with what felt like her large extended family.

Though scarred by the early deaths of her two sons, and years of struggle just to eat, Bhachiben, who never went to school, exuded a feeling of well-being and poise. This had come from 20 years of making enough money to live on through embroidery and serving as a leader and example to others in Vauva. Hers, I had to recognize, was an Indian success story, made possible starting at the age of 35 because of the Gandhian vision of Ela Bhatt, the tireless work of a young university graduate called Reema Nanavaty who came in to organize, and also because of the women artisans in the village who had learned how to pull together.

But for years before that, the struggle to survive was remorseless. As landless labourers, Bhachiben and her husband had relied on working on others' land. But when drought devastated the land, turning it into virtual desert, she and her husband were forced to migrate by foot to Surat in the south of Gujarat with a load of clothes and cooking utensils on her head. "We were nomads for four to five months a year doing agricultural labour and making 1 rupee and 25 paisa a day each, with one meal provided. We lived in the open fields or sometimes in straw huts provided by farmers," she said.

Later, after she had her two sons, they eked out what they could for four months in the Vauva area working a 10-hour day for 2 rupees and 50 paisa with two meals included as landless labourers working for other farmers. Two milk cows of their own provided them with milk. For the other eight months she had to find other work. When relief work was provided — digging earth for road building — she marched several kilometres with her children, and after digging deep into the earth she carted away loads of mud on her head.

"Sometimes when there was no work," she said, "I had to borrow handfuls of grain to feed the family." Eventually in desperation, like many other women, she sold her embroidery to traders for utensils or just a few rupees because she had no idea of the market. Interspersed with several cups of tea, Bhachiben's story took a long and harrowing time to tell.

At the end, as the sun was going down, Heena and I went back in the jeep with the SEWA driver to Radhanpur where we checked in to a $1.50-a-night residence run by a community of Jains. Like Hindus, Jains are vegetarians and believe in non-violence, but go so far as not eating onions because pulling up the roots kills off insects.

The residence provided us with our own Indian hole-in-the-ground toilet and off-the-floor comfortable beds with worn, lumpy comforters but no sheets. The night was chilly and there was no indoor heating so I slept in my salwar kameez plus two sweaters. The Indian breakfast was chili-laden, but with chickpeas, so I ate it for the protein and a need for energy, but I didn't have room for the pile of chapattis the servers loaded on my plate. Heena informed me that the Jains had a hard-and-fast rule against waste, so I had to force down the chapattis or pack them up and bring them with me, which I dutifully did.

Outside, the SEWA driver was waiting for us in his jeep. Unlike ordinary villagers I didn't have to brave public transport or a crammed-to-the-gills village taxi cart. That would come later....

As we approached Vauva, we stopped to let 150 milk buffaloes and their herder cross the road on their way to a grazing field. Milk cooperatives run by SEWA women were an example of another SEWA initiative increasing village prosperity.

Inside the village, master craftswomen Puriben, in a brilliantly coloured embroidered skirt and blouse, stood waiting for us in front of her concrete and tiled-roof house built a few months before for cash-down without a loan. This, she quickly explained, came from money she made from her salaried job in the Patan district as one of six "spearhead" leaders managing the embroidery production of about 500 embroiderers in five villages that she visited regularly.

Puriben had three married sons in their early 20s, all of them literate with some completed grades of high school. During the past season her sons and husband had earned a lot more money than usual from good crops of cumin on small packets of land they had acquired, renting out a tractor they owned, and selling milk to the cooperative. As a result they had been able to chip in on the house which cost 130,000 rupees, around $3,250 Canadian.

In the 2001 earthquake Puriben's mud and brick house had been destroyed and partially rebuilt and now her youngest son and his wife lived there. But because she had done so well, she and her husband were on their own in a safe and spacious concrete dwelling. Her sons and their families, which included three grandchildren, lived separately in other abodes. "I think it is better for each of my sons to live on their own so there are no arguments between the families," she later confided, even though she was going against the custom of living in an extended family.

She took my arm and ushered me into her living room that faced a sun-filled internal courtyard and a dining area where later we ate meals sitting cross-legged on the floor. She had electricity, ceiling fans, and a clock along with a bathroom with a hole-in-the-ground porcelain toilet and a bathing room with a large pail of water for washing.

From the edge of the courtyard I looked up to beautifully sculpted terracotta trim lining an upstairs terrace area accessible by a ladder pinned to the wall. Scattered around were jute bags of millet and mung, a kind of chickpea that her husband and sons grew on their small pieces of land.

A door from the living room led to a closed bedroom with a standing double bed with an embroidered quilt on top, shiny copper pots on the wall, and a handsome wood cupboard.

The house felt a little bare, mostly because there was no furniture in the wide-open living areas, but magnificent embroidery bloomed on the walls. A multi-coloured panel embroidered with mirrors that stretched across the door to the bedroom lit up the living room. Icon-like portraits of various gods and goddesses — the favourite being Lakshmi, the goddess of prosperity — gave the house a bejewelled feeling. From a tiny ledge for worship in the living room came a whiff of incense from the remains of a burning stick. It was a far cry from the flimsy two-room hut that Puriben had had to share with 11 people when she started married life in her husband's extended family and all the men had worked as landless labourers.

Waiting for us in the living room, her aunt Bhachiben and two of her daughters-in-law looked resplendent in vivid, embroidered skirts and blouses. The daughters-in-law, also embroiderers, sported wide embroidered belts and wore thin embroidered scarves in emerald and fuchsia on their heads that they sometimes discreetly dropped over their faces.

"Out of respect for the elders," Heena explained, referring to the presence of Puriben's husband, who without uttering a word, and appearing a shade dishevelled, moved like a ghost in and out of the living room in an ample white dhoti, loose blousy top, and white turban.

These girls looked lush and sensual in skin-tight bodices that revealed Scarlett O'Hara waists and gentle curves, and it occurred to me that in relatively close quarters, in the company of men, perhaps they were safer with at least their facial loveliness concealed. When their father-in-law moved away or when the daughter-in-law that was breastfeeding could put her back to him, she would remove her veil, throwing it over her shoulder and face only the women in the room.

The house quickly began filling up with female relatives and neighbours, many of them embroiderers whose lives had been changed by Puriben's leadership. One woman brought a child with a singing Barbie doll.

A few SEWA staff women from the headquarters in Radhanpur, where SEWA ran a regional office for a range of activities, drifted in, unfortunately with irritating cell phones that from time to time blared out martial tunes. One of the women was embroidery coordinator Saira Baloch. A stylish and talented Muslim woman with grade 12, she herself had had to fight her family and her community in order to be allowed to take a job with SEWA 20 years before.

Finally the village mayor, a young man who wanted to find out why a Western writer had come all the way from Canada to spend time with Puriben, dropped by. Several beds with "springs" made of braided cloth dangled on the dining room wall and immediately one of Puriben's sons retrieved one for the mayor to sit upon. The rest of us were seated on the floor.

The chatter in the room came to an end and I felt as though I were on television about to start interviewing a famous person. Puriben straightened up. Very poised, she smiled and waited a little. In response to my questions, she began to talk.

During the intense drought that lasted from 1984 to 1988, Puriben said that with her three sons she and her husband would migrate, like her aunt Bhachiben, from place to place mining salt, hollowing out pits for temporary ponds, and digging up earth for government roads for as little as 5 rupees a day, which at the time was about 50 cents Canadian.

"My sons, then six months, four, and five, couldn't bear the heat," she said. "So when I was digging earth I worked at night. I would dig a pit and put the three kids in it with the six-month-old in the arms of the five-year old. He was in charge. Sometimes we walked six to eight kilometers with the children to dig for temporary ponds." She found the heat affected her eyes and she developed a problem with night vision. "I became temporarily blind at night," she said.

When the drought let up, work was available from five in the morning to seven at night in the fields. "But it was difficult with three children, so I looked after them at home while my husband worked in the fields. We had just one income and were in debt. Out of desperation I sold embroidered kurtas to traders for 25 rupees each."

But then Reema Nanavaty, a 21-year-old microbiology graduate who had taken a temporary job with SEWA while she was waiting to be placed in the prestigious Indian Civil Service after passing entry exams, entered Vauva. The year was 1988.

Ela Bhatt first saw the village embroiderers' potential for earnings when she was asked in 1987 to meet with women in villages, including Vauva, in connection with an Indo-Dutch piped-in water supply project in the area. She had been asked to organize the women around the use of water but many had left the villages to find work. To organize around water, SEWA needed to stabilize the village by bringing in work.

While visiting the women still in the village of Vauva, she was taken aback by the beautiful embroidery inside their spare huts. "Their homes were bare, their possessions, few," she wrote in her 2006 book, *We are Poor But So Many*, "but still their houses gleamed...."

By tradition, women of the Ahir and Rabari communities that she was visiting worked in 13 different embroidery styles and made a dozen elaborately-embroidered skirts and blouse outfits for their daughters' dowries, but in between struggling to make a living they were also embroidering other items for their homes.

"The sharp contrast between the beauty and poverty in this desert land was glaring," Ela wrote. "The strong, dignified women had created riches with just thread and needle. How could such hard-working, tenacious, and highly skilled women be so poor?"

The women who had been selling their embroidered treasures for a song to exploiting traders were sitting on a mother lode of income if they could organize and find their own markets. To rally the women, she sent in young and enthusiastic Reema Nanavaty, who knew nothing about village life but was willing to learn.

By 2008, when I met her, Reema was chairman of the Trade Facilitation Centre overseeing the work of the embroiderers. She was also head of SEWA's multifaceted rural development program that included marketing of organic produce grown by thousands of SEWA farmers in several districts. She had learned by immersing herself in the life of villages and she loved her work so much that she chose not to enter the celebrated Indian Administrative Service.

"When Reema first started coming to Vauva," said Bhachiben, "we didn't trust her because she was an outsider. But one day she showed up with material and thread and asked four of us to produce 12 embroidered kurtas for 150 rupees each." At the time this would have been about $13 Canadian. "We could hardly believe it. My husband was making only about 150 rupees a month working in the fields."

"I was selling kurtas to traders for 25 rupees each," said Puriben. (At the time, about $2 Canadian). "Reema was offering six times that amount, and even more since she was providing all the materials."

The women took the material but were wary. They had been ripped off in the past, and why should they trust her? Some thought she might be just another manipulative trader.

A few days later Bhachiben and Puriben boarded an early morning bus to Radhanpur where Reema had rented a room. At 6:00 a.m., Reema heard a knock and was surprised to see the pair at her door. "Oh," she said, taken aback at the early hour of the visit. "Come on in. But why did you come so early?"

"That's when we could get a bus," said Puriben who was about 25 years old at the time. Bhachiben was 35.

"They had come to check me out," Reema told me later. "They didn't stay very long."

A week later, Reema, who was even younger than they were, was back in the village with money for the women along with more material and thread for kurtas after diligently tramping those eight kilometers on the cow path in from the main road. Still guarded, the women made her put the money on the table before they produced the finished embroidered kurtas.

Reema quickly placed more orders and her name spread like wildfire through the village until every embroiderer in Vauva and several from other villages wanted to work for this organizer from SEWA.

"When Reema came," said Puriben, looking back, "the work and the payment felt as though God had come to my house."

"After a while," she said, "Reema asked us to come to Radhanpur to the SEWA offices. Then she invited the two of us to stay at her house in Ahmedabad so we could learn about markets in the city." Later this expanded to include training in buying, selling, banking, and accounting, along with more formal management workshops offered in Radhanpur, Ahmedabad, and the villages.

"The caste elders in the village allowed us to go," said Puriben, "because Reema was always there, and we were meeting exclusively with women."

"Allowed them to go!" I almost blurted out, but I held my tongue. I was to hear the word "allowed" on a lot more occasions.

The market for the embroidery was craft exhibitions that attracted individual consumers and retail buyers. Embroidery from the women was pouring in and Reema asked Bhachiben, Puriben, and two other embroiderers to go with her and SEWA organizer Saira Baloch to Delhi to a huge handicraft exhibition.

"The village caste elders put their feet down and said we couldn't leave, and so did the mothers-in-law," said Bhachiben, "It was enough that we had gone to Radhanpur and Ahmedabad, but," smiled, "because we were bringing in money, our husbands said yes." And so the team took off to Delhi with a huge number of skirts, kurtas, blouses, pants, bags, quilts, and wall hangings made by 70 to 80 Vauva women.

Nevertheless, they left with caste elders threatening to fine the families of the women for defying them. They were gone for 15 days and Bhachiben said that her mother-in-law worried that she had gone for good.

At the Delhi exhibition they sold all the goods and came back with 100,000 rupees, an unheard of amount for these women.

When they returned, Reema offered to come to the village and tell the elders that it was unfair for the village to impose a fine because the women had gone to Delhi for livelihood reasons, but Puriben insisted that she could do it herself and she made sure that no fine was imposed.

"Slowly," said Puriben, "Reema built up our confidence."

Later, at another exhibition in Delhi, SEWA received orders worth

250,000 rupees (about $16,666 Canadian at the time), and it became clear the women had to create an efficient organization to turn out the items.

A union or a cooperative, which was how SEWA had usually organized women, didn't seem to fit, so Reema rallied the women to form groups under a program set up by the government's Department of Women and Children in Rural Areas (DWCRA) which helped women below the poverty line engage in livelihood projects.

Groups composed of 15 women were formed and DWCRA gave each a launch fund of 15,200 rupees. Each unit selected a leader and a committee of three that SEWA staff trained to handle the bank account, purchase and distribute raw materials, allocate tasks, monitor the work, and deliver the finished goods.

Puriben and Bhachiben, along with an impressive 17-year-old woman called Rasuben from another village, were the first leaders.

"It was all on-the-job training early in the morning or sometimes over dinner," Reema told me. "One day when I was with Puriben, who was very much involved with management of the Vauva groups, she told me that if I wanted to talk to her at any time, I could call her on her phone. I was living three days a week in Radhanpur and the rest of the time in Ahmedabad. 'Phone?' I asked.

"She told me she was earning so well with embroidery that she had enough money to invest in a phone for the scheduling of training groups and meetings."

Soon a craft development centre in the town of Radhanpur was created where embroiderers from all the villages met and took training. The centre, which also helped with marketing, served as a central point for picking up materials and delivering finished goods.

Dastkar, a Delhi-based voluntary organization that supported handicraft expansion, sent in designers who introduced new product designs and helped with marketing mainly through exhibitions.

Federal and state governments had created many programs such as DWCRA to alleviate poverty. Always practical, Reema and other staff learned how to take advantage of them.

In 1991, with help from the state department of rural development, a marketing outlet called Banascraft was established in Ahmedabad to sell embroidery. The state department of industries helped out with sales, promotion, and publicity, and the Gujarat State Handicraft Development Corporation agreed to purchase 200,000 rupees ($10,000 Canadian) a month from the embroidery groups.

Meanwhile the organization had expanded into Kutch district where I later went to a village and met Ranuba, an impressive non-literate embroidery leader that like Puriben was helping to transform her village. Ranuba had eight daughters, all on the road to becoming literate at a village school. To make sure they would all have a future, she had started a supplementary grocery business in her two-room hut.

Eventually Puriben and the other village artisans ended up working as embroiderers for SEWA for eight months a year, thereby becoming the main economic support for their families, and spent only four months working as day labourers. Along with running the household they usually looked after animals as well.

"We had to learn time management," said Puriben, who added that sometimes this meant refusing to do the bidding of the village elders. As an example she described how every year there was a community meeting in Vauva of Ahir elders from some 248 villages and the women were expected to prepare the food for it.

"One year," she said, "we had a tight deadline for a big order and we just couldn't take the time to do anything else. So Bhachiben and I went and told the head of our Ahir community that if we missed even one kurta the whole order could be cancelled and so we hired other people to cook."

"The caste hierarchy," Reema told me, "reacted by banning the Ahir embroiderers in the village from working for SEWA. I asked Puriben if she wanted me to address the caste panchayat, but Puriben said they would face the problem themselves."

Addressing the caste brass, Puriben and Bhachiben said: "So now that you've put this ban on us from embroidering for SEWA, will you now feed our families during the drought?"

Reema commented to me that Puriben was speaking on behalf of thousands of SEWA embroiderers in the region. "Some men supported us," said Puriben, "and the ban was lifted."

Over the years Puriben's experience as an embroidery leader gained her the kind of self-confidence that allowed her to try almost anything that would improve life in the village.

For example, on the water issue, the municipality had promised the village piped-in drinking water, and if not, tankers were supposed to supply it. In 2000, when the tankers failed to deliver, Puriben organized 200 women with empty water jugs on their heads to march in protest for 70 kilometres on the road to Radhanpur to the regional water board.

The result? "We got our water," said Puriben, proudly. After organizing so many embroiderers people were willing to follow her. "I was no longer just Puriben, wife and mother," she said. "People now say, 'That's Puriben's house.'" The people sitting around her at her house listening to her tell me her story nodded in agreement and so did the young mayor.

On another occasion, during a bad dry period, she went to Delhi and convinced the prime minister to send in fodder from other areas for a fodder bank that SEWA would organize so that milk buffaloes could be kept alive and milk cooperatives that SEWA women were running wouldn't have to close down. In the communities where they were active SEWA did everything ecologically possible to keep animal husbandry and farming alive.

"Ela Bhatt spoke, and then I spoke," Puriben said. "I was given four minutes to speak but I took 10 and the prime minister listened. We got our fodder banks."

Puriben also became a world traveller. From a woman who had been confined to her village, she not only went to cities in India to help sell embroidery, she also went to Washington and Australia.

"It was like a dream when I first went to Delhi," she said. "I had thought the entire world was huts and poverty and no greenery," she said remembering her experience 18 years before. "But I saw palaces, cars, and parks. Because I started earning, I could see other worlds."

But she wasn't entirely taken in by the world of cities. After being in Delhi, she came back with a certain appreciation of life in her village. "In Delhi people in the streets were running to the office and back and not talking to anyone," she said. "Here in Vauva, when we go out, we meet people and talk. I didn't see many people talking in Delhi. They just seemed to be running."

The world of money didn't tempt her either. In 2002 she went to Washington for a folk festival organized by the Smithsonian Museum that included a bazaar that resulted in 10.5 million rupees of sales ($338,709 Canadian) of SEWA embroidery and also included a demonstration of skills by Indian artisans.

"An official from the museum asked if she could buy what I was wearing," said Puriben who admitted she wasn't even tempted to ask what the museum would pay. "No," she said. "My mother made what I have on and I will never sell it."

In Australia, where she was also invited as part of a SEWA embroidery team, she was indignant when someone offered her money as an act of charity. Talking like the management professional that she had become, she dismissed the person with, "I am part of my country's delegation and I am taken care of."

A team effort that pulls together the talents of villagers like master embroiderer Puriben and design professionals like Villoo, the embroidery company would never have come to pass without the handholding of Reema Nanavaty and her determination to push the embroiderers into the 21st century.

For Puriben, and so many other embroiderers I spoke to, Reema's belief in their abilities and her reassuring presence as they moved into the unfamiliar world outside the village gave them the courage to move ahead.

A trio of disasters, first a cyclone in 1999, then a bad drought in 2000, and finally the earthquake of 2001, made it more and more clear to Reema how important embroidery was as an economic mainstay in the desert areas of Patan and Kutch.

"Under these circumstances craftwork which could be done under almost any conditions had become the only dependable way to earn a living. And 15,000 women were engaging in the activity," she told me.

"I felt we had to take the next step and become a viable business that used professional and up-to-date methods around production, sales, and marketing, but we didn't want to turn into a traditional garment factory. Between 2000 and 2003 we had many discussions around the roles of the grassroots artisans and professionals and the supply chain. The issue was really how the two groups could complement one another."

The answer in 2003 was registration in Ahmedabad of a non-profit company called the Trade Facilitation Centre.

Villoo Mirza at the National Institute of Fashion Technology had been recruited to train young women from Ahmedabad to stitch garments and become part of the production process that would make the basic items.

The village women would continue to embellish the items with their traditional embroidery and they received training by people like Heena Patel, who had a bachelor of commerce, on what it meant to become shareholders in their own company of 3,500 embroiderers with the goal of expanding to 15,000.

Through the World Bank's International Finance Corporation, a multilateral source of finance for private sector projects in developing countries, money was secured to get help in order to create a business model, do market research, and set up a management information system.

Finally in 2007, using funds supplied by a government program and a bank loan, the company bought and equipped the facility in Saraspur as the central location. The village embroiderers in their villages, however, remained the heart of the company, with representatives, including Puriben, on the board.

Profits would eventually be used for development of the areas where the embroiderers were located. "I would hope to see the company generate enough surplus revenue so that the two areas of Patan and Kutch can become self-sustaining in terms of jobs, and so that water and ecology can be improved along with health services and schools," said Reema. "The company should become a model for how the poor can run their own business and also contribute to regional development."

23
VEGETABLE VENDORS TAKE ON THE POLICE

A few days later, back in rough-and-tumble Ahmedabad, I was at the famous Manekchowk vegetable market in the heart of the old city watching row upon row of women on the pavement selling produce from baskets. I was with Savita Patni, the SEWA vendor coordinator that was providing background information.

Manekchowk was where Ela Bhatt first began to fight for the right of street vendors to sell without harassment from police and exploitation from loan sharks and middlemen. The SEWA street vendors union had 57,000 women members.

These vendors formed the backbone of India's informal economy where the majority of India worked, but municipal leaders in budding megacities like Ahmedabad were trying to replace the street vendors with malls.

Weaving through the cornucopia of vegetables laid out on mats and sellers in brightly coloured saris, we came upon Rajiben Parmar, SEWA's oldest street vendor. In an emerald-green sari, her ears bedecked with an astonishing row of earrings, she was perched behind an enormous stack of ripe tomatoes. Until the mango season started, tomatoes were her specialty. A woman of 60-plus, as she put it, she was among the first vendor activists. Along with her husband, all of her children were street vendors, including four sons and a daughter, all with some formal education.

Meeting Rajiben was like hitting gold. Not only was she one of Ela Bhatt's initiators into the world of street vendors, she was also one of the 15 promoters of the SEWA bank. Seated on a rag on the ground, we started talking in behind her tomatoes while her son took over selling. Her usual routine was to sell at Manekchowk from 8:00 to 11:00 a.m., then she left to recruit new SEWA members, collect membership fees, and work at the SEWA union offices. After that, she would return to the market to sell up to 9:00 p.m.

SEWA vendor Kaliben worked to improve the status of vendors at the Manekchowk market in Ahmedabad.

She talked about conditions in the early 1970s when she first met Ela Bhatt and police claimed the vendors had no legal right to sell on the streets. The original Manekchowk market was located in a large building with stalls but long before it had spilled out into the lanes and streets.

"Police were asking for bribes of 50 paisa (a half rupee) or some vegetables. And not only one policeman, but three or four a day." Fines for encroaching on public space were also being levied. "When the police came, we had to pick up our bags of produce and run. When we were organizing things here at Manekchowk, Ela Bhatt sometimes stayed with us day and night," she said.

After a series of protests and demonstrations, the municipality recognized a SEWA ID as a licence for selling, but this lasted for only three years.

Finally in the 1980s Ela Bhatt and some vendors filed a case at the Supreme Court claiming the vendors' constitutional right to trade was being violated. The court agreed and ordered the municipality to work out solutions to accommodate street vendors. The vendors had a right to sell at Manekchowk and the police harassment died out.

However, the municipality has tried to sideline the vegetable vendors at every turn. At one point officials tried to get them to move to the roof of a fruit vendors market up a treacherous winding staircase that I took with Savita. The vendors said they would need water, elevators, and storage space and rejected the idea.

Later, back at the SEWA union offices, out of the searing sun at the market, I settled down with Rajiben to talk some more.

"I've been vending since the age of 10," she told me. "My mother was a vegetable head loader at Manekchowk and I would go with her. Some vendors dropped vegetables on the road and never bothered to scoop them up. So I gathered up what I could until I had enough to sell. When I had enough money I bought my own scale and started buying my own vegetables."

In her family, where there was no father, she had two brothers and two sisters. "My mother supported us with the head loading." One brother finished grade 10 and the other grade eight, but she and her sister received no education at all.

As a child she learned how to set up a business and later she distinguished herself as a SEWA organizer helping to collect money from SEWA vendors so that SEWA women could launch their own bank.

"To buy our vegetables, we were borrowing money at 10 percent a day, or 300 percent a month from loan sharks," she said. "After we started our bank we could borrow at between 1 and 2 percent a month."

She took some sips of tea and sighed. Though deeply furrowed, her face shone with determination. Here was a woman who had been looking out for herself since the age of 10 and was still cheerfully vending as well as continuing to organize.

"To start our bank, I was collecting 10 rupees from members in Manekchowk," she resumed. In 1974 that was the equivalent of $1.25 Canadian.

"Some street vendors couldn't pay 10 rupees all at once and so I took 1 and 2 rupees at a time from the vendors. I collected the money in my sari. I was good at math and I just had to remember the names because I couldn't write them down. But I did remember," she smiled.

"I remember the night that Ela taught us how to sign our names so we could sign papers as promoters of the bank." She took a piece of paper and wrote a signature.

The interview had to come to an end because Rajiben had work to do. "You know," she said, looking me straight in the eyes, "without SEWA I think I would be dead."

The next day I was at the vast Jamalpur vegetable and wholesale market to meet Shantaben Parmar, a street vendor warrior and leader who, while trying to make a living selling vegetables, had had a history right up to 2006 of coming face to face with police wanting to clear her away.

At the edge of the Jamalpur market, next to a busy intersection with rickshaws, cars, and busses whizzing by, Shantaben in a bright turquoise sari presided over well-ordered baskets of colourful beets, tomatoes, carrots, green beans, okra, ginger, chilies, coriander, cauliflower, potatoes, cabbage, and onions. Steady streams of customers were picking out vegetables for their evening meals.

A large and imposing woman, Shantaben stood up and very graciously pulled out a cloth for me to sit upon. In order to talk we had to move back a little and let her daughters take over the selling. "I've been here for 30 years at this same spot, and I have no intention of leaving," she said with a bold toss of her head.

Street vendor Shantaben Pakmar is a SEWA union organizer that commands respect among police for her determination to fight for rights.

"I buy 2,000 rupees of produce a day and at the end of it I clear up to 500 rupees," she told me. That was about $13 Canadian. "Each day I save 50 rupees," a little over a dollar.

A non-literate woman of 58, she had been selling vegetables since she was 18, and was now doing a brisk trade along with two sons who had grade eight and two daughters with no education but plenty of business sense.

Police harassment, however, was always a threat. "I have my sticks and everyone knows I'll take them to the police myself if they start to harass," she said. She had had to learn how to protect herself. She described how

12 years before, in 1996, just before a big festival parade, a convoy of politicians prepared to roll by and police came to oust her and other vendors.
"We weren't in the way but we were seen as a nuisance," she said.

"I had 25,000 rupees of produce in baskets right here on the street
and the police threw everything into the road and crushed them. Then
they held me down and beat me."

They never beat her again. A SEWA member for 20 years, she eventually became a "campaign leader" at the top of the SEWA vendors union
with a history of going to a labour court about police abuse. "I trained
Savita," she said with some pride.

"Look," Shantaben said, talking rapid-fire in a no-nonsense way,
"there are 10 really strong women among the 1,000 SEWA vegetable vendors here at the wholesale market."

With a snap of her fingers, she indicated she could have a battalion
of vendors ready to respond to anything. As a result, she said, now police
and officers from the municipal corporation seek her advice. "Sometimes
they bring me tea."

The last big encounter took place in 2006, when police were trying to
move vendors from Jamalpur and SEWA got a stay order from a labour
court. "We can't be moved out and we won't be harassed. Police have
seen me at court and they know I have power," she said.

From the beginning, the SEWA urban union made street vendors
a priority, and support for them has taken many forms. One of them
was SEWA's Shop 40, a stall at Jamalpur which sells organic vegetables
from SEWA farmers at a commission of 5 percent as opposed to the
usual middlemen's 10 percent. "I buy my produce there," said Shanteben.
Thanks to the SEWA bank, she was able to sidestep loan sharks.

Unfortunately police harassment has remained a problem in other
markets around Ahmedabad. I attended a meeting where about 250
women screamed for an hour about police harassment at a number of
smaller markets around the city.

Rapidly-growing Ahmedabad was trying to build a reputation as a
modern super city, and police and municipal authorities had a habit of
treating the city's 100,000 street vendors as riff-raff from the past that
should step down to make way for big thoroughfares and classy boutiques.

However, with SEWA urban union leader Manali Shah at the helm, and feisty ladies like Shantaben on the ground, SEWA sellers were agreeing to accommodate the demands of a changing metropolis, but they had no intention of disappearing.

SEWA had hired an architect, for example, to block out spots for vending so that sellers would not disturb traffic and pedestrians. A SEWA vendors committee was making sure tidiness and cleanliness were always respected.

In addition, the SEWA vendors union was starting to buy up land for their own malls or bazaars, their plan was to have 27 of them.

The first one would sell organic produce from SEWA farmers and offer home deliveries to a target clientele of high-class Indian ladies that were willing to pay top rupee for quality. In order to create an appropriate milieu, prospective vendors were receiving guidance on how to cater to the niceties of this upper-caste market with tips on bourgeois demeanor; like quiet speech, impeccable finger nails, no spots or tears on saris, and a pleasant body scent.

But the traditional vendors on the street, who to me always looked like jewels and made the streets lively and attractive, could not be swept away. Across India 1 million street vendors were part of the country's small-scale economy where 93 percent of Indians worked, and they were determined to remain. There were, of course, growing numbers of supermarkets, the most notable in Ahmedabad being part of the Reliance chain, but my purchases there were restricted to bottled water and cartons of juice. Every day I saved an hour or so to buy a cup of tea and gorgeous-tasting fruit from a whole range of characters on the street that I had come to know.

Now it was time to meet SEWA women who had, over the years, taken up construction to help their families after the textile mills put over 100,000 men out of work. Working on preparing the riverbank to become a boardwalk of terraced restaurants and hotels, they had their own construction company and were learning new technologies that would keep

them up-to-date and marketable. I took a rickshaw to the embroiderers'
Banascraft boutique on classy C.G. Road. In my feeble attempt at protection from the blinding sun I invested in a light-coloured kurta in preparation for my tramp in the sand on the banks of the Sabarmati River.

24
DAUGHTER OF THE CONSTRUCTION GOD TO THE RESCUE

The blisteringly hot day began in an autorickshaw with Ramilaben Parmar, the president of Rachiata, a SEWA company named after the daughter of Vishwakarma, the Hindu god of engineering and architecture. Rachiata had been formed to give 200 female construction workers state-of-the-art construction skills and long-term employment so they could reap the benefits of Ahmedabad's construction boom.

Now through a special contract that Rachiata had negotiated, five women were upgrading themselves, making more money, and getting guaranteed work on a Sabarmati river project estimated to provide jobs for several years. I was going to meet them.

It was a day when I would later thank Vishwakarma that I didn't have to labour under a hot sun in the sand by a river bending and binding steel rods that would hold up a concrete foundation under a wall that I would have to learn how to build. We lurched our way through the traffic-jammed city filled with busses, limos, and cement trucks, along with Madison Avenue shops, wandering cows, goats digging for food, and camels carrying rocks.

Finally we swerved into a road that wound down to the river. We were now on a wide swatch of fine sand as thick as new snow and about as hard to negotiate; here and there we had to get out so the wheels of the little rickshaw didn't spin. My face was dripping and the rinse in my hair was leeching into my hat. My glasses were sliding off my nose. If I lost them I wouldn't be able to see a thing. We passed the Mahatma Gandhi ashram tucked up a rocky hill. From time to time I would escape there to get away from the heat and din of the city.

We came upon a colossal truck that was disgorging cement and a crew of men working around it. There was no room at all for our lowly rickshaw to pass. We sat and waited and waited. In its thrust to become a flashy Indian megacity, the Ahmedabad municipality was implementing a plan to widen the land next to the Sabarmati River in order to build a boardwalk dressed up with handsome gardens, outdoor restaurants, boutiques, and hotels. Small construction crews, most of them composed of men like this one, were at work on this long-term endeavor by the river. At the city's service were 500,000 construction workers, half of them women who often had to take the worst jobs.

The SEWA union, with 18,000 construction workers, was working to make sure their members could compete with the best and had also created an accident insurance policy for the workers. Now there was Rachiata and this was its second contract. The first contract gave 25 women 130 rupees a day for 12 days to level land, but this one promised long-term work.

The cement truck was still blocking our way. "We may have to wait a little," said Ramilaben, who pulled out a bottle of water and offered it to me. I opened my mouth, and Indian-style, without touching the opening, poured some down my throat, and gave it back to her.

SEWA's grassroots organizers were an incredible lot and Ramilaben, sitting patiently next to me in the rickshaw, was no exception. A woman with only grade five, she was working in a textile mill at the age of 10. When the mill folded she became a head loader of bricks, cement, and sand. Now she was a dynamic organizer and a wily negotiator with more knowledge about federal-level construction legislation than some of the Gujarat state's top civil servants.

Many years before, after carefully reading the newest federal legislation at a union meeting in the south of India, she had provided Gujarat civil servants in the labour department with information on welfare regulations regarding construction workers. Along with SEWA staff she was pushing them to set up a required welfare board.

We were still waiting for the cement truck to finish so we could pass by. I thought of Puriben and the other embroiderers in Vauva village that walked with bags on their heads if there was no transport. "Let's walk," I said, knowing that out of courtesy, Ramilaben, possibly seeing me as some weak Western creature that required transport, would never suggest it herself.

It was 12:45 p.m. and the women started their lunch at 1:00 p.m., which was when I could talk to them. We had to move. I looked way down the river. Off in the distance through the mists of dust turned up by rambling vehicles I could see some colourful figures that I knew were the SEWA women bar benders.

We marched briskly along and I watched a couple of naked young men from another construction site leap into the river. It was so boiling hot I felt like leaping into the water with all my clothes on and joining them. I had gone swimming in the Bay of Bengal fully clothed when I couldn't stand the heat there, but here it was definitely a bad idea since the drains from nearby slums up the hill emptied into the river, though the city claimed it would eventually clean it up.

I took another gulp of water. Stepping behind Ramilaben, who didn't seem to be suffering from the heat at all, I sloshed some water on my lobster-red face. As soon as we got close, the women who were expecting us rose up from their maze of rods, pulled out their lunches from behind a rock, and from some other place unfurled a large rag for us to sit on. We took off our shoes and started to talk. None of the women were wearing rough overalls or workpants. Like the Indian women working on their crops in the fields they looked colourful and feminine in saris.

Meet Kchanben Rathod, 32, petite, and pretty in a gold sari adorned with purple and red sunflowers and a red and blue scarf wound tightly around her head to protect her against the raging sun.

In the past she had gone to busy crossroads hiring halls hastily set up on Ahmedabad streets where companies signed up daily workers. But she said she had been lucky to get five to seven days' work a month and the pay per day was at most 80 rupees, or $2 a day Canadian. Now she had work every day for 25 days a month at 120 rupees a day.

She came from a family of road diggers, she said, and no one had any schooling. At 12 she started working in construction carrying bricks, concrete, and other heavy objects around on her head.

At a crossroads hiring location, a SEWA organizer encouraged her to join the construction union and this was the first training she'd had. Now she was eagerly learning to bend and bind rods and make rings. "I want to learn everything," she said. "I'd love to work every day, 30 days a month."

Work every day? I thought, but asked: "Why would you want to do that?" I tried not to sound dismayed at the idea of doing this back-breaking work every day of the week.

"So I can send my two sons, one aged 13 in grade seven and a second one who is eight and in grade three, to university," she replied.

Her husband was also in construction, and she felt she was better off than he was because she was in SEWA and learning new things. "My husband sees how good it is for me being in SEWA and encourages me," she said.

Now meet Manekben Rathod in a pink sari under a green jacket with a gold and pink scarf wound around her head and beads around her neck. She had been left a widow at 25 with four children. In order to eat they all worked in construction.

"There was a problem to get money," she said. "It was hard to get daily work." Despite the lack of education, her children were faring well.

Learning the trade on the job, her older son had become a master mason and made 250 rupees a day along with a free meal.

Her younger son Ashok, 20, was making 150 rupees a day as one of the 10 men that worked with Rachaita. SEWA included men in the team so that jobs requiring greater muscle and strength could be done. They were receiving training too. All of them were related to the SEWA women, so that the jobs and training stayed in the family, so-to-speak.

Maduben Makawana, in an azure sari with a baseball cap on her head, was the master mason, teaching the five female and 10 male trainees. She made 150 rupees a day.

Trainees Kchanben (right) and Manekben (left) with master mason and trainer Maduben (middle) belong to Rachiata, SEWA's women's construction company that allows the women to find better-paying skilled jobs.

She had received three months of training organized by SEWA in paving, bar bending, and concreting three years earlier. She had also become an expert at residential construction and could put together toilets. Before she was trained she had been a construction helper receiving only 80 rupees a day. Now she had the capacity to work as an individual entrepreneur as well.

As of March 1, 2008, a few weeks before I visited, she had begun training the five women for Rachaita on the Sabarmati River site under a contract they had won with M.S. Khurana Engineering, an important construction company. Once they were trained, she'd be training four more groups of five women along with new groups of men.

A widow who never went to school, Maduben had learned to read and write. Her two married daughters had no schooling but she had a son with a B.Com. and another son was finishing an engineering degree.

While I interviewed, as the sun moved, the women would stand up and move the rag into the shade, mostly to accommodate me, I thought, until finally it was time for them to get back to work.

Ramilaben stayed behind and a young boy that seemed to belong to no one and was eager for a tip escorted me up a hill where he could help me find an autorickshaw. I was whacked out by the heat, the walk in the sun, and imagining a life out there every day on the sand. At the top of the hill I looked down at the women back at work and reflected upon their hopeful expressions and their eagerness to learn. Thanks to a speedy rickshaw I was soon downing several litres of water, stepping into a cold shower, and, as fortunate that I was, lying awash in heavenly air conditioning. It was another day in Ahmedabad. Soon I would be back in Vauva with Puriben.

25
ON THE HOOF WITH PURIBEN

A few days later I was back in Vauva to stay overnight with Puriben and accompany her on her rounds supervising embroiderers in the villages. Neelam Shukla from the embroidery company's design department in Ahmedabad came with me to translate. We arrived from Ahmedabad late in the afternoon via a SEWA jeep I had paid for that took us from the city to the village in Western comfort. With us was Chandrika, head of the embroidery company's kits department. Usually Puriben met Chandrika and picked up material for distribution to the villages at SEWA's Handicraft Park in Radhanpur, a 70-kilometre bus or autorickshaw ride away, but today she was saved that jaunt.

Right away, on the floor of Puriben's house, the two of them got down to work. Chandrika had brought kits of white *dupattas* (the scarf that Indians wear around their necks) and showed Puriben what embroidery had to be done. Then she illustrated how mirrors should be inserted into a sari border and pointed out some mistakes that had to be corrected in a sundress that had been ordered by a Western buyer. A master embroiderer herself, Puriben picked up everything quickly.

Chandrika left in the jeep and suddenly we were deluged by a group of 30 village embroiderers who arrived at Puriben's house to have their own small meeting. There were over 200 embroiderers in Vauva that have become the economic mainstay of their families and Puriben was always on call. After conferring with them, Puriben went to her mini kitchen off her small internal courtyard and on a traditional grate over burning wood began cooking up a curry with pulses and vegetables and produced rotis made of millet. "All of it grown by my sons," she said, "and grown organically, too."

I nipped up the 90-degree ladder pinned to the wall to the roof terrace where sheaves of grain lay waiting to be shaken out. Puriben's three sons, all in their 20s, were up there, and they talked to me about yields from their crops and dairy cows. To get a bird's eye view of the village, I climbed in my bare feet up the sloping tiles of the roof. I wasn't up there a second before a crowd of children had gathered down on the road below to giggle and wave up at me.

Soon supper was ready. The sons went home to their wives and I climbed back down into the house. Cross-legged on the floor, we settled into a truly delicious supper that included kitchery made with rice, locally-grown mung beans, and cumin, which for my benefit was not laced with too much chili. Puriben's husband was away for a few days, so there was just three of us, along with three-year-old granddaughter, Hetel, who often stayed with her grandmother.

After supper, the house suddenly came alive with spirited village women, most of them embroiderers, a lot of them relatives, including Puriben's daughters-in-law and their children. In India, the only time I was ever alone was late at night when I was inside my hotel room in Ahmedabad. The rest of the time I was usually surrounded by a throng of people, and this was no exception.

Over tea we all curled up together on the floor, but with the high-pitched laughter and storytelling it was difficult to ask questions and get a translation, so I just sat back and enjoyed the colourful scene.

However, in response to some questions, the women did manage to let me know that girls in the village schools were flourishing.

"We want our girls to be educated," said one of Puriben's cousins, who was non-literate. "If girls from our village are not at their desks at school, the principal will come by to find out why."

"The Ahir now give importance to girls," said another woman, "but," she paused, "of course everyone needs one son."

Another chipped in with, "In the schools all the kids are together. Brahmins and Dalits. There is no child labour, and no casteism either."

Around 9:00 p.m. everyone trooped out and Puriben asked Neelam and me where we wanted to sleep. We chose the back room facing into the courtyard since that's where the braided-cloth cots were hanging on the wall.

Puriben could have slept with her granddaughter in her rather elegant bedroom, but since "together" is the way in India, Puriben set up four of these cots in a row, spread a thick quilt on the braided mattress bottom of each one, placed a sheet and quilt on top, and we all climbed in. With a fan on the ceiling to blow away mosquitoes and to keep us cool, and with a handy hole-in-the-ground toilet just a few steps away, I had a good night's sleep. A good thing, too, since the next day required energy.

The next morning Puriben served tea and biscuits which she picked up especially for us at a nearby road stall, and I went off with Neelam to meet one of two female teachers from the high school.

"When I came here three years ago in 2005," said Nehal Raval, the English teacher, "there were only nine girls in the whole of the high school; now there are 74."

She said that partly because of Puriben's leadership, more girls from the village were going to high school and not dropping out and that those now finishing high school were going on to junior college in Radhanpur.

We came back in the rising heat, and then the four of us, including three-year-old Hetel, set off to the village crossroads to board a rickshaw taxi for Puriben's visits to the villages. Puriben balanced a heavy bag on her head containing kurtas and dupattas for distribution and then took the hand of three-year-old Hetel, a good natured little girl who never cried or whined. We walked for three long kilometers.

We reached the corner to find a collective rickshaw taxi composed of a motorcycle with a large box cart attached at the back crammed with people and going in the wrong direction. We sat on some concrete benches to wait for a vehicle to take us seven kilometres to Jakotrya village where there were 60 SEWA embroiderers.

Puriben goes to work.

A construction truck approached, and with the agility of a gymnast, Puriben jumped into the road and asked the driver if he was going to Jakotrya. No, he wasn't. A rickshaw taxi looked available but it turned out to be going to another village.

Sitting under these sparse desert trees called *Bavad*, we waited in unbearable heat. Under normal circumstances Puriben would have set out much earlier in the day when it was cooler but I had wanted to talk to the village high school teacher so she had waited. I was feeling guilty and hot but Puriben looked cool and relaxed, the muscles of her lean body ready to respond to whatever was required.

"Usually I take a rickshaw," she said, "sometimes a truck if it comes, and if necessary, I walk," she said in the cheery way she always conversed.

I tried not to imagine what it would be like walking in this heat for seven kilometers on a bumpy road in flip flops with little Hetel. I was bathed in sweat and already exhausted.

To pass the time, Puriben talked to Neelam about her family. "The parents of one of my daughters-in-law want to know why I have to go to Delhi. What could I possibly be doing there?" she said with a grin. Many in the village were baffled and even a little envious of Puriben's comings and goings. She had last been in Delhi in connection with Hansiba, the embroidery shop named after her mother, who at 93 was SEWA's oldest member. The boutique, which was attracting many Westerners, was doing a brisk trade.

An autorickshaw travelling directly to Vauva came by, but that was of no use to us. While we were waiting Puriben exchanged a few words with a couple of men at the rickshaw stop. "That's unusual," said Neelam who pointed out to me that "women didn't usually talk to men that easily." Well, Puriben was obviously different; she was her own fearless person.

Finally another collective rickshaw cart en route to Jakotrya village lurched up and Puriben decided we'd take it. A couple of boys were perched on the roof of this hopelessly crammed cart the size of a giant cardboard box. It had thin steel benches on the sides packed with people, and a floor jammed so tight with travellers it was hard to find knee-room to edge in.

Someone cleared a few inches on a bench and I managed to lurch over, barely missing the head of a breast-feeding baby attached to a mother on the floor. Without an inch to spare, the pair tucked in between my legs. Meanwhile Puriben, her granddaughter, and her large cloth bag were neatly wedged into a side, and Neelam had to dangle her legs over the back and hope that when the cart barrelled over a large bump she wouldn't bounce onto the road.

The sun was beating mercilessly down on us but Puriben, with her granddaughter in her arms, was smiling. We were a compressed mass of about 20, including two babies, and I could feel steam rising up from us as we clattered along a dirt road flanked by scrappy trees on parched land. The ride was only seven kilometers but it seemed interminable.

I could have kept the jeep, but I opted to travel the village way because I wanted to get a feel for a day in the life of Puriben. I was finding out.

I travel with embroidery company barefoot manager Puriben on her daily rounds to the villages.
Photo courtesy Neelam Shukla.

She had a secure salaried job at 3,500 rupees a month and was paid well by Indian standards, but she had to oversee nearly 500 embroiderers in six villages, visiting them at least once a week. This was her usual mode of transport.

She was also responsible with Bhachiben for keeping track of the work and payment required for each embroiderer, but she was helped by the village embroidery leaders and Saira, the embroidery coordinator. Payment went from the Trade Facilitation Centre to a common account for the six villages and then to each village's embroidery account. Though non-literate, Puriben had learned how to do all this through courses in design and management provided over the years by the SEWA Academy and the SEWA Management School in Ahmedabad where Heena Patel worked.

Finally we arrived at Jakotrya, a village of 700 houses and 60 SEWA embroiderers. At a leader's house we sat in an open living room where we were treated to water and lunch. A few teachers from the local primary school dropped by to pay their respects to Puriben, who was obviously held in high regard.

Eager to get to work, Puriben began talking in earnest to group leaders Raniben Nakdama and Doshiben Ajabhai. The two women were wearing backless tops, and a young girl, also in a backless top, sat on the floor working on a skirt with a thick embroidered border.

Raniben had trained many embroiderers, but she was not used to making everything exactly the same. Puriben unloaded kits with dupattas for embroidery and pointed out nicely, but firmly, that to please an Indian retail store all had to be done exactly the same. In addition, Puriben spread out a white kurta in extra large that had already been embroidered and told her that larger ones like this required more embroidery.

Like Puriben, Raniben had done some travelling for embroidery and had gone to Barcelona and the U.S. for exhibitions. She had two sons in Bombay, one with grade nine and another with grade 12, working as salespersons in shops and a daughter that had completed grade five. Her husband was a farmer with his own land, and because of embroidery sales the family was doing well.

We left there and went off in another open cart in the blazing heat to Barara village, with 250 houses, about three kilometers away.

Puriben met embroiderers there in a grander house in an open living room with green and cream tiles with a flower border alternating with a chicken motif. On the walls were brilliantly coloured, painting-like posters of gods and goddesses including Lakshmi. A beadwork hanging stretched across the door portal.

I was seeing hard work in these villages but also signs that people had enough to eat. Children were in school, and like Puriben, they were living in more solid housing than they had had in the past.

We took off now to another town 12 kilometres away to get a car to go back to Radhanpur where the jeep for Ahmedabad was waiting for me and Neelam. Puriben came with us, out of hospitality, I thought, and this meant she would be delayed going to the next village.

On the road we saw a horrible accident. There had been a hit and run and two young men soaked in blood lay dead on the road, a crashed motorcycle beside them. This was also part of the new India I was experiencing where accidental deaths were frequent. Roads dominated by carts and bullocks or camels didn't require rules and tight controls, but highways with speeding cars, motorcycles, and trucks along with the animals did.

When we came to our destination it was time for me to say goodbye to my new friend that had opened up her life to me. We hugged each other and I watched as she took off with little Hetel to deliver materials to her third village that day. It would be dark before she returned to Vauva.

Puriben was of the village but also on the board of the Trade Facilitation Centre overseeing the work of the globally-oriented embroidery company. Together with a village embroiderer manager from the Kutch area she made sure the interests of the shareholder artisans remained front and centre.

As I rumbled back to Ahmedabad in a SEWA jeep along with Chandrika, whom we picked up at Handicraft Park, I thought of Reema Nanavaty at 21, with no experience but infused with Gandhian tenacity, marching into Vauva 20 years before with material and thread for those kurtas. Puriben and Bhachiben were just two among so many I met in the desert villages of Patan and Kutch that she personally empowered into becoming managers and leaders and pioneering a new chapter in village development.

Right from the beginning Reema Nanavaty had her eye on the larger picture. Starting with her work in Vauva, Reema had the determination to rally the women into producer groups, and later launch a viable company that will eventually include 15,000 embroiderers.

Because of the team of design, marketing, and business professionals she has assembled along with village artisan managers like Puriben, sales are steadily climbing and new designs with embroidery in garments, accessories, and home furnishings are selling to upper-middle-class India as well as to Western buyers. This new kind of company that is bringing the village into the global market is also part of the Indian success story.

To expand possibilities for as many Indian women artisans as possible, Reema worked to set up a task force on women and trade within the Indian government's ministry of commerce. Through this, the lace artisans of Andhra Pradesh may find a way to break out of the hold of middlemen. "We are certainly ready to help the lace artisans of Andhra Pradesh accomplish what we've done," said Reema.

Outside India in beleaguered Afghanistan, on the advice of the Indian prime minister's wife, she led a group from the Trade Facilitation Centre to visit Afghan artisans in Kabul to help them set up a collective based on the SEWA embroidery model.

Word of the SEWA achievement for the embroiderers is spreading. Now the Trade Facilitation Centre that Reema chairs is working with Women Together, an international organization promoted by the Queen of Spain that operates in the developing world to improve livelihoods by promoting access to Western markets and builds on the theme of fashion for development.

26
LAST THOUGHTS

At the world microcredit summit that I attended in Halifax, Canada, after my third trip to India in 2006, I saw how microcredit was being eyed by the large Western banks as a first class new way to make big money. Off whom?: off poor women in the developing world. Why?: because poor women around the world always pay back the money they owe. In India the women I met would beg or borrow to live up to their obligations. Unlike some companies, their default rate was extremely low.

Unfortunately, some Indian women who were up against it and not able to repay their loans on time resorted to drastic measures, just like some of the highly-indebted cotton farmers. In March 2006, in Andhra Pradesh, several women committed suicide because they could not pay repay loans to microfinance institutions that were leaning on them. As a result, certain branches of four microfinance institutions in the state were shut down.

At the Halifax summit, which I thought was supposed to be about reducing poverty through microcredit, I felt as though I were in a corporate board room. Rather than celebrating the economic and social changes women were attempting in their own countries as a byproduct of microcredit, participants from several institutions were talking about rules and regulations just like a bunch of beady-eyed accountants.

Because of these attitudes there has been a growing debate in many countries about the use of microcredit as an instrument of poverty eradication. I have even heard some Indians referring to microfinance managers and some NGO leaders as the new landlords.

Across the world, however, more and more women have been flocking to microcredit. In 2007, according to the Microcredit Summit Campaign, which reports on the activities of over 3,000 microcredit institutions, more than 100 million poor, 88 million of them very poor women, took loans totalling an estimated $15 billion U.S.

But in the summer of 2008, at the annual microcredit summit, this time in Bali, Indonesia, an alarm bell went off about the rise of gouging banks promoting microcredit to the poor at outrageous interest rates. Many pointed a finger at a Mexican bank that had been charging interest at 100 percent annually.

In response, Charles Waterfield, who had worked as microenterprise director for the international anti-poverty organization CARE, launched MicroFinance Transparency, an NGO to monitor interest rates for the use of consumers. A core group of participants signed up to make their interest rates public and push others to do the same. This group consisted of people like SEWA bank director Jayshree Vyas, Vikram Akula of India's SKS Microfinance, and Muhammad Yunus of the Grameen Bank.

In September 2008 at a Clinton Global Initiative meeting, a campaign for client protection in microfinance was launched by a group that included Women's World Banking and the Consultative Group to Assist the Poor (CGAP), an independent agency housed at the World Bank. The campaign is asking microfinance institutions to take an oath to engage in fair pricing, client privacy, appropriate collection practices, ethical standards for employees, and to resist over-lending to clients.

According to a report in July 2008 from CGAP, the average annual interest rate for microcredit around the world is 35 percent. India, which charges an average of 24 percent, joins Nepal, Ethiopia, Sri Lanka, and Senegal in demanding the lowest interest rates, while Uzbekistan and Mexico, which charge over 70 percent, sit at the top.

Even though most microfinance institutions and banks providing microcredit feel an obligation to help the marginalized, to be sustainable they must also make profits, and to serve poor women, they face considerable operating costs. Lending small amounts of money requires significant paperwork for trained professionals, many of whom travel weekly to villages to provide loan money and receive payments from small groups of women. Salaries for these loan officers and accountants have to be competitive.

As Vithal Rajan has underlined to me on so many occasions, you can't compare interest rates for poor women accessing microcredit with regular interest charged by banks. Because regular banks won't set up shop in villages and operate during non-business hours early in the morning and in the evening when the women are free, microfinance institutions and NGOs have been required as intermediaries. "On interest rates," he says, "the comparison must be made not to banks but to local moneylenders in villages and city slums who may charge 200 to 300 percent per year."

However, unlike what I experienced at the 2006 Halifax summit, at the microcredit summit in Colombia, which I attended in June 2009, the dominant theme was the need to reinforce the traditional social mission of microcredit. "Profits must always be secondary to social mission," cried out Muhammad Yunus to wild applause.

Despite the need for constant vigilance to guard against threats to the most vulnerable, in India I saw how microcredit can lead to major advances because of what women will undertake when they start meeting in groups. Once the village women clear away the nuts and bolts of taking loans and paying them back, discussion tends to turn to issues relating to social justice in their communities. A strong sense of solidarity and a belief in a better life for their children seems to be resulting in a greater commitment to education, health care, and smaller families. In addition, the women are surmounting cultural obstacles such as early marriage and are succeeding in operating as independent women outside the house and after hours, as the village sand managers did.

The Indian women I was privileged to meet were fun to be with and never thought of themselves as victims. Endowed with a fierce spirit, they believed in the wonder of living and the necessity of doing. In their dealings with nasty landlords and stubborn bureaucrats they demonstrated the kind of originality that came from a stinging sense of humour along with a desire for fair and equal treatment.

The women, I felt, always had their eyes trained on the future. Many of the non-literate women I came to know made great sacrifices so that their daughters could enter professions such as nursing and teaching. Models for these village girls can be found at universities in the cities of India where women make up half the graduates in the humanities and in medicine, and a quarter of those in science and engineering.

From what I observed, a fearless breed of village women leaders have been setting off alarm bells inside the Indian hierarchy. Most of them got their start in microcredit groups of the self-help variety. Important groups of strong and talented women, mostly through cooperatives, have advanced beyond microcredit and self-help groups to build up businesses that are propelling them out of an economic backwater and into competitive markets.

Basic microcredit continues to play an important role in pulling families out of poverty, but more is required if marginalized women are to ride the train to long-term development and participation in the mainstream economy. The Gram women with their budding dairy in Andhra Pradesh and the SEWA artisans in Gujarat with their embroidery company are shining examples of groups that are climbing on board. The lace artisans of West Godavari in Andhra Pradesh could be taking the same journey if the anti-poverty bureaucrats of the Andhra Pradesh government were willing to help the women rein in the oppressive middlemen.

Politically the village women are experiencing progress, partly because of a constitutional amendment passed in 1993 requiring that one third of village council seats be reserved for women. In India, 1 million women are now sitting on village councils, one third of which are headed by a woman sarpanch or mayor. Under these women more attention is being paid to girls' education, sanitation, reduction of domestic violence, and excessive alcohol consumption. In addition, elected village women have been more inclined than men to resist the demands for bribes.

Where they have organized, Dalit women, who have been so oppressed, are making themselves heard. In Andhra Pradesh, for example, Dalit cooperatives composed of neglected and oppressed women have become so prominent in rural areas that politicians of all stripes recognize that they are a force that cannot be ignored. Yet as N. Srinivasan points out in his 2008 report on Indian microfinance, throughout India, most of the hardcore poor and those in remote areas are still being excluded from the possibilities of microcredit.

When I first arrived in India in 2001, the fundamentalist Hindu Bharatiya Janata Party (BJP) was in power. But in the 2004 national election, the deprived in the villages and cities turned their backs on the business-oriented BJP government that had abandoned the rural and urban poor and resorted to ethnic cleansing. Politically-aware women meeting in groups in the countryside and in city slums played a role in the defeat of the BJP and the return of the Congress party in a coalition with leftist parties.

Since then women have continued to rise in importance on the national political stage. In 2007, Mayawati Kumari, a Dalit woman, was elected chief minister of the influential state of Uttar Pradesh, with its population of 160 million, for the fourth time. And Pratibha Patil, with a history of supporting poor women, was elected the first woman president of India after serving as governor of the state of Rajasthan.

In the 2009 election, the winning Congress party pledged to improve opportunities for women and in rural areas, expand education and health services, and improve infrastructure related to roads, access to water, and electricity.

In the daily life of villages, the advancement of poor women, often because of their own resourcefulness, is being revealed in all kinds of significant ways. The final village story I want to tell captures, I believe, the character of the new brand of village woman in India and also illustrates the nature of their progress. The tale was relayed to me by Smarajit Ray, the guru inside the Andhra Pradesh government who launched the state anti-poverty agency fashioned like an NGO, and who was always available to rural women.

Outside a simple thatch hut in a certain village two landlords were waiting under a tree for some Dalit women inside to come to a decision about leasing some land. One landlord had promised the women a lease on some land for a certain figure, but then he doubled the amount when he found someone else that would pay more. When the second borrower dropped away, the landlord returned to the women with his original offer. In between, a second landlord in deep financial trouble had come to the women with an offer to lease his land at way below the market price. His son was a pyromaniac who had burned down properties, and the landlord was desperate for cash.

The women decided that if they took the lease from the first landlord, they would give him only half the original price because he had tried to exploit them. If they took the offer from the second landlord they would pay him the market price because they didn't want to cash in on his troubles. Eventually they settled on the second landlord.

"What this story shows," said Mr. Ray, "is how power in the villages has changed. Never in the past would a couple of high-caste landlords be sitting under a tree waiting for the decision of some Dalit women."

Mr. Ray, who died in 2005, believed that the future for development in rural areas lay with women. This is why he pushed the Andhra Pradesh government to get into microcredit with what became Indira Kranthi Patham. Had he lived, I believe he would have pushed the *kranthi patham*, or revolutionary path, element a little more. Despite everything the empowerment of women in villages, combined with thatch hut justice of the kind illustrated by this land lease story, seems to be on the move.

During my final days of field work in Ahmedabad in 2008 I took the opportunity to talk to three dynamic women that are combining the promotion of microcredit with a determination to draw low-income women out of their cages of marginality into higher social, economic, and cultural spaces.

As I have already described, many grassroots women, using their own native intelligence, succeeded in breaking through the caste and male-dominated bastions they encountered in villages, business, and government. In the background, educated Indians committed to a more socially-just India were often facilitating this process, as I saw with Vithal Rajan who introduced me to the world of grassroots development by women in Andhra Pradesh.

In Ahmedabad, three facilitators that stood out were Joy Deshmukh-Ranadive, who directs the Indian School of Microfinance for Women, Jayshree Vyas, who moved from the commercial banking sector to head the

SEWA bank, and Vijayalakshmi Das, CEO of Friends of Women's World Banking. All have been influenced by the ideals of SEWA founder Ela Bhatt who played an instrumental role in the creation of all three organizations.

More than anyone, Joy Deshmukh-Ranadive, a Ph.D. in economics who is a mixture of writer, poet, academic, and microcredit school leader, allowed me to understand how the illiterate, or marginally-schooled, Indian women I met succeeded so brilliantly as business women, journalists, and union leaders. "You see," said Dr. Joy, as she was informally known, "there is education, and then there is information," and she proceeded to talk about how much of the education Indian students received in schools missed the mark, whereas the information they picked up, or systematically went after inside society, opened necessary doors.

This was something that had forcefully struck me early in my fieldwork in Andhra Pradesh when I met a group of village reporters with only grade six but with tremendous investigative journalism techniques and a thorough knowledge of their communities. I also thought of some of the SEWA women I had met, among them Ramilaben, the construction union leader with grade five who had been a child labourer, but whose knowledge of union legislation, combined with some well-placed activism directed at the government level, succeeded in bringing about important changes.

Dr. Joy, who insisted I call her Joy, pointed out that economic empowerment sparked by the benefits of microcredit was not automatically leading to shifting social norms, and that caste, religious, and family hierarchies could, disappointingly, remain the same. However, she felt that a clever use of information combined with the formation of women's collectives and the push for rights have been key factors in the march to break these down.

At her microcredit school for women — started in 2003 with some materials from the Coady International Institute in Nova Scotia, which is a recognized Canadian pioneer in promoting community development — she has developed training models designed to bring about "behavior change communication" that works at shifting socio-cultural relations in the communities of the women learning about microcredit.

Throughout my field work spread over seven years, I witnessed many examples of these shifts.

The experience of the Dalit women from Gram cooperatives in Andhra Pradesh, who performed so well running the sand contracts that higher-caste groups and even the men in their villages started respectfully calling them Madame, was one example of a caste and gender breakthrough. So was the fact that Muslims, Tribal women, and women from a range of higher castes accepted Posani, an illiterate Dalit woman, as the head of the Gram dairy.

In the small village of Vauva in Gujarat, male domination was broken when SEWA's Puriben succeeded in boosting the earnings of the embroiderers so that they became the economic pillars of their families. After that the male elders could no longer control the activities of the women or stop them from travelling outside the village or to Delhi.

Teen mothers in a self-help group under the organization Ankuram Sangamam Poram (ASP) in the village of Cherlapatelguda in Andhra Pradesh were initially so intimidated by their mothers-in-law that for two years they didn't dare take a loan in their group. But when they united to take actions to prevent their mothers-in-law from controlling money they wanted to borrow, they shifted the modus operandi within their traditional extended families.

In Hyderabad, poor Muslim ladies in full burqas belonging to the Confederation of Voluntary Associations working in the poor inner city had the guts to confront armed Hindu police outside a mosque and succeeded in preventing a riot. This highly successful action led to greater respect for Muslim women among the Hindu-dominated police force.

Jayshree Vyas, the SEWA bank director who helped the poor SEWA bank depositors build a foundation of social security, was the second path-breaker I met at the end of my stay in Ahmedabad. Under her, the bank went beyond basic savings and loans and into pioneering microfinance that promoted financial literacy and also set up health, disaster, and accident insurance as well as pensions. Both schemes were financed through the savings of the women depositors themselves.

A former financial analyst with a commercial bank in India, she joined the SEWA bank because she wanted to make a difference among low-income women. In 1991 she launched the insurance plan that she says has since then been copied by several microfinance institutions. In 2005 she was instrumental in starting a pension for women. "Women work until they die," she said. "They need some security in old age now that the nuclear family is growing and they can't depend so much on the extended family."

Pensions for employees of government and corporations cover only 7 percent of the working population, she pointed out, and widows' pensions for women below the poverty line are in the range of 200 rupees a month, or about 5 dollars Canadian.

The third member of the resourceful trio I talked to during my final week in the city was Vijayalakshmi Das who had shepherded me around Ahmedabad in 2002 and introduced me to the Citizens Initiative fighting the mob violence against Muslims when it wasn't possible for me to do my research at SEWA.

Vijaya is the chief executive of Friends of Women's World Banking India (FWWB), an affiliate of the New York-based Women's World Banking founded in 1979 by Ela Bhatt and other visionary women from across the world to provide poor but economically-active women in the developing south with financial services.

Under Vijaya, the Indian affiliate, which began in 1982, supports NGOs engaged in helping under-served groups such as Tribal women and promotes new kinds of livelihoods. Expansion of education and health is also a priority. For example, child labourers, some of them bonded workers, have been able, through special programs supported by FWWB, to sometimes go to schools while also working.

In recognition of the capacities of poor women when they are given a chance, now Nancy Barry, who worked at the World Bank on small enterprise programs and was for many years head of Women's World Banking, has come up with a project to expand employment for even more poor women. In 2008, she launched Enterprise Solutions to Poverty along with the Inter-American Development Bank.

Working in India, China, Brazil, Mexico, Colombia, and Kenya, the project is designed to help business schools and companies create business models capable of providing more income and work for increasing numbers of low-income people. The goal is to expand the incomes and social status of 50 million more people in the six focus countries over the next three years.

In India she is working with the Indian Institute of Management in Ahmedabad along with some top Indian companies. This, however, will operate in tandem with microcredit that can be expected to continue to play an important role in combating poverty and in mobilizing women around social issues.

I cannot conclude without a word about how NGOs and MFIs providing microcredit have been faring given the global credit crisis that began in the fall of 2008.

In the wake of the meltdown that started in the U.S I heard that some Indian banks were initially holding back on loans. But early in 2009, Vikram Akula, who heads SKS, said the situation had dramatically improved.

He has had no trouble getting money from Indian banks, which have a history of being cautious and well-regulated, or the Indian branches of foreign banks, including ones that in their home countries required government help. He is continuing to flourish. In November 2008, one month after the huge alarm about the credit crunch, SKS received an injection of $75 million U.S. in equity money. "Now," he told me quite matter-of-factly, "we can expand from 3 million women taking loans to 8 million women."

At the much smaller Indian NGO, Gram Abhyudaya Mandali — where women cooperatives with 47,000 members have launched a market-driven business in dairy and will soon expand into meat and poultry — prospects are so good that the Gram cooperatives that lend out money borrowed mostly from Indian banks have been able to drop interest rates from 24 percent to 18 percent.

Joy Deshmukh-Ranadive stresses that women depending upon microcredit must invest in property and lasting economic assets. Speaking as the economist that she is, in January 2009, she said that "to go back to the wisdom of Adam Smith who said that material things are the wealth of nations, it somewhere holds true for all times."

Referring to the financial meltdown in the West, she said that "with the advent of virtual transactions, there is often no real value or goods to back up the transactions."

Creating the necessary tools in India for economic development, education, and health, she believes, are crucial. "Ultimately," she summed up, "the best investment is in people and within people, in women and girl children."

In the current financial situation, created by the West largely because of greed and corruption, word is spreading that investment in microcredit is solid and carries a double benefit. First, there is a guarantee of a return because of the high reliability of the borrowers. But there is also the benefit of knowing that money invested is contributing to greater economic and social opportunities for poor women and their families.

A report in February 2009 by the Consultative Group to Assist the Poor (CGAP) and J.P. Morgan, a global financial services firm, says that the long term outlook for equity investment in microfinance is good.

According to a 2008 microfinance report carried out by CGAP that surveyed major donors and investors, 53 percent of money for microcredit globally comes from aid agencies, multilateral development banks, UN agencies, foundations, and international NGOs, but 47 percent comes from private sector investment. Within the South Asia group that included Bangladesh, Pakistan, Afghanistan, Nepal, Sri Lanka, Bhutan, and Maldives, India was receiving the most in both categories.

Blaise Salmon, president of Results Canada, a national network of volunteers committed to creating the political will to combat poverty in Canada and around the world, told the Canadian Press wire service in February 2009 that because most businesses that take microloans are successful, more and more people are looking upon microcredit as a solid investment option.

For example, the Citizens Bank of Canada, an online institution that specializes in ethical investing, has over 650 clients across Canada that support global microcredit programs through term deposits and RRSPs. In 2008 members invested over 6 million dollars Canadian in microcredit and in February 2009, deposits under their Shared World investors program for microcredit were yielding interest of 2 percent, which at the time was higher than several leading Canadian banks. To find out how their investment is helping women borrowers flourish, investors can also go to the bank's website.

The enterprising and community-oriented spirit that I saw in India's grassroots women is also flourishing in other countries of the developing south. In Africa, the Green Belt Movement in Kenya under Wangari Maathai, who won a Nobel peace prize for her work, is a good example.

The movement, which began in 1977, took off when Kenyan farm women established small nurseries that provided food and fuel and stopped soil erosion and desertification. As Wangari has pointed out, the movement has trained communities in human rights, democracy, and conflict resolution, and played a part in the reintroduction of a multi-party system in Kenya that led to her election to parliament in 1992.

In post-genocide Rwanda women are re-building their shattered country through parliament and various associations of women. For example, in the countryside a union of mostly women small farmers and animal breeders, led by a woman farmer, is supporting the spread of microcredit groups and producer collectives.

In Liberia, where Christian and Muslim women formed a peace-building network that helped end the civil war, Ellen Johnson Sirleaf, its first woman elected president and the granddaughter of a market woman, attributed her win to thousands of women who are marginal farmers. In May 2008, underlining the "extraordinary role African women play in economic development by farming, storing food, and selling it," she launched the Sirleaf Market Women's Fund to provide funding for the establishment of 50 new markets by 2012.

Women's World Banking provides financial services, educational programs, and leadership training to a network of over 50 microfinance institutes and banks who serve about 21 million small entrepreneurs in 30 countries. Mary Ellen Iskenderian, head of the institution, has said that in Africa "astounding progress" has been made around microcredit, and the organization is championing expansion in the Middle East and China.

Canada is supporting microcredit through a variety of institutions, including the Canadian International Development Agency, the Coady International Institute, and the Développement International Desjardins group from Quebec, which has been promoting microcredit and cooperatives in developing countries for 35 years.

Most recently a Canadian branch of Women Advancing Microfinance International, which began in 2003 to advance and support women working in microfinance, was formed.

Aside from the investment opportunities offered through an organization such as the Citizens Bank of Canada, ordinary people wanting to lend small amounts of money from the comfort of their home to budding entrepreneurs in poor countries can go to an organization called Kiva, which links with NGOs in developing countries, or to Microplace, a social business owned by eBay that makes it easy for investors to support small entrepreneurs all over the world.

In the West, support for women in developing countries has caught on among youth who like to travel and are learning about the world through the internet. For example, Canadian university volunteers under the World University Service of Canada affiliated with the Global Citizens for Change coalition are travelling abroad to work on community projects, sometimes helping women's cooperatives build their electronic capacity to sell their goods internationally.

But as William Easterly, formerly with the World Bank, likes to emphasize, local initiatives led and controlled by people accountable to their home communities provide the real keys to lasting long-term advancement. Outside aid that does not build in this component, he says, is usually wasted.

In poor countries, support for marginalized women in the informal sector must also be matched by assistance to women entrepreneurs in the formal economy. It is estimated that only 10 to 30 percent of microfinance borrowers graduate to higher-sized loans, and when they do they can face problems from the banks. To support women running small and medium-sized enterprises in developing countries, a consortium of banks called the Global Banking Alliance for Women, known to be open to women, had to be formed in 2000 and it is expanding.

Constant vigilance and support for women in developing countries such as India, it appears, will be required for a long time, but judging from my encounters with Indian organizers in the field, the rewards and excitement of work with grassroots people will continue to attract the necessary committed and energetic young adults emerging from Indian universities.

Yet, as N. Srinivasan points out in his 2008 report on Indian microfinance, microcredit has not yet sufficiently penetrated states with a large proportion of poor such as Bihar, Uttar Pradesh, and Madhya Pradesh.

In an attempt to reach the hardcore poor, the government of India passed legislation in 2008 setting up a Financial Inclusion Promotion Fund and a Financial Inclusion Technology fund to be administered under the National Bank for Agriculture and Rural Development (NABARD). Each fund has $125 million U.S. for projects to reach the destitute in the poor eastern, northeastern, and central regions of the country. NGOs, self-help groups, and local level associations are eligible to access funds along with banks, microfinance institutions, and even insurance companies.

N. Srinivasan, who served for many years as general manager of NABARD, believes that partly because of the extra costs and effort that would be required by banks and MFIs, grassroots organizations could most effectively use these funds to introduce microcredit to the neediest, especially those in remote areas.

Through my own field work I became so attached to India and the unsung women's movement driving development blossoming in the villages and some city slums that I started dreaming of reasons to go back to the country. I thought of how I might talk to eco-tourism interests in Canada that might link up with women's self-help groups in Indian villages that could launch their own local profit-making ventures. After giving a series of lectures at a journalism institute in Lucknow in 2005 I had been invited to teach there. If the students would concentrate on covering villages and rural questions, which are being neglected by the urban-oriented Indian press, I would enjoy that.

I also started to read about similar movements of women in countries forming the BRIC quartet consisting of Brazil, Russia, India, and China, which economists believe are countries to watch. The shores of Brazil and China began to beckon.

EPILOGUE

Eager to expand my horizons, it was with great anticipation that I accepted an invitation from Mary Ellen Iskenderian, president of Women's World Banking, at the end of April in 2009, to attend a Women's World Banking meeting in New York — the heart of world capitalism. This meeting would include their members from Africa, Asia, Latin America, and the Middle East as well as Eastern Europe.

Despite being in one of the world's most expensive cities, I booked a private room at a brownstone hostel on 55th Street right in the middle of the theatre district for only $70, including a do-it-yourself breakfast. The morning of the meeting, as I joined a clutch of vibrant back-packers in the kitchen, I thought how easy it can be to live more simply yet still have all the comforts one really needs.

But upon thinking of the women I had spent so much time with in India, I couldn't help reflecting that in order to pay for my room they would have had to spend two months worth of wages. After downing my cereal and coffee, it was with this sobering thought that I stepped into the street to catch a taxi to the offices of financial giant J.P. Morgan in a high rise building on classy Park Avenue where the meeting was being held.

Inside a reception room, I was suddenly in the company of an international group of about 200 people, most of them women, many in traditional dress, all working to connect poor women among the bottom billion of the planet to microcredit loans as well as propel them forward into economic and social empowerment. I was being included as a specially-invited observer for the first day of a four-day meeting that would end with a meeting of the women with leaders from the commercial financial sector so they could take advantage of new opportunities.

Right away I ran into Ela Bhatt. Jayshree Vyas, manager of SEWA's innovative bank, and Vijaya Das, of Friends of Women's World Banking India, both of whom I had also interviewed in India the year before, were also present. These women were among the most important pioneers of microcredit.

During panel discussions throughout the day on risk management, insurance, and savings mechanisms, I met an inspiring array of financially savvy women from all over the world who were pushing the limits of development in their countries by creating financial institutions designed to reach poor entrepreneurial women. Here was the other side of the capitalist coin where women with an impressive knowledge of money and investment could use their understanding of the financial system for the benefit of the entrepreneurial poor.

Meet Cecilia del Castillo, who created a Center for Agriculture and Rural Development for poor women on one of the major islands in the Philippines and has followed it up by starting a bank with over 211,000 borrowers.

From North Africa, meet Essma Ben Hamida who founded with her husband Enda Inter-Arabe, a microfinance institution in Tunisia that reaches out to 86,000 mostly poor women and has about $32 million U.S. out in loans.

From Brazil was Isabel Baggio, president of Banco de Familia, a Brazilian bank with over 6,000 borrowers and more than $5 million U.S. out in loans.

Add to these an impressive contingent of movers and shakers from Ghana, Benin, Burundi, Gambia, Kenya, and Uganda, most of them women but some men too.

Given that we were meeting only a few blocks away from Wall Street, where reckless and greedy financiers and their international colleagues had caused such world-wide financial havoc, yet were still looking for big bonuses, I felt moved to be in the company of these women — people who are using their financial talents and their commitment to community to put money and financial know-how into the hands of the poor of the world who are keen to set up viable businesses.

I was in a circle of not only Third World women but also of financial experts from the U.S. and Europe who had chosen a different path from the unconscionable money-makers. These experts know how to move around dollars and want to help. During one of the sessions I sat next to Inger Prebensen, chair of the Women's World Banking board of trustees. I asked this seemingly quiet and unassuming woman what her former job was. "Oh I worked at the International Monetary fund." And before that? "I ran a bank in Norway."

In addition there was President Obama's ambassador-at-large for international women's issues, a woman from the Gates foundation, and a woman and man from CGAP, the organization housed at the World Bank that is committed to alleviating poverty. There were also executives from financial rating agencies in London and Zurich.

A highlight of the day was a talk during lunch by Pedro Aspe, co-chair of an investment banking group and the former finance minister of Mexico. He spoke about the U.S. financial situation as seen from the Tropics. He finished by saying that now is the time for Women's World Banking to spring for some money from Washington, since investing in poor women that run real businesses, and also pay their loans on time, is a good deal. At the end of his talk, looking at Mary Ellen, who comes with experience from the World Bank and an investment bank, he said: "And I'm willing to help you draft your appeal."

Many of the women at the meeting have had years and years of experience, but I met some younger ones from Jordan, for example, that are organizers with a microfund that serves about 40,000 women borrowers. On the subject of youth, and looking to the future, I had a chat at the end of the day with Michaela Walsh, the first woman to head Women's World Banking, and a powerhouse of a lady that was the first woman manager at Merrill Lynch International. Still super active, she has created a Global Student Leadership and Enterprise Management program at a New York college and is training young women from all over the world to expand and eventually assume leadership roles in microcredit.

Before I left, I talked with Mary Ellen about exploring microcredit in the BRIC countries. "But maybe I should go to Africa," I said. "I can see from people I'm meeting here that so many exciting things are going on there." But from everyone I met, I know that the powerful and inspiring stories I heard in India will be found wherever women are getting together, no matter what the country. As soon as women form a microcredit group, and with a catalyst from their own country that knows how to work the financial system for their benefit, the stories of empowerment will be there for the taking.

December, 2009

APPENDIX
EXCHANGE RATES FROM THE BANK OF CANADA:
RUPEES TO ONE DOLLAR CANADIAN – YEARLY AVERAGE

Year	Amount of Rupees to One Canadian Dollar
2001	30
2002	31
2003	33
2004	35
2005	36
2006	40
2007	38
2008	41
2009	42

BIBLIOGRAPHY

Bhatt, Ela. *We Are Poor But So Many*. New York: Oxford University Press, 2006.

Burra, Neera, Joy Deshmukh-Ranadive, and Ranjani K. Murthy. *Micro-Credit, Poverty and Empowerment: Linking the Triad*. New Delhi: Sage Publications, 2007.

Bornstein, David. *How to Change the World: Social Entrepreneurs and the Power of New Ideas*. New York: Oxford University Press, 2004.

_____. *The Price of a Dream: The Story of the Grameen Bank*. New York: Oxford University Press, 2005.

Crowell, Daniel W. *The SEWA Movement and Rural Development*. New Delhi: Sage Publications, 2003.

Das, Biswaroop. *Role and Impact of Microfinance on Poor*. Ahmedabad, India: Friends of Women's World Banking, 2001.

Deshmukh-Ranadive, Joy. *Space for Power: Women's Work and Family*

Strategies in South and South-East Asia. Noida, India: Rainbow Publishers, 2002.

Easterly, William. *The White Man's Burden: Why the West's Efforts to Aid the Rest Have Done So Much Ill and So Little Good*. New York: Penguin Books Ltd., 2006.

Friedman, Thomas L. *The World is Flat*. New York: Farrar, Straus & Giroux, 2005.

Khilnani, Sunil. *The Idea of India*. London: Penguin Books Ltd., 2003.

Kristof, Nicholas D. and Sheryl WuDunn. *Half the Sky: Turning Oppression Into Opportunity for Women Worldwide*. New York: Alfred Knopf, 2009.

Kumar, Satish. *You Are Therefore I Am*. New Delhi: Viveka South Asia Editions, 2002.

Luce, Edward. *In Spite of the Gods: The Strange Rise of Modern India*. New York: Doubleday, 2007.

Mander, Harsh. *Unheard Voices: Stories of Forgotten Lives*. New Delhi: Penguin Books India, 2001.

Markandaya, Kamala. *Nectar in a Sieve*. New York: Signet Classics, 2002.

Narayan, R.K. *Malgudi Days*. Penguin Classics. New York: Penguin Books Ltd., 2006.

Rajan, Vithal. *Sharmaji Padmashree*. Calcutta, India: Writers Workshop, 2006.

_____. *The Legend of Ramulamma*. Calcutta, India: Writers Workshop, 2006.

Sachs, Jeffrey D. *The End of Poverty: Economic Possibilities for Our Time.* New York: Penguin Books Ltd., 2005.

____. *Common Wealth Economics for a Crowded Plant.* New York: Penguin Books Ltd., 2008.

Sainath, P. *Everybody Loves a Good Drought: Stories from India's Poorest Districts.* New Delhi: Penguin Books India, 1996.

Sen, Amartya. *The Argumentative Indian: Writings on Indian History, Culture and Identity.* London: Penguin Books Ltd., 2005.

Shiva, Vandana. *The Violence of the Green Revolution.* New Delhi: Other India Press, 1992.

Smith, Phil and Eric Thurman. *A Billion Bootstraps: Microcredit, Barefoot Banking, and the Business Solution for Ending Poverty.* New York: McGraw-Hill, 2007.

Srinivasan, N. *Microfinance India: State of the Sector Report 2008.* Thousand Oaks, California: Sage Publications, 2009.

Tharoor, Shashi. *The Elephant, the Tiger, and the Cell Phone: Reflections on India; The Emerging 21st-Century Power.* New York: Arcade Publishing, 2007.

Tharu, Susie and K. Lalita. *Women Writing in India: 600 B.C. to the Present; Volume 1, 600 B.C. to the Early Twentieth Century.* New York: The Feminist Press at CUNY, 1991.

____. *Women Writing in India: 600 B.C. to the Present; Volume 2, The Twentieth Century.* New York: The Feminist Press at CUNY, 1993.

Tully, Mark. *No Full Stops in India.* London: Penguin Books Ltd., 1992.

Yunus, Muhammad with Alan Jolis. *Banker to the Poor: The Autobiography of Muhammad Yunus, Founder of the Grameen Bank.* New York: Oxford University Press, 2001.

ACKNOWLEDGEMENTS

This book could not have been written without the magnificent coopera-tion of hundreds of poor grassroots women in India who were willing to sacrifice precious hours of their time, squeezed in between work and looking after their homes and families, in order to tell me their stories. Generous and welcoming, and always ready with a cup of tea, they more than anyone made me feel at home in village India. My heartfelt grati-tude goes first to them.

Special thanks goes to Vithal Rajan who opened the first doors for me into the world of marginalized Indian women on the march. A Canadian of Indian background who has spent the past 30 years as a development volunteer in India, he introduced me to the network of people that ush-ered me into the heartland of the "the India of the 600,000 villages" that most Westerners never experience.

Starting with Salome Yesudas at the Deccan Development Society in 2002 and ending with Heena Patel at the Self Employed Women's Association in Gujarat in 2008, I am deeply indebted to the many dedi-cated community organizers from the non-government organizations, microfinance institutions, and anti-poverty agencies that I chose to focus upon. They patiently translated for me and provided crucial context and priceless advice every step of the way.

Here at home I am indebted to the late Carole Levert from Libre Expression publishers who first advised me about the form my book should take. During the four trips I made to India she was always ready by email with words of encouragement and over lunch when I came back. Jim Moore, Geoff Adams, and Sheila McDonough of Scholars Circle at Concordia University, where I taught for many years, were also highly supportive. Concordia's reference librarians, particularly Susie Briere, provided quick and invaluable access to electronic sources. I am also grateful to writers Claire Helman and Linda Kay who read the manuscript and made suggestions.

I must thank publisher André Bastien and his dynamic team at Groupe Librex in Montreal for their steadfast guidance and loyal support which over the years has seen me through the publication of four books. For this book, I very much appreciated the work and commitment of Carole Boutin, in charge of contracts and rights, and of editor Romy Snauwaert. At Dundurn Press, it has been a special pleasure to work with editor Jennifer McKnight and other members of the group.

INDEX

OF RELATED INTEREST

Little Emperors
A Year with the Future of China
by JoAnn Dionne
978-1-55002-756-3
$24.99 £12.99

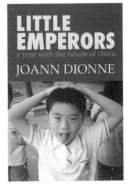

When JoAnn Dionne arrived in Guangzho, she
came prepared to live and teach elementary school
in a Communist country. She expected to see sol-
diers in the streets, people in grey Mao suits, and lineups to buy toilet
paper. Instead she found the world's oldest country, throwing itself head-
long into the future. She found traffic jams, neon lights, shopping malls,
and modern high-rises. And then she met the people who would live in
that future — her students. Along with crisp insights into Chinese culture
as seen through the eyes of a North American, Dionne provides a funny,
often poignant glimpse of a nation undergoing rapid transformation.

Porcelain Moon and Pomegranates
A Woman's Trek Through Turkey
by Üstün Bilgen-Reinart
978-1-55002-658-0
$24.99 £12.99

In this unique blend of memoir and travel literature, Üstün Bilgen-Reinart explores the people, politics, and passions of her native country,
whisking the reader on a journey through time, memory, and space. She
searches deep into the roots of her own ancestry and uncovers a family

secret, breaks taboos in a nation that still takes tradition very seriously, and navigates through dangerous territory that sees her investigating brothels in Ankara, probing honour murders in Sanliurfa, encountering Kurds in the remote southeast, and witnessing the rape of the earth by a gold mining company in Bergama.

To Timbuktu for a Haircut
A Journey Through West Africa
by Rick Antonson
978-1-55002-805-8
$26.99 £14.99

Historically rich, remote, and once unimaginably dangerous for travellers, Timbuktu still teases with "Find me if you can." As Antonson travels in Senegal and Mali by train, four-wheel drive, river pinasse, camel, and foot, he tells of fourteenth-century legends, eighteenth-century explorers, and today's endangered existence of Timbuktu's 700,000 ancient manuscripts in what scholars have described as the most important archaeological discovery since the Dead Sea Scrolls.

Available at Your Favourite Bookseller

DUNDURN PRESS
w w w . d u n d u r n . c o m